T0200750

heard, and turns them into an excitement and comfort you feel in your bloodstream. Inhale this book and you will inhale a life that finally makes sense on every level."

> • TAMA KIEVES, *USA Today*–featured visionary career catalyst and bestselling author of *Inspired & Unstoppable: Wildly Succeeding in Your Life's Work!* (www.TamaKieves.com)

"No easy feat to simultaneously engage both veteran seekers and those first dawning to their own light, but that is exactly what Roger Teel does here. His story-wisdom-telling technique invites readers to absorb their healing whole—like oxygen—or parse it out as a lifestyle technology by which process delivers result. Ultimately, Teel weaves sense out of the false dichotomy between 'life in the world' and inner peace by gently unraveling their connection at the core. Not only does this book hand over the keys to a successful life, it does so by tapping the spiritual courage to redefine altogether what that means."

> • DR. BARBARA E. FIELDS, executive director at the Association for Global New Thought and program director for Parliament of the World's Religions Centennial Celebration, Synthesis Dialogues, and Gandhi King Season for Nonviolence

"With such clearly delineated expressions of Spiritual Principle, Dr. Roger Teel brings forth an instant classic to the realm of New Thought writing. Each of his Seven Pillars of Truth and Nine Portals of Transformation provides greater understanding of the quintessential elements that exist within a meaningful and fulfilling life. What a joyous journey!"

> • DR. JOHN B. WATERHOUSE, president of Centers for Spiritual Living

"This powerful jewel of a guide for heart-centered living is a precious tool for each of us. It invites us—with intensely moving stories and life-changing spiritual principles—to live that perfect life of joy here and now. Read it and you will be changed at depth."

> • EDWENE GAINES, author of *The Four Spiritual Laws of Prosperity: A Simple Guide to Unlimited Abundance*

"Happiness, peace, and joy are spiritual concepts—and attainable. In this book, Roger Teel does a brilliant job in providing a gentle hand-on-your-shoulder road map. The truths and strategies outlined in this book are both simple and profound. Do not just read this book—put these principles into practice, and you will attain everlasting peace and joy."

> • AZIM N. KHAMISA, international speaker and author of *Journey to Forgiveness*

"This Life Is Joy is a treasure map of the soul. It is one of those rare books that truly reminds us of our spiritual heritage and assists us in fully embracing this experience called LIFE."

> • JAMES VAN PRAAGH, spiritual medium and bestselling author

"Mix powerful, poetic wisdom; invitations to deep self-exploration; a pinch of humor; and keys to self-mastery, and you have an amazing book by Roger Teel. This Life Is Joy is a wonderful, step-by-step guide to living an awakened life."

> • CYNTHIA JAMES, author, speaker, and coach

"Here is a book I loved and deeply valued from integrating its content. In it, Roger Teel masterfully brings clarity and heart to anyone and everyone's life journey. Woven with fascinating stories and illustrations, a host of universal truths rise up and usher the reader into higher dimensions of understanding about life and one's self. A MUST-READ!"

> • REV. HOWARD CAESAR, senior minister of Houston Unity

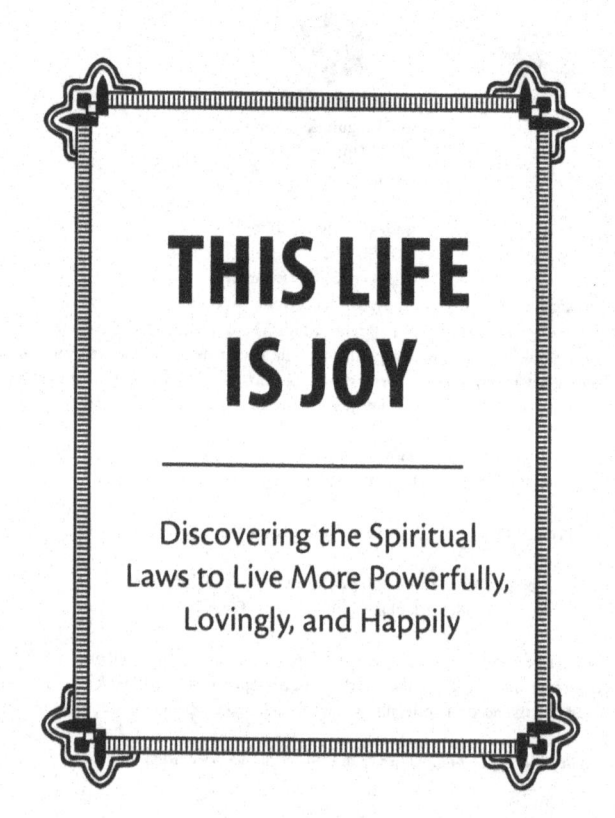

THIS LIFE IS JOY

Discovering the Spiritual
Laws to Live More Powerfully,
Lovingly, and Happily

Roger Teel

A TarcherPerigee Book

tarcherperigee

An imprint of Penguin Random House LLC
375 Hudson Street
New York, New York 10014

First trade paperback edition 2016

Most TarcherPerigee books are available at special quantity discounts for bulk purchase for sales
promotions, premiums, fund-raising, and educational needs. Special books or book excerpts also can be
created to fit specific needs. For details, write: SpecialMarkets@penguinrandomhouse.com.

The Library of Congress has cataloged the hardcover edition as follows:

Teel, Roger.
This life is joy : discovering the spiritual laws to live more powerfully, lovingly, and happily / by Roger Teel.
p. cm.
ISBN 9780399165870 (hc.)
ISBN: 9780399174957 (pbk.)
1. Spiritual life. 2. Religious life. 3. United Church of Religion Science—Doctrines.
4. New Thought. I. Title
BL624.T445 2014   2014018548
204'.4—dc23

Printed in the United States of America

Book design by Lauren Kolm

For Erica . . .
and
To the Glory of the
Universal Spirit!

CONTENTS

FOREWORD

I am overjoyed and honored to comment briefly on Roger Teel's brilliant book that you now hold in your hands. I have known Roger for more than three decades now, and I know him to be one of my all-time favorite ministers. The one thing I have always observed about Roger is how much he is loved—rather, adored—by all of his parishioners. This book reflects that inner sense of divine love on virtually every single page. Originally, I was going to skim through this book and provide a testimonial because I have been such a close friend and colleague of Roger for so many years. I had frequently encouraged Roger to write his own book because he has been such an effective communicator of the essence of spirituality in his many sermons and workshops that he has conducted for the major portion of his adult life. Once I began reading, I was hooked. Not only does Roger provide a stellar blueprint for living one's life from a place of higher spiritual awareness, but he provides fascinating examples that bring home the points he is making in a practical format.

This Life Is Joy is the perfect title for this book. This one statement reflects precisely the kind of man that Roger has always demonstrated himself to be. It's all about choosing to live our lives from a place of love and gratitude. I have heard Roger deliver many stirring presentations over the years, and always his message was about finding contentment within, and living each day by surrendering to our universal source of being, which is an energy of kindness, peace, divine love, and, of course, JOY. We all come from a place of pure well-being, a place of oneness, a place where no opposites exist, because oneness cannot be divided or carved up in any way. There is no opposite of Joy when we are completely connected to our source of being. The very beginning of our life is pure Joy—no sadness, no misery, no fear, no hatred, just Joy. After taking on the pitfalls of a false self, and listening to this ego attempting to convince us of our limitations, we leave that world of oneness and take on a host of absurd beliefs that cause us to lose our divine connection to God. It is here where Roger's writing will be most helpful in assisting you to fully live each day. This book outlines in highly readable prose how to master the essential spiritual laws and apply them in your daily life. It is filled with great stories and a virtual treasure house of stimulating quotes.

Congratulations, my dear friend and colleague. I have long anticipated a book for my library that reflects your kindness, humor, and scholarly career as a minister of spiritual truth. I have been so privileged to stand on the same dais with you and speak to thousands and thousands of your parishioners about the things that stimulate my soul. Now you have created a masterpiece that I will consult regularly. You have helped so many people over the past forty or so years in your ministerial work and your timely lectures all over this planet.

Now, with the publication of *This Life Is Joy*, people all over the world will be able to drink in the wisdom of this man whom I've admired for so many years. I love this book and I encourage you to read it slowly and take notes on it as you read, as I did, from beginning to end. I have long loved and respected Dr. Roger Teel, and my admiration for him has now expanded exponentially since having read and studied this insightful and practical guide for living a spiritually uplifting life. I have been a firsthand witness to the love that so many people have for my friend and colleague, Dr. Roger Teel—and now the people of the world will get to see for themselves why he has engendered such affection from everyone he touches. I enthusiastically endorse this great work and am proud to lend my name in helping as many people as possible to receive the benefits of what is written here.

LOVE,
I AM, Wayne Dyer

PREFACE

The book you hold in your hands is a beautiful, powerful invitation: to remember what your Self has always known about you and how, moment-by-moment, it tenderly escorts you into the luminous and seemingly dark places where, with a courageous heart, you walk the hero's journey, the spiritual warrior's journey, the Christ's journey, the Buddha's journey to awakened awareness. In *This Life Is Joy*, Roger Teel intimately shares the fruits of his many years of spiritual practice as well as the personal victories of individuals who turn to his heart of compassion and wisdom for guidance on their path.

In the opening paragraph of his classic *A Tale of Two Cities*, Charles Dickens might easily have been describing aspects of our postmodern society when he wrote, "It was the best of times, it was the worst of times, it was the age of wisdom, it was the age of foolishness . . . it was the season of Light, it was the season of Darkness . . ." Graffitied across our mental landscape is society's message that our self-worth is measured by the size of our television screen, the latest gizmos of electronica we possess, and how many followers we have on Facebook. The universal principles articulated in *This Life Is Joy* are essential for reclaiming what is sacred and true about every man, woman, and child gracing our beautiful planet: our ultimate worth is our inherent birthright to awaken to our true nature of love and wholeness, of enlightened awareness.

Through examples from his own inner explorations, Roger shares with us the spiritual practices that have contributed to his creation of "The Seven Pillars of Truth" and the "Nine Portals of Transformation" that form the heart of his vital message. With deep insight he emphasizes that behind every human aberration there lies a spiritual aspiration waiting to emerge in, through, and as each one of us. The completeness of his trust in the fundamental goodness of the universe provides evidence that our life's challenges and those times when we enter the dark night of the soul are not saboteurs; they are the clear mirrors revealing the next step in our evolutionary progress. Having the courage to come face-to-face with ourselves is the portal through which we can view the pristine features of our Original Face, which include the qualities of unconditional love, compassion, peace, joy, creativity, and contentment of being.

For many years now I have had the privilege of having Roger as a colleague in the New Thought–Ageless Wisdom tradition of spirituality and serving with him as a member of the Leadership Council of the Association for Global New Thought. We frequently recollect how the honor of hosting His Holiness the Dalai Lama at some of our annual conferences and receiving the transmission of his wisdom and humor have graced us with skillful means for sitting under the Bodhi tree to nurture ourselves and give thanks for being spiritual beings having a human incarnation. Roger brings those principles to light, illuminating the unique, individualized expression of our Creator Source that is the essence of all sentient beings. I encourage you to read these pages slowly, take their wisdom to heart, and then reread them to fully embody their transformative energy. Above all, practice them and your life will be blessed.

Michael Bernard Beckwith
Agape International Spiritual Center
author of *Life Visioning*
June 2014

PART ONE

Openings into Life Mastery:
A Short Story

He was a seeker. Always had been. Earlier in life his all-consuming search was for more . . . more recognition, money and possessions, friends and lovers, opportunities and advancement, pleasures and satisfaction—what he had come to believe was "the good life." And he had achieved a fairly good measure of success in most of these areas. Lately, however, he could no longer run away from or deny a desperate feeling of hollowness that saturated most of his waking moments. Everything acquired thus far not only failed to deliver much joy, it seemed only to intensify his yearning. Now he began to search for something beyond . . . for a better way, higher meaning, greater fulfillment. He worked hard at his labors and tried to live a good life, yet he was haunted by the beckoning of this something beyond. He couldn't quite define it, but it was real in his heart.

Sometimes he felt close to the discovery, but lately it felt more out of reach than ever. This seeming lack of progress was unsettling, disheartening, frustrating. Self-doubt washed over him and he wondered if the searching was mere fantasy or a ceaseless dissatisfaction with life. Maybe it was time to give up, let it all go, find a way to make do.

Then he heard the news: an awakened one—a keeper of the mystic keys to truth, happiness, and freedom—was traveling in this region. Few, they said, had been allowed to speak with this lofty soul, but many had been comforted and blessed just by being in this one's presence. The seeker's heart leapt. He knew he had to sit at the feet of this master, no matter what it required of him. Though his pursuit took several weeks of arduous travel, his determination brought him successfully to the awakened one's encampment. The seeker pleaded so fervently that the attendants were moved to convene a special council. Finally they announced that the seeker would be granted an unprecedented audience the next morning. He rejoiced and hardly slept at all.

At dawn's first light, he was ushered away from the main camp to a clearing in the forest. Sitting by a small fire was the great sage, enfolded in a hooded white robe. The seeker knelt on the other side of the fire, lost control, and began to sob. Then he caught his breath, composed himself, and told of his lifelong searching . . . the passion, the relentlessness, and, lately, the frustration.

When finished, he felt pangs of embarrassment from this uncontrolled litany. He looked up in time to see the great one pull back the hood of the robe. The seeker was stunned. The master before him was a woman, and her radiance immediately sent waves of warmth flooding over him. Her features expressed the essence of feminine energy . . . gentle yet powerful, ageless, wizened, compassionate. It was not what he had expected, yet somehow he knew it was exactly what he needed.

She began to speak, but not of simple answers. Instead, she offered him an opportunity if he was up to it, a chance to challenge himself beyond anything he'd attempted thus far. Would he be willing to be placed in a situation in which he would have to find a way out . . . an experience that would force him to find a different approach? There was a risk, she explained. He could get lost in this experience, languish, or even perish in it. As he considered her invitation he felt a tightening of fear . . . followed by a greater quickening of anticipation. He agreed to submit himself to this unknown trial. After all, how could it be worse than the constant gnawing he felt most of his days?

Sensing the seeker's sincerity, the awakened one rose and moved slowly before him. She lifted her hands and placed them upon his forehead. The seeker was immediately plunged into an alternate reality. He felt himself accelerating beyond control down some sort of passageway or corridor. After a while he slowed, but was then thrust into a very dark space. When he fell to its floor, the space closed all around him and he lay stunned in a cavernous darkness. When his eyes adjusted, he could barely make out that he was, indeed, trapped in a cave. Where was the lesson in this? he wondered.

After a while he began to look for a way out of this place. His hands groped all over the walls, looking for an opening of any kind. But he couldn't find any. Just when he thought he was lost and destitute, a minimal serving of food and water appeared as if by magic. This sustained him as he continued to search for a way out. He lost all track of time and marked his days by the appearance of his meal. At one point, he began to climb up little crevices in the wall, thinking that an opening might be near the ceiling of this cave. But again he found nothing and several times fell back to the floor. Day after day he searched. He scoured every inch of the place to no avail. He felt totally trapped and bruised in so many ways.

As dark as was the cave, after a while the seeker stumbled into an even darker place within himself. He became uncontrollably angry. He shouted, cursed, and railed against God, against the sage by the campfire, against life itself. Then he turned on himself, verbally lacerating himself as a miserable, lost, worthless being. No wonder he was cast into this living hell. After ranting for who knows how long, he collapsed in utter dejection and hopelessness. He felt like he was melting into the floor of the cave, into nothingness.

There was no more fight in him.

It was then that he realized something that gave him his first sense of relief in a long time: it wasn't his entrapment that was the real problem; it was the nature of his searching . . . forceful, controlling, violent in its own way. He came to understand for the first time that this kind of searching was futile, even damaging. It made finding an opening more elusive than ever. It was getting him nowhere, wearing him out. And . . . it was preparing him for something else.

Having played out so much within himself, he now felt empty . . . in a good way. No longer did he scrutinize the walls, ceiling, and floor of the cave. He closed his eyes and became still. He asked for help and surrendered his resistance to the unknown. He made his awareness pliable and let go of his certainties and judgments . . . about everything.

Then it began: The seeker perceived a light gently glowing within him. How had he not seen this before? He took his whole attention there and gave himself to the light's allure. He felt himself moving again but in a different way . . . expanding. The cave could no longer confine him. He didn't leave it, really; he grew bigger. The cave of darkness began to shrink into a small space within him while, at the same time, he began to enlarge as an extension of the light. The illusion was that he was within the cave; now he knew that, in truth, the cave was within him, and at that very moment, he was free. His opening was found not through overcoming, but by becoming . . . becoming more than the dark place. It was the realization of realizations: The way out was not "out there" but "in here." A portal to a more expansive and powerful reality, a Light, was within him—then, and in every situation, all the time, no matter what.

He relaxed and opened his eyes. To his surprise, he was sitting by that campfire again in the presence of the revered sage. He looked deeply into her eyes and she smiled knowingly. Now he understood. A deep and marvelous Joy surged forth from the wellspring he had discovered within himself . . . and he, too, smiled.

As with most teaching stories and parables, this is my story, your story, everyone's story. We are all seekers, not because something is missing that we must struggle to find. We search for more because we are made of more, so much more than we usually know. We are participants in greater dimensions of reality than we realize when trapped in worldly, ego-oriented awareness. There are times when human experience is really difficult and painful. But have you ever sensed that something in your approach might be making it even more troublesome . . . and that there is a pathway of life mastery that could not only free you but also evolve you? Have you sensed a deep calling to discover and master more enlightened ways?

Consider this: in our hardened world and our busy lives . . . amid our problems, issues, and troubles with others . . . there are openings. These openings are higher realizations that create inner actualizations. When we see the opening's light, even as an inner ember, and let these higher realizations have their way with us, we are ushered into greater frequencies of awareness and expanded dimensions of life mastery.

It is then that we experience more lofty and powerful aspects of the authentic Self, our spiritual nature, and its profound capacities.

It is then that we have the wherewithal to open to more effective responses and answers.

It is then that we know, with certainty, that there is that Something within us that is always greater than anything facing us.

It is then that we expand and transcend.

It is then that we can find light in the darkness and open up to a limitless storehouse of opportunities and possibilities.

It is then that we become the healers and peacemakers that God, the Creative Source of all Life, has designed each of us to be.

It is then, as a mystic put it, that we "let God be God—in, through, and as us."

When circumstances seem very dark, it is transforming to remember that all things are more than they seem to be . . . and that *you* are more than you seem to be. There is a way to find openings into life mastery that are different from the "usual" approaches. It is not found by aggressive searching or by fighting, resisting, or attacking whatever is going on. It is not found by hiding or suppressing aspects of ourselves. In the language of integral philosophy, the more powerful approach is to transcend and include. It is being willing to grow larger in awareness than the dark spaces, ever mindful that though the dark spaces may be reduced, they do continue to reside within us. In the language of spiritual psychology, this is embracing the rejected or disowned parts of us—the shadow—just as the seeker finally quit fighting parts of himself. In this way, we embrace all that we are and are freed to expand into greater dimensions of awareness and livingness. A greater light guides our way into newness, wholeness, and mastery.

There are times in life to push forward, to make things happen, to take a dominating approach. This is the masculine dynamic in full expression, and it is also the foremost strategy employed throughout most aspects of Western culture. In fact, to take any other approach is very often ridiculed, much as introversion is often erroneously held to be inferior to extroversion. However, our cultural imbalance toward the masculine has produced significant shortcomings and challenges. Since every person is a composite of masculine and feminine qualities, true mastery calls for a balancing of these modes of being. There are, equally, times to cease resisting, to allow, to expand, to become more—engaging the wisdom of the feminine—rather than to demand, attack, or coerce things. Most inner growth occurs when the feminine dynamic is introduced to balance the masculine, and it is becoming more and more clear that the most powerful arrangement is for the feminine aspect of each of us to be in overall leadership on our path, with the masculine toolkit being utilized wisely to bring forth results when this is appropriate. At the collective level, a renewal of the leadership of the divine Feminine is now essential for the evolution of humanity as we seek openings into greater peace and well-being for all.

Most often, the caves that trap and limit us are our definitions and judgments of things. By insisting on these limiting definitions and judgments, we stay trapped, frustrated, and bruised. The opening is found by discovering and embracing a more expansive realization of what is going on and who we are. By dissolving the illusion that life's fullness and greatness is missing, we free ourselves from the unyielding and debilitating search for more and better. Then a greater potential can be birthed, suppressed magic can be unleashed. Situations begin to transform as awareness expands. Miracles, healings, and serendipity emerge without all the struggle and aggressiveness. What unfolds is of a higher order than what otherwise would have been. There is the wondrous realization that, in this process, we have become instruments of something greater—call it God, Spirit, Love, Truth, or whatever you choose. This is the next stage of human evolution, for we are the enlightened ones we have been seeking. That is what this book is all about.

What follows in the next two parts is a rich set of opportunities to move from searching to becoming . . . to discover and move through life-empowering openings. These openings complement one another and can lead us into the experience of powerful new dimensions of mastery. This mastery is not acquiring something missing, nor is it a conquering of opponents or obstacles; it is an empowering of our awareness of what life really is, who we really are, and how we can create a masterful relationship with anything that might seem to block our progress. You will learn how to go from resistance to transcendence.

Part Two will support you in moving through openings into truth . . . giving you a more expansive and empowered understanding of reality that alone can change and up-level everything. Then, Part Three will give you the keys for transforming the difficult situations we all encounter on life's journey. You will be equipped with insights and tools to enhance your awareness. You will be shown how to grow beyond old limitations and how to create openings for healings and blessings greater than you might ever have imagined. Each chapter begins with "The Essence," core realizations about that particular opening . . . followed by "The Experience," how that opening has been discovered or used in life experiences . . . and then "The Expression," ways you can activate and move through each opening.

It is all about moving into the masterful You! The spiritual teacher and writer Ernest Holmes offered a pivotal reminder: *That which you are searching for . . . you are searching with.* Twentieth-century Indian guru Ramana Maharshi also declared: *There is no greater mystery than this . . . that we keep seeking Reality though, in fact, we are Reality.* May the teachings in this book become for you dynamic openings into all things great, gracious, and glorious! And may your pilgrimage to enlightenment bring you into the presence of your very own Awakened Self.

———

(Author's Note: Throughout this book, I capitalize certain words, such as Love, Truth, Self, etc., to designate the divine, spiritual, or universal dimensions of these terms, as contrasted with their worldly, human, or more limited scope.)

PART TWO

Seven Pillars of Truth

Essential Spiritual Principles
for Building a Powerful
and Beautiful Life

1. THIS INSTANT IS LOVE

God is Love; and they that dwell in Love, dwell in God, and God in them.

—1 JOHN 4:16

Love is the central flame of the universe, nay the very fire itself. . . . The essence of Love, while elusive, pervades everything, fires the heart, stimulates the emotions, renews the soul and proclaims the Spirit. Only Love knows Love, and Love knows only Love.

—ERNEST HOLMES

– The Essence –

On the pathway toward awakening, there is a Great Prayer that every soul eventually prays in words unique to each heart. My heart prays:

Free me, O God, from the deep trance . . . the web we humans have spun and in which I am now caught . . . the illusion that your Love is somehow distant or absent from this world, from my life . . . and that I am no longer what you made me to be. Free me from this trance and initiate me anew into the vast

and ever-present Reality of Your endless and all-embracing
Love . . . that the fountain of my heart might open up again and
overflow onto parched and barren human-scapes that cry out
for greening. Yes free me, O God, that I might realize:

— This Instant IS Love. —

Everything shifts and transforms when you activate the awareness that this very instant *is* Love. This is the supreme opening into greater peace, power, and plenty. This is so much more than romantic, emotional, or sexual love. This is divine and unconditional Love. It is the ultimate and only Reality. It is God in essence and expression, and our highest path is to continually open to greater experiences of this Love so that we might become Its instrument and messenger. Love is who you really are, and this Love is ready to flow whenever you are willing to give yourself to the opening that is your heart.

Throughout our history, humankind has distorted and diminished the essence of divine Love so completely that many have lost their comprehension of It, though they are always and forever an expression of It. We are taught that Love is a commodity, something "out there," just as many have been taught that God is someone or something "out there." When Love is distorted in this way, It becomes for many something to get, control, and use to personal advantage. Furthermore, whenever we form a word label for anything, we limit and objectify it, thus separating ourselves from it. Divine Love is more than any word, label, concept, or commodity.

Noted spiritual teacher and author Brugh Joy was an angel in my life. He was a deeply intuitive, creative, and transformative spiritual facilitator. I'll share more about his impact later on in this chapter. In his book *Joy's Way*, he adds clarity to the awareness of divine Love:

To be quickened by Love, the unconditional radiance that emanates from the heart, moves even the most skeptical person into the Transformative Process. It is the energy that uplifts downcast eyes, heals the pain of years of struggle, nourishes the soul in its venture to unite with the Spirit. It is the essence of the cohesive force that binds all things to God. This Love is nonemotional, nonsexual, and nonmental. It has the power to spiritualize instantaneously, imbuing each individual with an expanded experience of universal relationship and universal values. The sensation is one of Divinity, and it does not matter whether rational states comprehend. This Love is the energy that sweeps one toward home, a return to the embrace with God.

To move into the power of Love, know that it is the most elemental aspect of reality of which you can be aware: this holy instant, this very moment. Divine Love includes all we can see, touch, or comprehend, yet it is so much more. It includes all people and sentient beings, yet it is even more. It includes the earth and indeed the entire cosmos, yet it is even more. It is the Reality and Beingness of this very instant. With this awareness, you will gain the keys to the kingdom of unconditional, spiritual Love. This transforms everything into progressively higher states!

True Love

A wedding at which I officiated in the mid-'90s stands out in my memory. It wasn't so much the wedding but a conversation I had with the bride before the ceremony. We were sitting in the bride's room in a beautiful hotel about thirty minutes before we were to begin. I remember congratulating her on her "big day," and this seemed to create an opening. She began to share with me that she had been a young adult with no life. She had acne and thin hair. She carried about twenty-five more pounds in body weight than was good for her. She hid herself away, had few friends— mostly just acquaintances—and was very insecure and bored. She went on to explain that on a particularly dreary day for her, she happened to be watching a puppy at play. The puppy was incredibly cute but odd and homely at the same time. This little dog was romping around so confidently, so blissfully, licking her face and lavishing her with unconditional Love. Her heart was won over . . . and in that moment she realized that Life was delivering her a powerful message via that puppy: it was time for her to destroy the list she maintained of personal deficiencies, truly love herself, and just go for it in life. It was time to let her light shine and to live her life confidently, no matter what anyone else might think. It was a defining, transforming moment.

She told me that she took action from that day forward. Did she start going to a gym, get a makeover, or work with a dermatologist? No, not at first. It was clear to her that her first steps were not about repairing appearances but restoring self-assurance. She began resolutely changing her thoughts and feelings about herself, and then she began to shift her behaviors, day by day, step by step. She was determined to *be* the love she so deeply yearned for, the same love she could gift to her world. She admitted that she did eventually do a number of practical things to support her appearance, but these things weren't done to try to make her acceptable in her own mind, but as further expressions of her love for herself and her new life. The biggest change, she stated emphatically, was to love herself and to let that love flow to others. Her life changed progressively and rather quickly. And now here she was, at age thirty-two, moments away from marrying someone she loved profoundly. Her story moved me deeply. I couldn't help thinking that we were about to witness her second marriage; the first was an inner marriage . . . saying "Yes" to the indwelling Beloved.

Every one of us is a potential master in the expression of Love. It is the essence of our true Nature. Yet it is so very easy to lose track of this, to cover it up, and to distort its expression. Since we have so powerfully honed the intellect, it is most tempting to intellectualize Love and think we really know and understand it. There is a teaching story that tells of an acclaimed professor who saw two doors. The first led directly to Love. The second led to an auditorium where a lecture on Love was being given. Without hesitation, he darted into the door to listen to the lecture!

The greatest error, however, is placing Love outside ourselves. Then it becomes something we have to prove ourselves worthy to receive, and we begin to work hard to get it. We mold ourselves to others' expectations and needs so that they will find us acceptable and give us the love we feel we need. This neediness grows, and so does our attachment and clinging to the objects of love. Then whenever we get hurt, it sears and wounds so deeply because we've erroneously concluded that love has been taken from us, and we have long since forgotten how to apply the healing balm of real Love. That's when we pull back from intimacy and confident living. We might try to act indifferent—"Who needs that so-and-so!" Then it's typical to heap up the righteous judgments and resentments. It's a short step to becoming irritable, jealous, and reactive. The heart has become walled off and tightly closed. We lose sight of the true essence of Love and block Its amazing empowerment. C. S. Lewis sums up this kind of scenario:

> To love at all is to be vulnerable. Love . . . and your heart will
> certainly be wrung and possibly be broken. If you want to make
> sure of keeping it intact, you must give your heart to no one,

not even to an animal. Wrap it carefully round with hobbies and little luxuries; avoid all entanglements; lock it safe in the casket or coffin of your selfishness. But in that casket—safe, dark, motionless, airless—it will change. It will not be broken; it will become unbreakable, impenetrable, irredeemable. To love is to be vulnerable.

True Love is unconditional love. This is Love unburdened from the common distortions . . . the neediness, expectations, price tags, judgments, demands, bargains, manipulations, and dependencies. Unconditional Love is the core essence of the Divine, of God, of the Spirit. As expressions of this God-Life, our deepest, truest essence must also be this pure, unconditional Love. And when we take the momentous step of loving without conditions, profound healings and blessings are revealed. To love unconditionally is to remove all demands and prerequisites for the giving and receiving of love. It is loving the true essence, not merely the outer appearances or justifications.

A teenager shocked everyone around her when she took an overdose of sleeping pills. Her parents, especially, couldn't believe she'd do this. She was so popular, successful, loving, and obedient. When she regained consciousness, for a while she'd speak only with her doctor. With her permission, he later shared the daughter's feelings with her parents: "She knew that you thought she was perfect, and she felt that she had to *be* what you thought she was. But that kind of love isn't enough. You can't exist as a reflection of someone else's needs or dreams. You have to be supported in being your own person." The lesson: be sure the people in your life know that there is no price tag or demands on your love!

Omnipresent Love

We have been told that the Kingdom of God is within us. This kingdom is omnipresent Love—in us, around us, through us, as us . . . and as all creation. When you verbally or even silently declare, "This Instant Is Love," a profound opening is made available and you begin to move back into the "kingdom." You will likely feel a shift, a quickening of your heart, a relaxing and a peacefulness, an expanded sense of vision and meaning. You have moved yourself into this field of spiritual reality that can then guide you and express itself through you. You may notice changes, progress, even healings by simply maintaining this awareness silently yet devotedly. Boundaries and obstacles will soften. Higher realizations will emerge in the alchemy of this Love awareness. Connections of Oneness become palpable, for we are all One in Love, as Love. You will be steadily opening your heart chakra, the center of divine Love in your being and body.

This is the most fundamental and powerful step on the pathway of life mastery. It is, however, not a onetime achievement nor is it a destination. To anchor masterful consciousness and livingness is to dedicate oneself to continually opening the heart and to practicing this "instant Love." (A powerful heart-opening exercise is available to you in the concluding chapter of this book, "This Mastery Is Heart.")

As we activate the truth—This Instant Is Love—and feel it quickening the heart, moving us into Its opening, we deliver ourselves out of the trances of separation, worldly limitation, and ego-mindedness. We immerse ourselves in a solvent that progressively dissolves the years of distortions that placed Love outside of ourselves, others, and each instant. We embrace the most essential healing of all, and gain the capacity to become emissaries of Love and Oneness. We begin living the heart-centered life.

The Love that is God is an ember in each of us that will never go out. It awaits the surrendering of aggressive forcing, the releasing of fear and neediness, along with the fresh air of the open heart so that It may be kindled into an amazing energy for Good. Our lives are masterful and blessed to the degree that we realize:

— This Instant IS Love. —

– The Experience –

Early in my life I was given the realization that Love is the only Reality. Then I forgot it and had to relearn it later. This is the way it is for most people.

I Was Six Years Old

It was a beautiful summer day. My father had just finished mowing the lawn. It felt so good to lie on that warm, freshly cut grass, to bask in its musky fragrance. I remember gazing up at the blue sky and the occasional clouds that were spread like brushstrokes. Then it happened. It was as if I was no more; I was pulled totally into the scene, and the worldly Roger was gone. Now I *was* the sky and the clouds and the lawn and the sunlight. I have no idea how long this immersion experience lasted in chronological time; however, the depth of the experience felt timeless. When I was thrust back into my local self, my personal awareness, I felt so completely disoriented and shaken that I clenched the grass tightly with both hands just to get a sense of stability. It felt like I had died, but obviously that wasn't the case. When I stood up I felt light-headed and wobbly. For the next several days I continued to feel slightly disoriented. At that age there was no way for me to understand this experience and I was frightened that it might return. It seemed so unusual that I hid it away and told no one.

Years later I felt drawn to study the experiences and insights of mystics throughout history. I was struck by their accounts of an occurrence that was quite common among them. In their own unique ways, they described their experience of the collapse of the subject/object paradigm, and with that the experience that some called "no self." In their poetic, mystical language, many of them proclaimed that this "no self" was actually an experience of their "Universal Self," their true Self. Reading this, I now had a basis to understand what had happened to me on that summer day when I was six. Since I was so young and was less attached to the three-dimensional framework of things, I was able to let go and stumble into a unitive experience. The most significant thing about it was that the experience left me changed. From that time on I remember absolutely knowing that there is an Ultimate Source, Spirit, or Life permeating this universe and It is Love, a Love that is wondrous and within all of life. Though I couldn't articulate this in my younger years, it was still an inner certainty. I didn't know how I knew it and I certainly had no way of justifying it then, but nevertheless I knew. Furthermore, I was given a knowing that this omnipresent Source was safe and caring beyond anything that could be explained. It was as if all this was downloaded into me. Interestingly, in talking about this experience over the years, others have shared with me that they had similar spiritual experiences in their youth.

It wasn't long after that experience on our front lawn that I told my bewildered parents that I was, all of a sudden, very interested in spirituality and wanted to attend church. They weren't churchgoers at the time, but they allowed me to walk to any of the many churches in our neighborhood. I didn't really understand much of what was said, but I enjoyed the atmosphere of Spirit. The older I got, however, the more I felt a dissonance. The traditional theologies I was hearing did not match the energies and knowingness that had been seeded in me. I had experienced something that would not let me go and would compel me to continue to search.

I Was in Love, or So I Thought

It was 1981 and I was twenty-nine years old. I was in the early years of my ministerial career and had been in a three-year relationship with a beautiful girl. Just before the Christmas holidays, we decided that early in the New Year we would announce our engagement to family, friends, and my congregation. My soon-to-be fiancée then went to Ohio to share Christmas with her half sister. When I picked her up at the airport after this holiday trip, however, she seemed distant. *She's probably just tired*, I thought. Several days later I came home after work to discover that everything of hers had been removed from my townhome, and there was a note from her. She wrote that our relationship was over and that I was not to try to call her or connect with her again. It was, plain and simple, over.

I was stunned, shocked. I couldn't believe it. Maybe it was a joke, though not a very good one. So despite her instructions, I called her anyway. Her mother answered and told me that she didn't know what had happened, either, but that her daughter was very clear. Indeed . . . it was over. The disbelief then turned into intense grief. I was engulfed in a pain that was enormous, more than anything I'd ever experienced.

After about six weeks of despair, my pain began to alternate with bouts of immense anger. This devolved to the point where I proclaimed openly that she had been unbelievably cruel and that I flat-out hated her. My awareness was becoming more and more toxic. I wasn't sleeping well and my appetite was hit or miss. My prayer life was at a standstill, and my creativity had evaporated. This went on for four or five months. I put on a good public front but, in truth, I was a mess, and I was endangering my well-being and my cherished career in the ministry.

A really good friend will tell you the truth. That's what saved me during this downward spiral. I was having a beer with a buddy—a true friend. He was enduring yet another of my tirades of victimhood and self-pity. Finally he reached his limit. When I paused to catch my breath, he seized the moment. He said, "You know, Rog, you share some profound and powerful spiritual teachings and tools. Maybe you ought to try using some of them!" My initial instinct was to knock him off his barstool. How could he be so callous of my feelings, so insensitive to my wounding? But deep down, I knew he was right. It was high time for me to explore the deeper meanings in this experience. It was time for me to find an opening for healing and growth.

I began to consult with professionals who could assist me in sorting things out. The first realization of great impact was my admission that the relationship with this lady wasn't all I was touting it to be. In truth, it was more a relationship of convenience and dependency. (And she was a really gorgeous woman, at that!) But I had deluded myself because I couldn't imagine letting the relationship go since I felt so needy of her love.

Beyond that, I also began to realize the nature of most of my relationships up to that point. Truthfully, those I was in relationships with couldn't get very close to me. I controlled the intimacy levels continually and expertly through superficial activities and my workaholic tendencies. When anyone tried to press through this, I found one way or another to end the relationship.

This led to the crowning and transformative realization that through the course of my young adulthood—and especially following my parents' divorce—I had walled off my heart. I was a loving enough person, and I talked a lot about love. Nevertheless, my heart was highly protected and mostly closed. I began to realize that what had seemed like the most brutal of betrayals was actually an invitation to a reconnection with the Love I had come to know at age six on my parents' front lawn. It was an invitation to the greatest opening . . . the opening of my heart.

There's a lot of truth in the adage that when the student is ready, the teacher will appear. When I reached this point in the healing process, my heart was already in its early stages of opening. But I needed more help. Serendipitously, I became aware of the work of Brugh Joy, whose major emphasis was on the activation of the heart chakra. I felt ready to take the leap. I booked myself into his two-week transformational experience held in the high desert of California.

You Want Me to Do What?

That was my initial reaction when Brugh announced midway through the two-week conference that I and the other thirty participants were to go out into the desert for two full days and nights. We were to fast and to drink only water. Also while in the desert, we were to find "our teacher" out there in nature, whether it be an animal, a cactus, or whatever. I was flabbergasted. *I paid good money for you to be my teacher!* I thought. *And you want us to hang out for two days in that godforsaken desert? And fast?* My anger surfaced anew. I grabbed some water and my sleeping bag and stomped out into the surrounding desert. I kicked up dirt, threw rocks, and screamed angrily. I didn't know where to go so I just wandered for hours as I cursed the whole experience over and over again.

As night fell, I also fell . . . into the pits of depression. Nothing seemed to matter or make sense anymore. At one point, I noticed a rabbit running by in the fading dusk, and thought, *You don't matter, rabbit. In a few months you'll probably be dead. What will it matter that you lived at all?* I cried off and on. I yearned for a sense of God's Presence but couldn't seem to feel it. I felt drained and empty . . . much like the seeker in the opening story when he could fight no longer. What would become of me, and where was my life going?

I slept off and on that night, mostly fitfully. At daybreak, I felt numb but no longer angry.

I meditated for a while while then wandered some, then prayed and meditated some more. By midafternoon, I felt a shift. I no longer resented the desert. In fact, I was beginning to notice its beauty and life energy. Then this intensified. I could see the life energy flowing as everything, much as when you can see waves of intense heat, though it wasn't hot enough that day for heat waves. No, these were waves of essential energy at the heart of everything, and I could see it and feel it. Everything took on heightened life for me. That night I lay in my sleeping bag looking up at the stars with tears rolling down my face. It was all so utterly magnificent to me. I had reentered the heart and soul of life, in me and all around me.

Brugh had instructed us that we were all to meet at the top of a hill at dawn of the third day. We were to chant "OM" as we celebrated the sunrise together. As I joined the group on that hilltop and entered into the chant, my heart chakra flew wide open. Waves of Love cascaded through me. It was a familiar Love, but an experience I had blocked for far too long. It was one of the most rapturous experiences of my life. It left an unmistakable and enduring mark within my awareness. Love would forever mean so much more to me, more than words can adequately convey. Mark Twain once wrote: "The two most important days in your life are the day you are born and the day you find out why." This experience became a touchstone for what became my personal mission, why I came here this time around: heart-centered living.

The ego defends against love. This faulty sense of self fears losing control, fears risking true intimacy lest the depths of inadequacy were to be found out. When we give ourselves to Love, however, everything changes for the better. Following the conference with Brugh, so many blessings began to fill my life. As I maintained a heart-opening practice, my relationships improved dramatically, and eventually I opened myself to the incomparable love of my wife. Then our family became a glorious opportunity for fulfilling love. My experience of the Divine, the infinite Beloved, continues to expand and deepen. My ministry has also continued to grow to levels I would never have imagined. My joy in life is more steady and unshakeable. I know "the peace that passes all human understanding."

This has been my journey, coming full circle back to the fulfillment of that initiatory experience at the hands of Love at age six. This journey has taught me, ever so clearly, that I could not be more loved. Think about this for a moment: *You cannot be more loved!* Unfathomable Love surrounds and indwells us all, and this Love never has to be earned and cannot be lost. To take this in—really allow it in—is to immerse oneself in the greatest mystery and miracle of all. There is nothing more healing than this experience, and from this place of being loved flows all true happiness, creativity, joy, and peace. Our only job is to learn to keep our hearts open, activated, and warmed. The highest and best will then take care of itself in the most powerful and blessed of ways.

Emmet Fox, a great metaphysician and prolific author, proclaims the radical wonder of divine Love for every person who is ready to attune to Love in any instant:

There is no difficulty that enough love will not conquer;
No disease that enough love will not heal;
No door that enough love will not open;
No gulf that enough love will not bridge;
No wall that enough love will not throw down;
No sin that enough love will not redeem.
It makes no difference how deeply seated may be the
 trouble . . .
How hopeless the outlook, how muddled the tangle,
How great the mistake;
A sufficient realization of love will dissolve it all. . . .
If only you could love enough,
You would be the happiest and most powerful being in the
 world!

And Pierre Teilhard de Chardin, the excommunicated Catholic priest, mystic, and author of *The Phenomenon of Man*, proclaims the radical wonder of divine Love for our shared future:

Someday, after we have mastered the winds and the waves and
the tides and gravity, we shall harness for God the energies of
Love. And then, for the second time in the history of the world,
man will have discovered fire.

– The Expression –

To Establish Yourself in an Ever-Increasing Expression of This First Opening into Life Mastery, Here Are Three Practices:

1. Make this first opening a mantra of empowerment. Throughout your day affirm, *This Instant Is Love.* Be sensitive to the inner shift that

occurs. Look through the eyes of this perspective and follow its energy with your choices. If you choose, set a timer or a soft alarm to go off on the hour or half hour. Let the tone signal you to return to this freeing awareness. And especially if you find yourself in difficulty or conflict, let that remind you to initiate this opening and to remain with great dedication in its space of mastery.

2. Perhaps you'll find further inspiration from considering a poem that came to me:

> **Peacemaking**
>
> When I embrace my wounds and allow them to heal . . .
> I have no impulse to injure you.
> When I understand my desire to be lifted up . . .
> I refuse to tear you down.
> When I think rightly about myself . . .
> I need not make you wrong.
> And . . .
> When my cry for love opens my own heart's doors . . .
> I no longer close you out.
>
> — ROGER TEEL

Each day, after reading this, reflect upon:
the state of your wounds . . .
your desire to be lifted up . . .
your thoughts about yourself . . .
and your cries for love.

Then close your eyes and sense that you are filling up with divine Love and spiritual Assurance . . . and that any hollowness that might distort your experience of Love is being dissolved. Envision yourself as complete, beautiful, peaceful, and masterful. Feel this deeply and for several minutes.

Hear the words "Thou art my beloved child in whom I am well pleased."

Bask in this Love, and realize, your picture is on God's altar!

Then open your eyes . . . and carry your Light into the world!

3. I'll say it many times throughout this book: Find a way to serve and care for others. No other action moves us back into a consciousness of Love more powerfully or reliably than heartfelt giving to another or to a cause that makes a difference!

2. THIS BEING IS LIGHT

You are the Light of the world. . . . Let your Light so shine . . .

—MATTHEW 5:14

Then it was as if I suddenly saw the secret beauty of their hearts, the depths of their hearts where neither sin nor desire nor self-knowledge can reach, the core of their reality, the person that each one is in the eyes of the Divine. If only they could all see themselves as they really are. If only we could see each other that way all the time. There would be no more war, no more hatred, no more cruelty, no more greed. . . . I suppose the big problem would be that we would fall down and worship each other.

—THOMAS MERTON

– The Essence –

So much of humanity has been "conned out of the kingdom"—the kingdom of spiritual realization. We have bought into the reports of the senses, the assumptions of the intellect, the fears of the ego, and the broadcasts of mass thinking. Based on all this limited and distorted input, most people believe that reality is material, three-dimensional, and limited to the constraints of space and time. The greatest tragedy in all this, however, is the down-leveling of our concepts of others. This is the belief that other people—indeed, all beings—are essentially physical, worldly life-forms. Then we memorize the other's history, wrap this up in our judgments of them, and place the bow of their current experiences on top to complete the package. We assume, then, that we really know them, when what we mostly know is our collection of images, judgments, and assumptions about them. Extrapolate this to the social and collective levels, and it's no wonder there is so much conflict, injury, and heartlessness in our relations with our fellow human beings upon this planet.

Some aspects of institutionalized religion, though usually birthed from a pure motive, end up compounding these distortions by declaring, in many cases, that God—the Source of all that is—also considers people to be simply the sum of their life experiences. Thus they are to be judged accordingly and could, quite possibly, be found to be unworthy, unlovable, and potentially dispensable—that is, unless the one in question converts and conforms to the ways and teachings of that particular religion. Those who refuse these means, or don't know of them . . . well, they're just out of luck. Add to all this the religiously incited or sanctioned wars, the inquisitions and crusades, the persecution of those who have thought "outside of the box," the oppression of women, gays, lesbians, and those from different cultures, the blatant disregard of the earth . . . and it becomes readily apparent, to those who are willing to free their minds and open their hearts, that much within religion—with the exception of the high teachings of the mystic masters across traditions—represents not God-consciousness but human littleness.

There is sacred, healing work to be done! Mastery in its many facets calls us to transcend the superficial, simplistic, ego-driven, and worn-out assumptions of mass or materially based thinking. It calls us to perceive a deeper truth in other beings. Just as it is a transformational opening to realize, This Instant Is Love, it is equally powerful to pause and to know deeply, This Being Is Light.

Could it be that the halo phenomenon expressed in so much Renaissance art, along with the centuries-old perceptions of auras, are true and accurate representations of the essence of human beings . . . when they are awakened and expressing Love? Consider that we are all Light Beings temporarily occupying physical forms on this earth so that we might rediscover and apply spiritual Truth while also sharing our Light and giving our gifts.

Start with yourself. Do you know yourself as more than simply your past or present circumstances? Do you know that your past actions represent not who you really are, but where you were in the development of your awareness at that time? Have you sensed something more within you than the world supports or some others perceive? Do you remember peak experiences when you realized yourself as free and pure Spirit? Do you sense that this is not the first time you have been in bodily form, and that your essence is a Light that continues to shine when your current body shall be released? Yes, I invite you to contemplate these things and to connect with your authentic Beingness . . . to look at yourself in the mirror and proclaim, "This Being Is Light!"

Then you can extend this gift to others that you meet on your path. Yes, human interactions can get complicated and troubled. We forget easily and react from this forgetfulness. The worldly trance states are powerful, indeed. This is why we must remember these openings into life mastery . . . and this mastery is a way of being—moment by moment, day by day—and not a destination. This is precisely why Jesus, the greatest of the wayshowers and master teachers, regularly departed from the confusion and suffering he encountered, so that he could pray, reconnect with the Divine, and reestablish his mastery over the human condition. He then returned to the mainstream seeing beings of Light wherever he went. I believe that it was the Love he emanated from this high vision that was so compelling to people, so profoundly healing.

Many of our unskilled behaviors and actions stem from a distorted sense of self. Most people, especially in our Western culture, are taught early on that their worth is suspect and that they matter only when they achieve impressive results. Thus many people are driven by the need to justify themselves in all they do, to confirm their worthiness. *Go out and make something of yourself,* many of us were told. What was being deeply conveyed is that we did not matter much as we were in that moment. From this basis we concocted a way of living as "human doings," rather than spiritual beings. We launched out on a path of seeking . . . rather than becoming.

Early on in my life, I marched to that very drummer. I carried a deep, somewhat unconscious sense of inadequacy into early adulthood. I felt driven to accomplish so that others would see me as acceptable, maybe even wonderful. Later I realized that this drive for worthiness was my unskillful means of proving my worth not to others, but to myself. From personal experience, I know that this is a very painful way to live. I didn't realize then that we drive away success when it's based on this motive. So the wins were fleeting and there was very little confirmation of self to be had. And when there were the occasional victories, the voice of inadequacy continued to need more proof. I was just like the seeker in the opening story . . . doing everything I could to find an opening in my doingness that would only be found in my beingness.

This I have learned: my life will rise only to the level of my own self-concept. As deep healings unfolded along my path, I experienced an enormous epiphany:

"I am who I am . . . and that's enough!"

Furthermore, who I am is the Love of God shining forth as great Light. When I move to this opening and allow this Light to shine, I find peace and unparalleled empowerment. Spiritual Self-Love is an opening into masterful living that shines forth in a multitude of ways . . . especially the ways of caring, sharing, building up, and healing.

You'll confirm this opening for yourself if you'll just pause in the midst of any interaction with another—even if it's contentious or unpleasant— and remember, This Being Is Light. Sense the deep shift that occurs, along with the options that emerge for that interaction. Oh, and remember one other critical thing: this other being is also a mirror reflecting you back to yourself. When you perceive the other as the Light they truly are, you will be opening up to the grace and powers of that same Light in yourself.

As a being of Light, you are an individualized expression of the One Power, the One Presence, the One God-Life. As you take this in, giving your heart to it, I invite you to receive and embrace a paramount realization:

"I am whole and complete . . . where I am . . . as I Am."

Indeed, the spiritual Life and Light in you is the I Am, an expression of the divine, the *I Am that I Am*. It may not be possible to entirely avoid carrying a self-concept shaped, to one degree or another, by the past and by the evaluations and dictates heaped upon you by others and by yourself. It is, however, absolutely possible, and essential, to discern a higher self-concept, a spiritual foundation for being, and to employ this expanded awareness as a new manifesto for your being and becoming. The worldly self-concept may linger and occasionally become a nuisance as you reorient your awareness and life vision. However, that personal, spiritual manifesto becomes, more and more, the guiding, directing, healing, and empowering agent upon your path. It generates our marching orders and healing opportunities. Ultimately it sets you free . . . to be.

As Eckhart Tolle declares, "Whenever you are present, you become transparent to the light, the pure consciousness that emanates from this Source. You realize that the light is not separate from who you are but constitutes your very essence."

The Reality that I am, that you are . . . is Light!

– The Experience –

A special experience on my path etched itself on my heart as a compelling example of the Light Divine in each person.

And the Steak Flew!

I had never been quite so nervous. It was my first high school prom. I had worked up my courage and asked a really cute girl to be my date and, to my genuine surprise, she said "Yes!" Well, at one level I was proud and delighted; at another level I was not only intimidated at the prospect of this prom experience . . . I was flat-out scared. It was one of those "good news/bad news" situations.

I busied myself making all the preparations: renting a tuxedo, making a reservation at a nice restaurant, and ordering a corsage. Early on the day of the prom, I even washed my car, inside and out—something not very often granted that car. As the day wore on, I got more and more nervous.

I'd been dating only about a year and this was the biggest date I could imagine.

It seemed like I scrubbed myself raw in the shower, then I got dressed—the first tuxedo I'd worn since serving as a ring bearer in a wedding when I was about seven years old. I went over in my mind the entire agenda for the evening: picking her up, driving to the restaurant, having dinner, going to the dance . . . and maybe even the after-party. My paranoia prompted me to consider every detail I could imagine. I was dressed and ready. There was nothing left but to venture forth. If only I could stop perspiring!

I said hello to her mother, shook hands with her father, and posed for pictures—lots of pictures. She seemed delighted with the corsage. As we left her house, I felt like things were going just as planned . . . except that neither of us knew what in the world to talk about. One after the other, we took painful stabs at a conversation, but they were pretty short and quick. The silent spaces were agonizing. *It'll be better at the restaurant*, I thought.

I had gone all out, booking our dinner at a great Denver restaurant in those days called Top of the Rockies. It was on the top floor of a tall building with great views. As we stepped out of the elevator, the maître d' welcomed us and proceeded to show us to a table right by the window, just as I'd requested. I was so happy that he didn't make a big deal out of us—how cute we high schoolers were all gussied up for a prom. *Things are looking up*, I thought. And I was right. Our conversation seemed to take off. Our shared nervousness evaporated and we began talking nonstop. My confidence was soaring.

The waiter brought us menus and we ordered. She got a shrimp dish, I ordered a steak (the manly thing to do, I imagined). We enjoyed our salads and our chatting. I began to think that she might just really like me. This was going to be an awesome evening! Then our entrées arrived. For the first time all day I actually felt hungry. Wanting to use the best of manners, I gently poked my fork into the surface of that big steak. Then, with big strokes, I began to saw on it with the steak knife.

All of a sudden everything seemed to shift into slow motion. To my horror, the steak slid off the plate and flew out just beyond our table. I remember that it seemed to hover over the floor, seemingly chiding me for having the audacity to conjure up any sense of confidence on this date. Then the slow motion ended and the steak plopped down onto the carpet about two feet from our table. In the nanoseconds that followed, I distinctly remember my sincere desire to die . . . or at least to become invisible. I also instantaneously became every bit as red as the ribbon in my date's corsage, and that damned perspiration oozed from every pore. My date, equally shocked, halted her chewing and gazed at me with fright-filled eyes.

Almost instantly—certainly no more than fifteen seconds elapsed—that maître d', who'd been standing at his station about twenty-five feet away, swooped over to our table, bent down, and grabbed that fallen steak with a white towel that had been draped over his forearm. Then he began to apologize profusely to me. "How could the kitchen have done such a thing?" he proclaimed. "How could they have served you a steak that wasn't on a steak plate? I am deeply sorry, sir. I'll have them prepare you another steak immediately, and this time I'll bring it to you on a proper steak plate. I am so very sorry to both of you!" Then off he went to the kitchen. He'd done all that so quickly and gracefully that few people in the restaurant had noticed the incident.

My shock had taken on many nuances, but I had enough sense not to miss the moment. I turned to my date and, as calmly as I could, said, "Can you believe that! That a place this nice would serve me a steak on the wrong plate? Of all things!" God bless her, she played along saying something like, "Yeah, that's amazing. Pretty dumb on their part. And you didn't even get to start eating your steak. I'll eat slow 'til your new steak gets here." "Okay," I said, "but they better not take too long. We've got to get to the dance." Thankfully, the blushing and perspiration began to subside and I was back to acting as cool as I could.

In about ten minutes, the maître d' returned with another steak, this time perched on a peach-colored plate. "Now," he said, "you'll have better luck with this plate. Again, sir, I am most sorry. I'll make sure this never happens again." With just a twinge of smugness I remember simply saying "Thank you." I've never eaten a steak more carefully than I did that second one. Then we had dessert, I paid the bill, and we got up to leave. As we passed by the maître d' at his station, he simply said, "Enjoy your evening." Again all I could muster up was another "Thank you."

I pushed the down button and we waited for the elevator to arrive. Just as the doors began to open, I remember glancing back at that maître d'. Something was exchanged between us. He smiled slightly yet so kindly, transmitting an invitation for me to hang in there, stay confident. I imagine he had memories of his own embarrassments or blunders, how devastating they can feel in the moment. I'm certain he could sense my unspeakable gratitude and relief.

I never knew that man's name, but I see his face as clearly as yesterday. I will never forget him—his instant kindness; the radiance in his eyes; his communication of Love, compassion, and respect; and his intention to be a force for blessing. I share all this because I now realize how brightly his Light shone that night. Now, we all know that there's no such thing as a steak plate. Actually that evening, I wasn't entirely sure, but if it was an invention on his part, I would have deemed it a holy one. He had options. He could have made fun of me, made a big deal of my faux pas, poured salt in my wounds. But he chose to cushion me in a most vulnerable and painful moment. He was an angel right then, the light of his soul shining into what could have been such a dark, dark experience. To this day, I occasionally pray for him ... that he receive ever-increasing blessings for the magnitude of his gift to me of support and Love.

Whenever we shine our Light into another's life, it leaves a timeless mark, a lasting radiance. The Light from that maître d' shines in my heart to this day. It teaches me how we can heal our world. It reminds me that Love and Light are real; everything else is illusion. It hearkens to an ageless lesson: We all need each other's Light, more than we may choose to admit ... for Light shared stirs up the embers of compassion, the greatness of Spirit that is everyone's true gift to this world.

– The Expression –

Here Are Some Practices to Anchor an Ever-Increasing Awareness of the Light of Your Being, and Everyone's Being:

1. Ponder these questions that can take you beyond lesser estimations of yourself:

   - *Who am I ... when I stand in God's image of me?*
   - *Who am I ... when I get out of the way and allow Spirit to shine?*
   - *Who am I ... when I let God be God—in, through, and as me?*

2. Commit yourself to being a messenger of light. All this requires is a clear intention and the willingness to trust the Wisdom and Power that can flow through your open heart. Rabbi Lawrence Kushner writes the following:

We understand that ordinary people are messengers of the Most High. They go about their tasks in holy anonymity. Often, even unknown to themselves. Yet, if they had not been there, if they had not said what they said, or did what they did, it would not be the way it is now. We would not be the way we are now. Never forget that you too—yourself—may be a messenger.

3. Whenever you are concerned about another, especially someone very close to you, I invite you to pray a prayer that was given me many years ago. I never knew the author, but I am certain of the Truth it proclaims. Though it is quite beautiful to invoke for anyone, it is especially powerful as a prayer for children.

Child of Light

Child of Light, I bless you, I think of you, I pray for you . . . not in terms of what I think you need, or what I think you should do or be or express. I lift up my thoughts about you, I catch a new vision of you. I see you as a Child of Light. I see you guided and directed by an inward Spirit that leads you unerringly on to the path that is just right for you. I see you strong and whole. I see you blessed and prospered. I see you courageous and confident. I see you capable and successful. I see you free from every limitation and all bondage of any kind. I see you as the spiritually perfect being you truly are.

— Child of Light, I bless you. —

3. THIS WORLD IS CONSCIOUSNESS

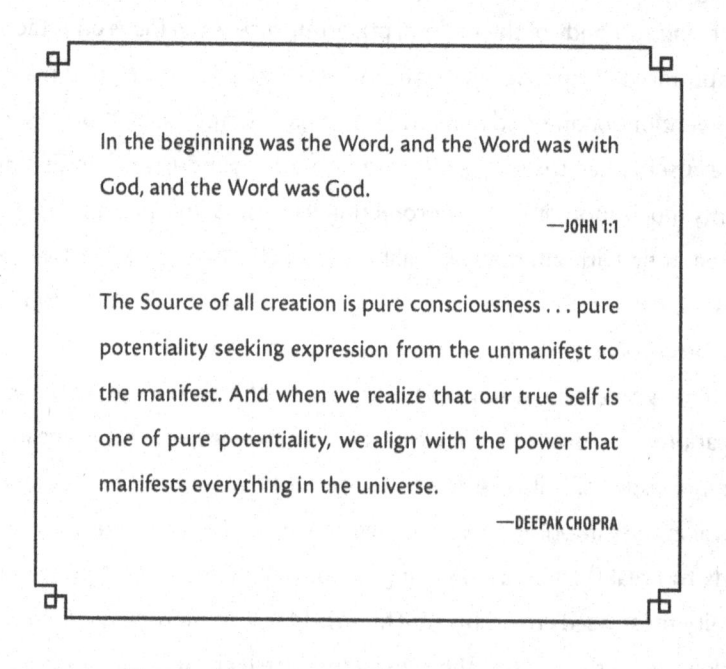

In the beginning was the Word, and the Word was with God, and the Word was God.

—JOHN 1:1

The Source of all creation is pure consciousness . . . pure potentiality seeking expression from the unmanifest to the manifest. And when we realize that our true Self is one of pure potentiality, we align with the power that manifests everything in the universe.

—DEEPAK CHOPRA

– The Essence –

There is a widely held belief that this world is primarily an arena of dense matter, dominating forces, and rigid mind-sets. Holding this viewpoint, the world can seem like that cave in the opening story . . . dark, unyielding, oppressive, and suffocating. There seems to be no way out and our efforts often tend to cause additional problems or injury. But the lesson in this is not easily learned. Most people doggedly persist in attack mode, bashing up against the obstacles and resistances they encounter in the world, then licking their wounds when worldly forces retaliate.

Take a fresh look at the power structures that currently prevail and you'll see that they are an extension of this underlying worldview. Consider Western medical approaches, for example, which tend to downplay, even disregard, therapies that work with the invisible healing energies within the being and body of the patient, preferring instead to focus on attacking symptoms at the physical level with substances, procedures, and material interventions of one kind or another. This narrow approach, though sometimes useful, has turned health care into a megaindustry that, at times, seems much more intent on protecting its profits and interests than on cooperating with alternative healing approaches that, in a creative partnership, could save billions of dollars and innumerable lives. To top it all off, the costs to the public of traditional health care have skyrocketed.

There is an essential principle at the heart of life mastery: when a chosen approach ceases to work well—if it ever did—explore other means . . . even, or especially, if they seem counterintuitive, radical, or contrary to prevailing assumptions. The courage to apply this principle very often leads to breakthroughs. This brings us to one of the radical insights humanity most needs to embrace: This World Is Consciousness!

Now, from the outset, the senses and intellect fight this notion. The material world we perceive with our senses seems so real, so unquestionable. Yet who can deny the limits of the senses to give us a complete report? We know there are sounds we can't hear with our ears, bandwidths of light we can't see with our eyes. Thankfully we also can't see all the microorganisms that crawl all over us. Our physical senses are wonderful instruments but they don't even do a complete job of telling us about this physical realm, much less helping us to perceive the invisible realms. There is so much more to life than our senses alone can reveal. If we can accept this, then it's easier to open to an inner reality system that produces this outer world we but partially perceive.

The realization of the world as fundamentally invisible consciousness is not new. This has been proclaimed throughout much of human history, especially by the mystics and enlightened masters. In addition to this body of ancient wisdom, quantum science now asserts that matter emerges out of a quantum field that is characterized as energy and information. This has also been called the field of pure potentiality. Thus the leading edge of science has moved into agreement: reality is nonphysical; it is primarily consciousness. Some call this ultimate and ineffable consciousness Spirit, or Creative Mind, or the Indwelling Beloved, or Truth, or Light. Thomas Hora, founder of Existential Metapsychiatry, coined a phrase that also works well: *Love/Intelligence.* Whatever name is used, this consciousness is the Life that conceives, animates, and indwells all beings, all things.

Now some go to the extreme of suggesting that this makes the material world an illusion. I'm not sure this is a truly helpful notion. It's not that the material world isn't real. All dimensions and expressions of Life partake in Reality. It's just that matter is merely the tip of the "reality iceberg." Supporting materiality "beneath the surface" is infinite, invisible consciousness in more frequencies, layers, and subtleties than we have fully fathomed. Reality is a spectrum that flows from the invisible to the visible . . . and back again. This world we do perceive is a temporary outpicturing of initiatives in consciousness. All creations in form are the end result of a nontangible creative process.

It is also essential to understand that the invisible intelligence that creates anything continues to dwell both within and around that creation. Therefore, we all dwell within the dance of the invisible, creative Genius of this universe. Our bodies and our personal awareness are expressions of this infinite Oneness. This is why it states in the Bible that in God "we live, and move, and have our being." We are part of—one with and within—the divine Mind, the creative Energy, the One Presence and Power that forms, sustains, and, at the same time, transcends this material, three-dimensional world.

This brings us to extraordinary openings into greater life mastery. Since we are conscious beings and can work creatively with our awareness and our thought, we have the capacity not only to interact at the gross level of the physical world but also to access and create within the metaphysical world. Here's why this is so powerful: this wisdom gives us the wherewithal to shift from the limitations of reaction to the expanse of creation. We are initiated into the inner realms of ever-expanding vision and creative intention. We are empowered to open to higher inspiration and to seed our insights into a creative process that is limitless and all-powerful.

Embracing this spiritual worldview of reality also deepens and vitalizes the experience of our higher Identity and our higher role in the world. Ernest Holmes hints of the possibilities:

> There is a greater Mind within each which may be called upon. There is nothing too small or too great for this Mind. Listen! Be receptive! Believe absolutely! Be convinced! The one with a great purpose in life is always consciously or unconsciously holding this purpose up to the universal influx, thus causing an outpouring of divine wisdom through his or her own individual mind. . . . The infinite wisdom becomes human knowledge in such degree as the human furnishes a channel through which it may flow.

What is this "consciousness" in operation in our lives? It is what we have accepted and molded within awareness. It is the *content* of our deepest beliefs, acceptances, and expectancies . . . coupled with the *energy* of our overall awareness . . . the quality or vibration of awareness. For example, a person might be said to have a low prosperity consciousness. This would indicate that there is deep and significant mental content supporting this . . . perhaps scarcity concepts drilled into the person at an early age, or a belief system centered on struggle and loss. Adding to this, it is probable that this content is energized by fear and a sense of personal inadequacy.

Belief content + energetic frequency = personal consciousness.

In our own experience, then, our consciousness is the creative template for our lives . . . the causal seeding that becomes the harvest of our experience. Consider these wisdom teachings:

> *"As thou hast believed, so be it done unto thee."*
> —MATTHEW 8:13

> *"When you pray, believe that you have received,*
> *and you shall receive."*
> —MARK 11:24

> *"Our life is what our consciousness makes it."*
> —ERNEST HOLMES

> *"By your choice dwell you now in the world which*
> *you have created. What you hold in your heart*
> *shall be true, and what you most admire, that you*
> *shall become. . . . You are life, inventing form."*
> — RICHARD BACH, *ONE*

Quantum physics further adds that our individual consciousness affects everything. Studies have shown that the expectations of scientists have affected the outcomes of experiments. This "observer phenomenon" demonstrates that there is no such thing as a passive observer . . . that we each affect material structures around and within us. Actually, it is a mental illusion that there is an "out there." The world we see is the world we stand in the midst of and create around our selves.

Thus our consciousness is the link between the invisible and the visible, between the potential and the actual, between the subjective and the objective . . . *and* it can actually melt the boundaries between them. Our consciousness is the most precious gift of our existence, and our lives only begin to work and evolve when we discover our relationship to consciousness . . . and use it creatively and beneficially. For as we sow in consciousness, so shall we reap in our experience!

The most common tendency, however, is to simply try to change things at the level of effects, to change the surface circumstances—the things, situations, conditions, people, our bodies—without changing the consciousness underlying these effects.

Consciousness is the dominant causal energy in our experience, so we're dealing only in temporary Band-Aids when we seek to manipulate the conditions around us without enhancing our consciousness. For instance, imagine that future technology develops a way to switch bodies and life conditions with someone else—"Beam me into another body, Scotty!" So you make a switch and get everything you have deeply desired, all the things and experiences that have seemed so elusive. Great deal, right? Actually, probably not . . . because it wouldn't be long before your consciousness would reorient and rearrange your life back to the way it used to be. And all that great new stuff would fall away, because you would already be experiencing it *if* your consciousness were capable of generating and sustaining it. It might be fun to try on a new life for a week or so, but only changes in consciousness produce lasting shifts and changes in experience.

Shel Silverstein wrote a humorous poem titled "Fancy Dive." It features "Melissa of Coconut Grove," who dives off a diving board and executes numerous fancy, exotic, and amazing flips and contortions. The final line is telling. It declares that Melissa "then somersaulted nine times and a quarter . . . and looked down and saw that the pool had no water!"

Most people seek to live impressively, powerfully, and effectively. But the thing we most often forget to check is our consciousness. And it's the most important ingredient. If you desire to change and enhance your life, you cannot sidestep the enhancement and empowerment of your consciousness!

Core Ideas and Stories

The elements in consciousness that have the greatest power to block or limit us are core ideas and "stories." Each of these represents deeply accepted and limiting "mental models" of ourselves that are usually embedded in the unconscious dimension of the mind. There, they operate by pure habit and without our conscious invitation or permission. They just assert themselves because they have been given that incredibly powerful force of conviction, of belief, and are fueled by correspondingly compelling and restrictive feelings.

Debbie Ford, in her book *The Right Questions*, calls these core ideas our "underlying commitments" and gives us a greater sense of how these acceptances operate to block or impair our experience:

> Our "underlying commitments" drive our thoughts, our beliefs, and—most important—our choices. They are unseen forces that shape our realities. Our underlying commitments are responsible for the discrepancy between what we SAY we want and what we're actually experiencing. These underlying commitments are formed by unconscious decisions we've made in the past.

She is saying we may imagine that we're ready to receive our next steps or greater blessings in life . . . but in our unconscious depths, deeper commitments may be declaring: "NO WAY!" Many of these underlying commitments can be discerned by coming to grips with "our stories"— the stories we tell about our life and our possibilities that we have been proclaiming and reinforcing, over and over again. In most cases, we have told these stories so often and with such conviction, that we have given them the power to sabotage us, to close us off, and to drive away our newness and progress.

I categorize these limiting stories that block our greater Good as:

The "OLD" . . . The "COLD". . . and The "TOLD."

THE OLD: Our stories were usually formed in response to early setbacks and painful experiences. They are deeply rooted in our past . . . *and* we have told them about ourselves for so long that they have become "our truth." Once they become our truth, we unwittingly work to reinforce and justify our stories. But we seldom realize that our stories are just that . . . our composed responses to events and experiences, *not* necessarily the final Truth.

What old stories have you been telling about yourself . . . so much so that you don't even give them a second thought? What causes lots of people to get bogged down in life are stories that often begin with phrases like these:

> *"The reason I can never get ahead is . . ."*
> *"Something I'll never get over is . . ."*
> *"The part of me that always gets in the way is . . ."*
> *"If only I had [such and such] . . ."*
> Or, *"If only I hadn't done [such and such] . . ."*
> *"I never get any of the breaks . . ."*

"I don't feel worthy to receive my Good, because . . ."
"I love to give, but I never receive in return . . ."

Old stories continue to show up in our actual experiences because we give them that power. We neutralize conscious, creative, and powerful choosing by retelling our old stories, our composed interpretations of our life. These stories become our personal myths that will continue to run our lives until we deliberately choose to create and empower a new story . . . one that inspires, heals, and opens up possibilities.

THE COLD: These are the stories about ourselves and our prospects that have no heart, no compassion. They are usually the most harsh and unkind interpretations of some event or aspect of life, or of life in general. What are the most belittling stories you continue to tell about yourself? They are painful and carry a sting, but they also have the payoff of jerking you back from the starting line of risks and new adventures. There are always different interpretations, different versions, for every experience. Why not choose one that empowers rather than deflates?

"The Cold" stories are also ones that are not connected to our deepest passion and to our genuine caring. The heart is the source of our passion and our true Power . . . so if the stories we tell are old and cold, we're going to stay stuck!

THE TOLD: These are the stories that have been told about us . . . ones that people have proclaimed about us that we ended up buying into, accepting. They are also the stories and acceptances of limitation that people are telling about life, or about the economy—or whatever—ones we are also apt to embrace.

Author and growth facilitator Dawna Markova speaks to this: "When the inner walls to your soul are graffitied with advertisements, commercials, and the opinions of everyone who has ever known and labeled you, turning inwards requires nothing less than a major clean-up."

Have you ever felt like the walls to your soul were graffitied by all that has been told about you and accepted by you? She continues: "When you have the courage to shape your life from the essence of who you are, you ignite, becoming truly alive. This requires letting go of everything that is inauthentic."

Is it time to clean off your inner graffiti . . . to release all "The Told" stories?

Consciousness Empowered

Later on in this book, I'll share a really important point in greater depth: Outcomes are not the ultimate or the "end all" in this life. When we believe that it is all about the outcomes and we don't create a desired outcome, the tendency is to form harsh, belittling, and disempowering stories. Then these stories get told so frequently that they become knee-jerk reactions. At this point they have become ensconced in the subconscious mind where they will continue to assert their limitations until we transform them.

Instead of outcomes, our lives are really about "value received." You have the capacity to receive value from any experience, even one that falls way short of the desired outcome. When you choose to receive value from your experiences, you automatically become a winner in every instance. You know more and have a stronger ability to move forward with greater effectiveness. Compassionate personal stories are not a glossing over, or a rationalizing of things. Instead they tap into the genuine gold in every experience, the opportunities couched in even the most difficult or devastating experiences.

Life invites us to cocreate a new story, a higher story . . . the "gold story" of our key life experiences. There is untold power in moving from "the old . . . the cold . . . the told" stories . . . to the "gold," to new portrayals of your life experiences that reveal the precious and God-inspired You . . . the you who has always been trying, learning, and growing as best you can. The gold story about every experience allows you to create sturdy pillars of consciousness, for remember, your consciousness is the sum total of your most deeply accepted beliefs (your stories) and the dominant energies that permeate your awareness. Author and anchor your gold story, and from it will unfold many "bold stories" of enthusiastic, courageous, and committed living.

Consciousness may seem exceedingly elusive and subtle. For some it seems like focusing on consciousness is foolhardy and a waste of time . . . better to get busy making things happen. There is a time for constructive action, to be sure. However, building up one's consciousness of Life, Truth, and Self is the highest order of priority and greatest key to true Power. For you are not only Love and Light; you are consciousness in expression.

A Vision for Higher-Consciousness Living

You are so much more than a material, time/space organism. You are the I Am . . . a being of Light born from, living within, and giving expression to universal Love/Intelligence.

As you walk in this awareness, the world no longer has the power to intimidate and manipulate you. Obstacles and dilemmas become opportunities to listen deeply and to make yourself available to a vast inner guidance.

You no longer fall prey to as much discouragement or disillusionment with the world. You are becoming keenly aware of the forces of thought and the quality of consciousness at play in the human condition. Moreover, you realize yourself as a spiritual change agent, capable of bringing forth higher perspectives and transforming blessings.

You take your place within the causal dimensions of life. Instead of feeling victimized by circumstances and effects, you step forth to set new causes in motion by exploring and expanding consciousness—in you and in the world around you.

Your awareness that all people are Beings of Light and that This World Is Consciousness becomes a way of life, and you progressively stabilize your awareness of that nondual Presence and Power of Love, Wisdom, and Harmony. This is so much more than a temporary high. It becomes the conscious fabric of your being.

You realize ever more deeply that you are at home in a friendly universe, that all is well. The imaginary hole of "not-enough-ness" not only fills up but dissolves, and with this comes the unshakeable conviction that you are complete and whole in the Mind of God, now and always.

You center yourself in practices of Spiritual Self-Love. There is also the growing realization that the endgame of spiritual unfoldment and practices of mastery is not self-love—this is only the beginning. Once you have this as a base, vibrationally, you grow from there into the leading edge of creativity, of purposeful expression, of manifesting and building up the kingdom of heaven on earth.

This becomes a joyful exploration into who you are as a spiritual being . . . always being surprised at that which is springing forth from you as expressions of beauty, depth of wisdom and creativity, love, elegance, and enthusiasm—all the eternal verities of the Spirit that are within you and within all.

And . . . you are no longer being dragged along. You are a "Yes" to Life's invitation to copartner in the next stages of unfoldment and evolution, both in yourself and in the world. You realize yourself as a conduit for continuing revelation, the means by which the One Life, the Spirit, is advancing and celebrating Itself.

———

Realizing these things . . . this opening into life mastery offers such glorious empowerment, such a vast opportunity to continuously remember that there is so much more to all beings and to life than meets the eye! This is the unparalleled adventure of taking a spiritual quantum leap . . . right into the heart of the quantum universe, within and all around. One of the greatest secrets is now revealed: this world is infinite, invisible consciousness!

– The Experience –

I share with you another personal experience that illustrates the invitation to higher consciousness . . . especially a consciousness of our connection with the Source.

Deeper Roots!

In my early thirties, I found myself in tough times. What was going on is not important. What matters most are the insights that came to light . . . when I was ready to receive them. In the midst of what was going on, I decided one day to go for a hike in the beautiful Rocky Mountains, which spread out on the western edge of Denver. After a while I found a couple of boulders that made for a great place to recline. I lay there and looked up at the towering pines and the beautiful aspens. Nature is such an awesome teacher. Some key realizations flowed to me: First, I realized that despite the grandeur of these majestic trees, I was seeing only half the story. I was underappreciating a critical dimension—an unseen dimension each of the trees had to have to survive and thrive—*their root systems*—their essential, unseen growth structure.

Now, this probably seems a bit elementary, yet in that moment it stood as a deeply powerful lesson for me. I began to wonder about my own roots—not my ancestry, but my real roots . . . that unseen dimension as vital to me as roots are to a tree. Trees need to be grounded in a medium of stability and nourishment. So do I. So do you. None of us created our lives, and without that greater Love/Intelligence, we couldn't sustain ourselves for even a second. A larger dimension sources and resources us—the spiritual soil in which we "live, move, and have our being." Perhaps this is why the Psalmist affirmed, "And he shall be like a tree planted by the rivers of water, that brings forth his fruit in his season; his leaf also shall not wither, and whatsoever he does shall prosper." As a "tree" planted by the rivers of water—water often serving as a symbol for the Spirit—I began to understand that it was time to tend to my spiritual roots.

Reclining there on those rocks, I had another realization: The old-growth pines and spruces towered over all the rest. What a root system they must have! Later I read that each of these gigantic wonders has a root system at least as deep as the tree is tall. The principle became clear: the more majestic and evolved the life expression, the deeper the roots must be. Again, I wondered about myself. Was I tapping into the Source of my stability, nourishment, and growth? Was I putting down deeper roots into Spirit? There is a means in consciousness to draw from and to rely upon the Source so as to grow our lives . . . but it's up to you and me to develop the capacity to receive—and this is a capacity only of consciousness.

I also remembered a principle in gardening: If seeds aren't given something to work against, their roots stay shallow and underdeveloped. The plant is weaker, less magnificent, and could quite possibly be washed or blown away. So a good gardener pats down the soil so that the sprout has to work hard, put down deeper roots to support its drive upward. Now if a seed had a conscious mind like we do, it'd no doubt grouse, complain, and come to resent the obstacle . . . even though it is the key to its success . . . even though it is prompting the inbuilt Intelligence in the seed to rely on the soil and to grow deeper roots. I began to realize how often I would subtly, and sometimes not so subtly, tell a story of resenting my difficulties, when from a higher perspective they were offering me the opportunity to discover and express more of my inner capacities.

The spiritual wisdom of the ages declares to all who can hear, there is a God-seed in all beings—a divine Idea held in the Mind of God, a perfect pattern of Being. This God-seed is the True Self planted in Omnipresent Spirit. On that day in the mountains, the Love/Intelligence within nature sent me a clear message: deeper roots are the most essential elements in consciousness. And tough times are usually serving to promote deepening. The trials and difficulties in life do not squash the inner seed of perfection. Instead they cause greater strength and beauty to be revealed.

Now in the presence of great life challenges, the most common tendency is to neglect inner growth and to focus on outer results or solutions. The ego surmises that the answer is to simply develop some more "branches," to increase our surface elegance or importance. But there's a problem with this approach: the winds of life will blow us over so easily when we've mostly got a lot of pomp and fluff but insufficient roots. And the really effective results or solutions are most often birthed through quantum leaps in consciousness . . . purposefully using the resistances or problems to deepen consciousness so that a higher order of ideas can flow into awareness. We often end up sabotaging breakthrough ideas and their impact by focusing on practical measures . . . rather than spiritual treasures. Always begin by working with your consciousness!

That day in the mountains, the deepening process began for me. I took a stand to trust the nourishment from my "inner roots." I chose to stop telling life-limiting stories of victimhood and struggle. I began receiving a growing sense of assurance that what I was facing had a hidden purpose—to deepen and empower my consciousness of the omnipresence, omniscience, and omnipotence of God-Life so that I could become more deeply rooted, like "a tree planted by the rivers of water" . . . and a vessel to receive the guidance and wonder-working ideas of the Spirit.

If somebody should ever tell you to "take a hike," my best advice would be to do it!

– The Expression –

1. There is no such thing as "drive-through consciousness development."

Growth in consciousness must be nurtured over time and with devotion. There is a powerful exercise in "The Expression" portion of the next chapter. It will assist you in developing a lifestyle of consciousness cultivation.

In addition to this, I invite you to practice daily heart-opening exercises, such as the one at the end of this book. Begin by taking many deep breaths and relaxing. Then remember that This Instant Is Love . . . and that you are a being of Light. Let your heart continue to open as you feel waves of healing love pouring through you for you. Practice receiving this love, basking in this Love, and understand that you are having a spiritual experience . . . an experience of the Reality of the Divine, within and all around you.

Complete this process by realizing that you are a being of Power and Love . . . that you are here by Divine Design. Ernest Holmes writes "God has need of you, else you would not be." Feel blessed, reassured and strengthened.

2. Consciousness Test Cases

Whenever you hear yourself talking about your life—your past, your current experiences or challenges, your future prospects—be alert to the nature of the stories embedded in this sharing. If something tenses within you, it is probably a higher wisdom cringing at this "lesser story." Especially notice this material when you are dealing with an area of your experience that has been difficult. Often our greatest obstacle is ourselves, most especially our stories.

When you happen on to an "old, cold, or told" story, get out a journal and write your "gold story." This is the story about the value received from the experience and your determination of its creative impact for you going forward. As you write this "gold story," be prepared to confront "naysayer voices" within you. These are the voices that would proclaim that you're fooling yourself, that you had the correct version of the story already . . . that you are not a magnificent being capable of learning from everything . . . capable of soaring. Simply bless these spoiler voices and write on. They do not have lasting power.

As you continue to write, you will begin to reveal powerful and freeing insights for your life. Cherish these. And practice telling your new story until it overrides and dissolves the old, limiting ones and becomes your bold story!

3. Count Your Blessings

Using whatever means you desire, make it a regular practice to focus upon the wonders and tremendous blessings already in your life. Move beyond stories of "not enough," of what author and teacher Eric Butterworth describes as "onliness"—"I only have this, I only have that"—and energize profound appreciation for that which *is* in your life . . . as well as that which is available to your life through an expanding consciousness. This is becoming *abundant* in consciousness . . . for a sense of our present blessings is a great developer of consciousness. This is tapping an "attitude of gratitude" and letting it prosper your life!

Spiritual philosopher Robert Russell writes: "The ultimate goal of all spiritual practice is to be so fully conscious of God's presence that you are unconscious of anything unlike God. Since God is the source of all supply and the giver of every good and perfect gift, the closer you live to God, the more spiritual benefits you will share. The best method for living closer to God is the practice of whole-souled gratitude."

Gratitude opens our minds to receive more and more Good. The grateful mind accomplishes . . . it is tireless, joyous, and alive. The thankful mind always looks for the best in people and situations and so brings the best out of them. The thankful mind lives in the *now* and is contented from within. The grateful heart is established in a sense of abundance and thus stimulates abundance in increasing measure. The grateful soul heals, unleashing a healing force to balance and bless discordant situations.

4. THIS IDEA IS SUBSTANCE

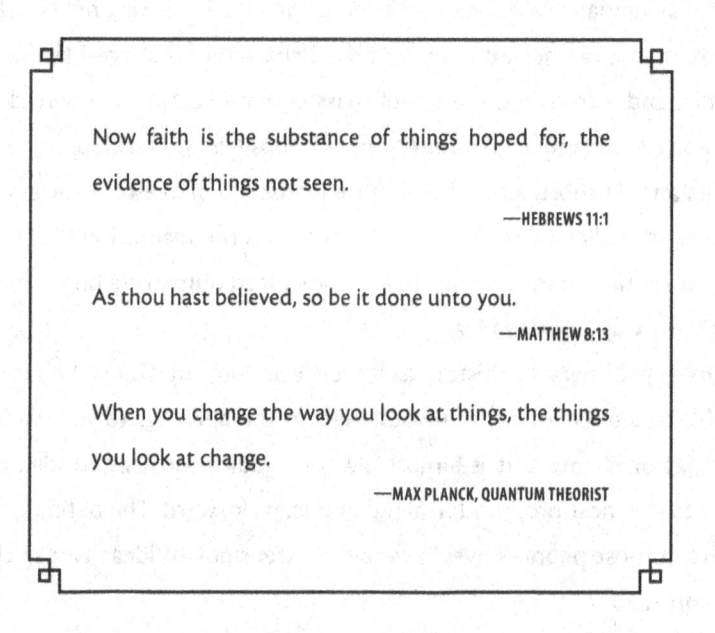

Now faith is the substance of things hoped for, the evidence of things not seen.

—HEBREWS 11:1

As thou hast believed, so be it done unto you.

—MATTHEW 8:13

When you change the way you look at things, the things you look at change.

—MAX PLANCK, QUANTUM THEORIST

– The Essence –

By realizing that the world is consciousness, we ready ourselves for another essential opening into a life of greater mastery: This Idea Is Substance. Discovering this opening moves us beyond the superficial conclusion that an idea is basically just a hollow notion . . . airy, fleeting, weak, and powerless. Instead, we are primed to realize that in a world of consciousness, ideas become crystallized building blocks that are essential to initiating and sustaining manifested forms.

Just take a look at human history. It has always been an idea—a passionate, timely, innovative, rigorous, lofty, or even shattering idea—that has changed things. In the fifteenth century, Gutenberg came upon an idea. He unveiled to Europe the printing press, one of the most significant of all human inventions. It opened up an ever-increasing flow of ideas into human awareness. It anchored the Renaissance, enlarged the Reformation, and introduced the era of mass communication. It uplifted the masses, tested and sometimes toppled those in political or religious power, and, in short, altered the entire landscape of Western society. All from an idea allowed to take form. Add to this the realization that every other invention or movement that has advanced human life began in this very same way . . . as an idea.

Survey your personal history as honestly as you can. You will no doubt be able to see the impact of pivotal ideas at the openings to your various passages or chapters. It is almost always a radical or resisted idea that initiates the most profound healings and leaps forward. The defining moments in most people's lives have been extensions of ideas whose time had come.

Grasping the impact of an idea upon experience can sometimes move us into a bit of smugness. "Look at what *my* idea produced!" or "*We* came up with an incredible idea!" As wonderful as it is to acknowledge the power of an idea, it's even more important to recognize the source of transformative ideas. Ralph Waldo Emerson puts this so clearly and powerfully:

> We lie in the lap of immense intelligence, which makes us receivers of its truth and organs of its activity. When we discern justice, when we discern truth, we do nothing of ourselves, but allow a passage to its beams.

This is a humbling clarification but one that is equally exhilarating and empowering. We don't create or author higher ideas. Each of us is a unique center of awareness within Divine Mind capable of embracing and championing the ideas to which we become receptive. As we make welcome higher ideas, we are equipped to put our unique, personal spin on them, yet they flow to us from that "immense intelligence" at the heart of this universe. As individualized expressions of Spirit, of Love/Intelligence, each of us lives within an infinite ocean of possibility. At any moment, we can open to, receive, and cultivate a transformative idea beyond anything we have ever realized before.

Let's return to the Bible quotes from the start of this chapter. The first states that faith is substance, the evidence of things not yet seen. Many people are confused about faith, having been taught that faith is an unusual or unlikely strength of believing; that some have it, many don't. Nothing could be further from truth. Faith is a state of consciousness we all can master. It is stated so clearly: "God has given to every man the measure of faith" (Romans 12:3). Faith is the elevation of an idea to the level of total conviction. Faith emerges when an idea is activated then embraced and embodied. Put another way, our role is to take an idea into our hearts and then move it from conjecture or possibility into ownership and complete believing. And when you have done this, the second quote tells the rest of the story . . . "so be it done unto you!"

This is one of the greatest spiritual principles of the ages: an idea at the level of faith is substance. Early writers in the field of New Thought, progressive spirituality, frequently wrote of this spiritual Substance as a precursor to matter. When an idea is taken to the level of faith, it becomes Substance for the form inherent within it. It moves out of possibility and takes on its quantum birthright. I like to put it simply: empowered thought "thickens" into things. It is an awe-inspiring opening to know that an idea is Substance that, through a Power greater than we are, can become form, matter, or experience.

The creative process in the universe, and in the individual, is a progressive movement of ideas into form. Any aspect of creation is an idea in a material or worldly state of itself. Take the example of water, H_2O. Your initial image of water may be of that fluid you frequently drink, or that you enjoy as it flows in a river or lake. But this is only one of the modes of expression of this life-giving substance. It also has a mostly invisible state, which we experience as humidity or feel as steam rising during boiling. Cool down the process, and the fluid state emerges, and you can pour this liquid into any container or mold. Cool it still more, and it becomes a solid that maintains the shape of the mold you provided it . . . until eventually the process returns H_2O to its invisible state. This is how an idea moves into expression: it begins as a pure possibility (like humidity or steam); then when it is declared or owned, it becomes fluidlike . . . spiritual substance that can take any shape our creative intentions assign to it; then through the crowning step of full conviction or faith, it becomes a tangible, observable form or experience in the world (as in the temporarily solid ice). One phenomenon in three states of itself—idea as possibility, idea as substance, and idea as form or experience.

The entire cosmos is a testament to this creative process. Every thing, every form, was first an idea that became substantial and eventually a thing. In the metaphor of the Genesis creation story, it suggests that God brought forth various levels of creation by first activating and proclaiming the idea: "And God said, 'Let there be . . .'" such and such; then it says "and there was" such and such; and "it was good, and very good." The phrase "Let there be" suggests the activating or empowering of the idea. Then the thing itself emerges and in an impeccable form, for it all was "good, and very good." How could a divinely inspired creation be otherwise! All creation has an impeccable idea and a divine goodness at its center—and this includes you and me.

I've always loved the story of the three baseball umpires. They were having lunch together and talking about their beloved craft. At one point, one of them proclaims, "There are balls and there are strikes . . . and I calls 'em as I sees 'em!" Hearing this, the second man disagrees: "There are balls and there are strikes . . . and I calls 'em as they are!" But then the third ump ends the conversation by declaring: "There are balls and there are strikes . . . but they ain't nothin' 'til I calls 'em!" Everything takes on what our ideas declare them to be. It's always our call. In the wisdom of the quote from quantum theorist Max Planck at the beginning of this chapter, "When you change the way you look at things, the things you look at change."

We become artisans within this creative process by entering back into the truth that the world is consciousness and that we are beings of Light and, with this God-awareness, "all things are possible." Then, buoyed by this Truth, our next step is to "energize and normalize" a new idea. We have to work with the idea until it's a natural, acceptable, and believable inner reality, instead of merely a "wish and a hope." Ideas have varying degrees of conviction energy behind them. A new idea may seem really attractive, and we may have some degree of conviction about it; but that doesn't mean that we have fully embraced it and elevated it to a place of conviction and believing. As the man with the epileptic son admitted to Jesus, "Lord, I believe; help Thou my unbelief" (Mark 9:24).

We move an idea up the ladder of greater believing by taking it to the core of ourselves and actually becoming it. There are two suggested practices at the conclusion of this chapter to support this process: Affirmative Prayer and Inspired Visualization. These serve the very important function of moving the idea to a place of *feeling*. The creative process responds to what we *feel* is true and real now . . . not just what we think is true. It is not done unto us as we think, wish, hope, fantasize, or complain. *It is done unto us as we believe . . . and believing is knowing and feeling that it is so.* We must feel that the idea is not only possible, it is real now; it is who we are now; it is done . . . right now! It helps to remember that everything is "twice-created": first, as a clear idea anchored in faith; then, secondly, as a manifested form or experience. First creation is part of our spiritual job description, and this is not completed until the idea is fully established in conviction and feeling as a spiritual prototype, an idea-seed that is now Substance of things intended and evidence of things not yet seen (but on their way into form).

What is not part of our spiritual job description in this creative process is trying to make the end result happen or stipulating the means by which it must happen. Instead, we create clarity of faith through feeling. This moves the idea from head to heart, where it becomes deeply rooted into our very being. Then we turn it over to a Power greater than we are. This Power—sometimes called The Law of Mind, or simply the Law—does the work of secondary creation. This everywhere-present Power is all-intelligent and fully equipped to accomplish anything. It is the same Power that has formed the manifest universe according to the blueprints of Divine Ideas. It knows how to accomplish in the highest and best ways. How comforting to know that within an idea of Substance is the Intelligent Power that will bring it into form. A great English metaphysician, Thomas Troward (1847–1916), wrote, "Having seen and felt the end you have willed the means to the realization of the end."

The ways and means to the realization of the end are automatically assured when our idea is anchored in faith as Substance.

We can also work with this opening from another angle. Every current experience has at its center some core idea that was its genesis.

When experiencing something undesirable, it is most typical to feel guilty for it, and then to seek change by attacking the situation or condition. We move into a higher degree of life mastery when we choose the more powerful approach of working at the causal level. If a believed idea was the starting point of the unwanted situation, then that idea can be neutralized and replaced by an idea of greater quality. It has been said that what thought has done, thought can undo. In the process of recognizing the faulty or worn-out ideas that need changing, there's no need to heap guilt upon oneself. Ernest Holmes reminds us that "Honest self-assessment is the first step in healing." It is an act of great self-love to recognize honestly and compassionately our own misguided or ineffective ideas or perceptions . . . and then to revise or replace them.

The formation of our life experiences is usually a subtle process. Sometimes it's evident that an individual had an obvious role in creating or inviting an experience into his life. At the most fundamental level, the seed and substance for such an experience was some core idea. For instance, there is a particular core idea that creates enormous havoc and can attract a huge array of difficult or painful experiences into a person's life, often without his conscious awareness; *it is the deeply ingrained idea of inadequacy or unworthiness*. So much pain and disruption can be traced back to this erroneous core idea. Because of this, it is always a good idea to focus on building up spiritual self-love.

Sometimes, however, it's not clear how one's internal processes could have given rise to an experience. Perhaps it was a subconscious thought process that simply made the person available or susceptible to the experience. Other experiences seem to barge into our lives largely as a result of the choices and actions of others. Whatever the case, remember this: we are most masterful when we seize the reins of the creative process and craft the most life-giving, growth-supporting responses. It is far more masterful to do something powerful with an experience than it is to analyze how it came into your life.

One of the greatest growth paths is to take responsibility for the quality of awareness, for the ideas that are being empowered. For many, their inner thought life is unexamined and undisciplined . . . until the choice is made to embrace a higher mastery in life. Indeed, this is one of the great gifts we've all been given: choice. We are constantly choosing how to perceive and interpret experiences, how to react or respond, and what ideas will be established as "our truth." All we have to do is take stock of the results that follow these choices. We can opt for self-pity, self-loathing, victimhood—the kinds of inner choices that actually call more pain and difficulty into our lives—or we can carefully and dynamically choose in different, more effective ways such as inspired intentions, self-love, and compassionate responsibility.

Always remember that you are in charge of your consciousness and that you are a being of Light. Even if you have spent many years filling your mind with self-limiting rubbish, remember that you are not your thoughts, even though you have given them power. You are the one who can step back into the observer mode—I call this the "wise witness" state—and assess these thoughts as they automatically crop up out of sheer habit. You can learn to "be still, and know that I am God" (Psalm 46:10) . . . meaning, in your stillness to know the I Am of you that is God-Life. Then when you have stilled the "gerbil wheel" of your mind and soaked in the reality of your Being, you can summon higher awareness and initiate new, powerful, enlightened ideas. You can give yourself to them, taking them from head to heart, integrating them fully into the conscious and subconscious dimensions of your mind. You can move into your world living in new ways that are totally congruent and in alignment with these higher ideas. You will have become masterful and a person of faith . . . one who continually transmutes the lower into the higher. It is this reservoir of higher consciousness that will sustain you through life's changes and challenges while also inspiring those around you who have "ears to hear and eyes to see" (Proverbs 20:12).

In his *Long Walk to Freedom*, the late, great Nelson Mandela shared a heart-stirring example of the journey of an idea from impossibility, to possibility, to substance, and then into form. As a great leader who dissolved the apartheid system in South Africa, Mandela was sentenced in 1964 to life in prison with hard labor. When apartheid began to break down, however, his sentence was remanded—after more than twenty-six years of labor, incarceration, and separation from his family!

Regarding that time, he said, "I learned to work with my mind. In the mind is the great freedom. In the mind is the great prison." And he explained the process he developed: "I had to move from 'It's not happening' to 'It can happen,' and take 'It can happen' to 'It will happen.' And when I got to the place of beginning to think 'It will happen, it will happen; I just don't know how, but it will happen,' I moved to a place of 'It IS happening. It's happening through this. It is happening right now!'"

This inner process had to be key to Mandela's survival and to the progress of his movement! Notice the progression of the idea: Great ideas usually show up as ideas that are outrageous and improbable—if not "impossible." These ideas wait for someone to claim them anyway. This is usually a bold act of total heart . . . the love of a higher ideal becoming irresistible. Nelson Mandela was convinced in his heart that equality for all South Africans was an idea whose time had come. How else could he have risked his life, how else could he have endured more than a quarter century of agonizing imprisonment?

Once an idea is conceived, the "long walk" begins. At the beginning, most of us find ourselves struggling with "It's not happening." The obstacles seem too enormous, the idea too radical, our efforts too meager. This is a critical point. Many simply give up, and the idea goes back in waiting for its next pioneer. The essential next step for any idea-possibility is for it to evolve into "It can happen." We get to this point by putting aside any and all concerns about *how* it can happen. We simply have to commune with the beauty of the idea along with its ripeness, the seeming yearning of the universe to birth it, not later but right now. It needs us to continue to love the idea and simply accept that "it can happen," admittedly in ways beyond our understanding. Mandela had to get to this point, and by arriving here he began to gain momentum.

It's a great step to unequivocally believe that a great idea *can* happen. By further developing our consciousness, the next step is available: "It will happen!" Once again, to get to this place, we must not look to worldly circumstances to confirm or prove this. We have to commune with the Life Force within the idea . . . sense the evolutionary impulse that calls it into being, and practice *knowing* that it will happen regardless of current situations or events. In fact, contradictory situations or events can actually hasten the actualization of a timely idea. So we must not become discouraged by "what is or seems to be." We must remain compelled and impelled by "what can be."

The full flowering of empowered consciousness occurs when the idea-seed is energized by the realization "It *is* happening." Anytime you anchor an idea in total and passionate acceptance, then it *is* happening . . . first, as it gestates and gains momentum in consciousness—individually or collectively—and finally, when it reaches its tipping point and breaks forth into full manifestation in the world of form and experience. Though Mandela was physically imprisoned for twenty-six years, I believe that he first became free when he reached the crowning realization "It *is* happening." It would only be a matter of time before he was freed from prison and apartheid would finally crumble.

Some ideas are the limited projections of the human shadow—the unawakened self, the fearful ego. These ideas have no ultimate staying power; they are destined to reveal their inherent flaws and be swept away into the backwash of progress. When an idea has no power of Truth within it, it is certain to crumble and give way to a greater revelation of the Love and Light of Source. The greatest obstacle to the progress of humankind is an attachment to obsolete or heartless ideas, belief systems, and practices. What may have been expedient, popular, or comfortable for a time must inevitably yield to possibilities and ideas of a higher and more life-giving order. The good news is that "we lie in the lap" of the Source of the most powerful ideas we could ever require. All we have to do is to throw ourselves open in total acceptance, admitting that we really don't know what is next or what is best. In this childlike vulnerability we are then ready to ask . . . open . . . and receive.

In Supporting Personal Growth, the Question Is Not Just "What No Longer Works Well in My Life?" There Are Even More Powerful Questions:

- *What in my experience no longer represents the Truth of my Spiritual Nature or the mandates of my heart?*

- *What is the Spirit-Inspired possibility for my life that a part of me is afraid to comprehend?*

- *What would I be doing if money and know-how were not issues?*

- *Lying in the lap of God's "immense intelligence," what next step seeks to be conceived in my awareness and incubated in my heart?*

Ask these questions . . . and listen. Your greater experience and higher Good are but an idea away—a Spirit-led idea.

Throughout his writings, Thomas Troward suggests that the immense array of life-forms on this planet exist for the purpose of providing increasingly effective and dynamic outlets for the intelligence and livingness of God, the all-originating Spirit. What a privilege it is for human beings to provide the One Life, the Spirit, with such magnificent opportunities for divine expression. It says in Genesis that God made man and woman in "the image and likeness of God." I believe this would be more accurately translated, "made in the image and nature of God." May each of us step more fully into our divine nature and cocreate with the all-originating Spirit ever more glorious revelations of the divine Imagination. We are equipped to do this when we clearly realize that This Idea Is Substance! This opens us to the full miracle of who we are within the panorama of creation. I saw a poster with an inscription that touched my heart: "If you don't believe in miracles . . . perhaps you've forgotten you are one!"

– The Experience –

A New Sidewalk

Years ago I was told about a fascinating article published in a major newspaper. It interviewed a man well advanced in age. He'd been living in the same little house in that city for many decades. He told the reporter that one day he stood out on his front porch and surveyed his humble property. He became troubled by the condition of the sidewalks running both along the street in front of his house and the one extending up to his porch. The concrete was crumbling badly and weeds were growing through the cracks. He realized that these walkways were a significant hazard. So the man did a prayer right on the spot. He talked to God as though God were a good buddy standing right next to him. He conveyed the situation to God, asserted that it was high time for there to be new sidewalks, and that this was surely no big deal for God. After all, "with God all things are possible" and "It is the Father's good pleasure to give you the kingdom." He finished his prayer, declaring that it was a done deal.

Then he went back into the house and called his children. He arranged for his sons and some of his grandchildren to break up all the concrete and haul it away. Then he had them smooth out the ground that remained. Next they bought some two-by-fours and laid these eight-foot lengths of wood end-to-end along the outline of the walks, secured by stakes pounded into the ground. Thus they had created the forms. When all this was finished, the man had another talk with God, confirming that he had done his part, now God was to do the rest.

About a week later, a cement truck came barreling down that man's street. The driver needed to turn right at the street corner next to this man's house. But the driver was going so fast that in trying to make the turn he turned the truck over on its side instead. It would be a while before cranes could right the truck, so it became crucial to off-load the cement before it hardened inside the truck's big barrel. Our homeowner simply and happily told the driver that he could just deposit that cement right where he had prepared for it . . . and by the end of the day, the man had his new sidewalks.

An idea becomes substance when we have embraced it so completely that we have created "the form" in Mind. The universe will pour in the Substance to fill the mold we create in Mind.

An Expensive Rejection

A young clerk who worked for a hardware store many years ago got a wild idea to get rid of some excess inventory by putting up a table in the middle of the store to sell off a few of the oldest items. Everything was priced at ten cents. The sale was a success, and the store owners did it several more times.

The young clerk then had another idea: to open an entire store that would sell only nickel and dime items. His boss scoffed at the idea, said it'd never work. The young man went ahead with his idea and was enormously successful in his day. Later, that boss lamented: "As nearly as I can figure out, every word I used in turning Woolworth down cost me a million dollars!"

Beware of letting current mind-sets destroy new possibilities. Remember, most good, new ideas seem outrageous and unlikely at first. Make sure to give ideas some breathing room before discarding them. Some years ago in meetings with my staff, we established a rule made popular by Dr. Phil McGraw: *Every idea is a good idea for at least fifteen minutes.* So for at least fifteen minutes we had to consider and protect a radical new idea before allowing it to be assaulted by the many considerations and reasons "why not." Because of this practice, I sense that we saved many good ideas from an early demise.

We do not suffer from a lack of ideas.

We suffer only from a lack of imagination and receptivity.

– The Expression –

As avenues for moving an idea to the level of Substance, I offer two essential and powerful practices. Both are grounded in the wisdom of Richard Bach as expressed in his classic book, *Jonathan Livingston Seagull*:

*"You must begin by knowing
you've already arrived!"*

1. Affirmative Prayer

Many people carry lots of old baggage about prayer . . . that it is pleading, begging, demanding, arguing, bargaining, bribing . . . and that it is unlikely to produce any results unless they are "miracles." Many turn to prayer only when things are most bleak—911 prayer, I call it— and would honestly admit that they've experienced few results from their prayer life. This is not because prayer is ineffective but because, as Jesus declared, "You pray and receive not, because you pray amiss." For these, an entirely different approach to prayer beckons.

True prayer is meant to be a vital process that transforms the consciousness of the one praying. It is *not* something we try to do to God or to a problem or need. It is a spiritual shift we cultivate entirely within ourselves. Remember the seeker in the cave. He frustrated himself by attacking the cave in search of an opening. Having exhausted these efforts, he surrendered and discovered that the greatest opening was within him . . . a Light in his Heart. Realizing this, he began to expand and transcend. This is exactly what prayer can do for us: it brings us to the point of real Power . . . the capacity of consciousness to realize Truth and to expand into unlimited dimensions of awareness and livingness. This is "seeking first the kingdom"—which is within us all—and everything else is then added unto us. The all-powerful Law produces new results along the lines of the new acceptance in consciousness that becomes established within us.

In true prayer, we stop forcing or trying to make things happen. *Prayer is meditating upon and feeling higher Truths . . .* Truths that move us out of fear and into the Love, Wholeness, and Givingness of the Divine. The purpose of prayer is to awaken inwardly to the Presence and Power of God so that our consciousness can become empowered to accept the Good of God already given to us. This does not require immense skill or effort. Prayer calls for clarity, willingness, and heart. It is giving ourselves fully to a higher perspective of Life, orienting our awareness to the Power and Reality of Truth. Doing this opens us to unlimited blessings in both our inner and outer lives.

There are several stages or phases to Affirmative Prayer that have been articulated in many ways . . . but let's keep it simple. Here's an easy way to remember the steps and move through the basic process using G. I. F. T. as an acronym.

AFFIRMATIVE PRAYER IS A G.I.F.T.

To begin: Take several deep breaths . . . begin releasing fear, confusion, and turmoil . . . and move to the quiet center of your awareness.

Step #1: God-Consciousness . . . "God Is"

Bring into your awareness the realization that This Instant Is Love . . . and realize that God, Infinite Love/Intelligence, is all there is. Everything is an expression of the Life Divine, and everyone derives his or her life and being from this ultimate One Life. Move your awareness from a surface sense of separation into an inner realization of unity. *Feel this Divine Reality in and all around you.* Know that this Reality is all Love, Light, Possibility, Power, Wholeness, Beauty, Joy, and Peace. Bask in this sense of the mighty Presence of the Living Spirit: "There is only one Life, Power, Presence . . . God, the Living Spirit. This Life Divine is perfect and whole. God-Life is all there is, the only Reality." Stay with this step until you are experiencing and feeling its peace and empowerment.

Step #2: Identification . . . "I Am"

From the foundation of the first step, intensify your realization of the Truth of your Being: "I and my Source are One. I am Pure Spirit. The 'I Am' of me is the Wholeness, Completeness, Love and Light of God." Feel a depth and peace within you, an integrity of being, and claim this fully. Know that you are, now and always, a spiritual Being. Realize that nothing in the world of conditions, circumstances, or effects can alter your eternal Truth of Being. Imagine seeing yourself in a mirror and proclaiming, "This Being is Light!" Sense the Light of Spirit that you are, and accept that this Light is radiating into your body and into the body of your life experiences. Know that nothing in or of the world can diminish the Truth of you . . . that you are a child of the Infinite and Holy One. *Feel all of this . . .* as Love, Wholeness, Peace, and Joy.

Step #3: Formulation

In the beauty, peace, and power of the first two steps, you are now ready to formulate clear ideas of your accepted Good. As you will learn in the chapter on Desire, we do not pray *for* them but *from* them. Craft a clear concept of your ideal experience, remembering that before you ask, "It is already given." Establish the clear idea of your Good and affirm that it is yours *now*. In the Mind of God, it *is* yours now. "I am guided . . . prospered . . . healed and uplifted . . . inspired and fully blessed." You are crystallizing the higher idea-seed and bringing yourself to a full acceptance of it in this powerful moment of prayer. You are not asking God for it; it is already "the Father's good pleasure to give you the kingdom." Instead, you are accepting and anchoring an idea as Substance. Make sure this idea is based on the overall good you seek and the clear experience you are accepting. Avoid specifying how your idea is to come into form, and make sure that you always are willing to accept "that . . . or something better." Accept your highest and best in the focus area of your prayer, remembering that Infinite Mind has options, along with ways and means, more vast and perfect than we can understand.

Step #4: Thanks . . . and Take Over!

Having owned your idea as Substance in the high consciousness of your prayer, it is now time to celebrate this creative process and turn the prayer over to the infinite Power of the all-creative Law. This is the manifesting Power that executes and forms the Word of Spirit. It is the Power that operates upon Ideas of Substance and establishes them in form and experience. So at this point, we are giving thanks and releasing the prayer into a Creative Process that is unlimited in its Intelligence and Power: "In full faith and acceptance, I now turn this prayer over to the wonder-working Power of God, knowing that it is done unto me as I believe . . . and all is well. I am so grateful for this Truth that is made manifest for the highest and best in my life and in the lives of all involved."

"And so it is!"

As you practice this pathway of prayer, it will become more and more natural to you. Always remember that it is not the words that matter as much as the *feeling* tone you establish . . . the consciousness that all is well and your Good is established. It is bringing yourself to the state of full believing. You should leave a prayer time feeling profoundly peaceful, joyful, and assured. Know that as a part of the perfect activity of the Law, you will be guided in all your ways . . . what to say and do, whom to meet, how to proceed. Enter into affirmative prayer every day as a way to keep your awareness on course and to continue deepening your acceptance. And enjoy the "gift" that is affirmative prayer!

G: "God Is"

I: "I Am"

F: Formulation

T: Thanks . . . and Take Over!

2. Inspired Visualization

Another very effective tool of consciousness development is Inspired Visualization. This can be utilized separately or within the formulation step of affirmative prayer.

Becoming very still, release all stresses or concerns. Then visualize or imagine yourself in the full accomplishment of your higher ideal, your desired state. Make this imagery vivid in every way: sounds, colors, smells. Hear what you would hear, see what you would see, say what you would say, sense all that you would sense . . . in the full experience of your goal. Moreover, *feel* what you would be feeling in the full attainment of your ideal.

As you immerse yourself in this visualization fully and with great feeling, imagine also that accompanying you in this experience is a being of Light. This Being may be one you're aware of—an enlightened master you admire—or this Being may have no particular identity that is familiar to you. Know that this Being is of the highest consciousness . . . all Wisdom and Love. As you move about in the powerful scene of your accepted Good, sense that this Being is walking alongside you . . . imparting wisdom, reassurance, insights, greater and greater clarity. Sense that this Being is championing you and evolving your awareness and personal power. Cherish this sense of spiritual partnership and glean the wisdom and assurance that flows forth. When it feels complete, gratefully release the visualization, knowing that this kind of inspiration is always available.

Remain in this visualization for a significant period of time . . . enough time to deeply anchor the experience of "believing and having" . . . of looking and praying *from* the desired experience. The inner reality you are creating will become actuality in your body and in your experience. Substance shall be made manifest.

5. THIS RELATIONSHIP IS ONENESS

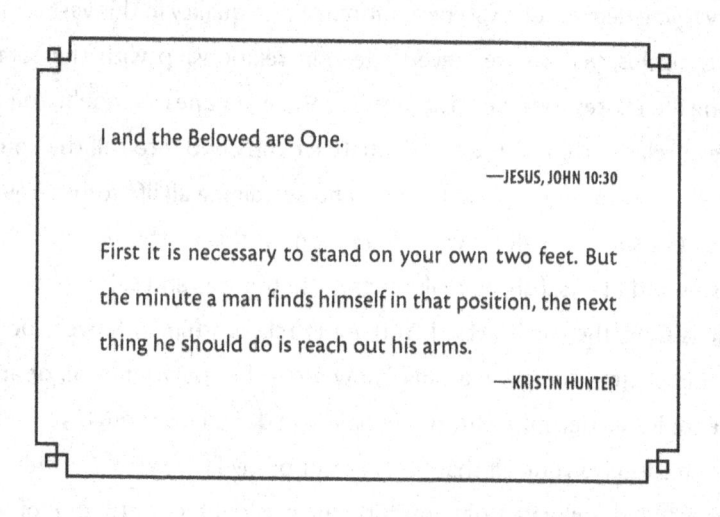

I and the Beloved are One.

—JESUS, JOHN 10:30

First it is necessary to stand on your own two feet. But the minute a man finds himself in that position, the next thing he should do is reach out his arms.

—KRISTIN HUNTER

– The Essence –

It seems to me that to be alive in this world is to have said "Yes" at the soul level to advanced placement studies in an upper-level curriculum titled "Growth and Becoming Through Relationships." It is an intriguing program of study, though seldom an easy one, and these classes are never electives; they're always required. Just when you think you've finally completed most of the courses in this curriculum, another is introduced that's more demanding than ever. This is because the areas and opportunities for applying the wisdom gained are just about endless. So, since there's always higher-level work to be done, who knows if we'll ever finally graduate. This is definitely the aspect of life and mastery where we are all lifelong learners!

Though we'll never finish these studies, there are some key realizations flowing through every "relationship/course" we register for in this program. The first principle that eventually becomes apparent is that we are all in relationship with everyone and everything—no exceptions. There are varying degrees of awareness, intimacy, and quality in this vast array of relationships, yet we are, nevertheless, in relationship with the totality of the life expressions we encounter . . . and even ones we don't. You and I are in relationship with God, or whatever you choose to call the Source, Love, Energy, or Intelligence birthing and sustaining all life-forms. You are in relationship with all aspects of creation on this earth: the birds, trees, grasses and plants, fish, animals, bugs . . . all the seas and substances . . . as well as Gaia, the earth herself. You are in relationship with every person on this planet, though you only know a small population well, or at all. You are in relationship with the people you don't like, though you might want to deceive yourself that "they're out of my life." What you still have is a troubled, unhealed relationship, but it is definitely still one of your relationships. You are in relationship with the entire cosmos, known and not yet known. Hopefully you know that you are also in relationship with all the facets and dimensions of yourself. Realizing all this, it's no wonder there's no end to the studies.

The next principle that eventually surfaces is that a relationship works best when we are conscious of it and available to it. We are responsible for the quality of each and every one of our relationships. It's fairly common to be blissfully unaware of certain relationships. Sometimes we just neglect them or take them for granted and, in many instances, we opt to distance ourselves or deny some slice of our relationship pie. However, relationships need tending, and if we deny our relatedness to anyone or anything, that particular relationship will, in one way or another, grab our attention eventually by becoming some sort of limitation or problem.

Now here's one of the more challenging relationship principles to embrace: every relationship with another is actually designed to teach you about yourself. That's why all our relationships are essential and unavoidable. They are all in service to our growth and becoming. In fact, we could not know ourselves at all if it weren't for relationships. Imagine that you were the only one in the entire universe. You wouldn't be able to know yourself more completely—or at all—because there would be no one and nothing to reflect you back to yourself. It's true that we contribute our uniqueness and gifts to others in the orbit of our close personal relationships. But the fuller truth is that our gifts to them are still an experience of themselves that they are having. (You might want to keep that in mind the next time you're shopping for that expensive gift!) Bottom line: our relationships are essential to knowing and growing ourselves.

However, the paramount relationship realization is . . . This Relationship Is Oneness. Though every one and all things seem unique, different, and "not us," the deeper reality is that we are all of the One . . . we are all expressing the same ultimate, universal Life, or Spirit. All life-forms are the One Life, God-Life, expressing as that being or that thing. This means that the unimaginable variety and multiplicity of creation is joined at the deepest level in an eternal, indestructible Oneness.

We are all one, *and* we are also unique and essential expressions of the One. Unity does not mandate uniformity. The incredible wonder in this is that the One Infinite Creative Life can express in such innumerable and glorious ways, and we are privileged to open our minds and hearts to the magnificent array of Life's celebration of Itself! This brings us to a crucial opening into life mastery: the high practice of celebrating uniqueness while, at the same time, honoring Oneness.

Ken Wilber, one of the world's best thinkers in the areas of consciousness, new science, and transpersonal psychology, wrote, among many milestone books, one that I feel is especially relevant and important: *No Boundary: Eastern and Western Approaches to Personal Growth*. In it he points out that the apparently solid boundaries we believe in and live by are actually invented . . . produced by our skewed vision:

> *The ultimate metaphysical secret, if we dare state it so simply, is that there are no boundaries in the universe. Boundaries are illusions, products not of reality but of the way we map and edit reality. And while it is fine to map out the territory, it is fatal to confuse the two. . . . All of the battles in our experience— our conflicts, anxieties, sufferings and despairs—are created by the "boundaries" we misguidedly throw around our experience. Each boundary we construct in our experience results in a limitation of our consciousness—a fragmentation, a conflict, a battle.*

Now considering his words, we don't have to look too hard or far to see the damage caused when we worship false and limiting boundaries. These invented boundaries are barriers that produce separation, isolation, and the basis for shallow understanding and a lack of compassion. In fact, a belief in some boundary causes us to make two very destructive assumptions: first, that whatever is outside the boundary is "not me/us," and, second, whatever is on the other side of the boundary "doesn't really matter."

The most basic "boundary illusion" is that we are separated selves, and this is why many people assume that everyone and everything outside the boundary of their concept of self is "not me" . . . and usually "doesn't really matter."

Our lives and our world suffer immensely from the illusions of boundaries. This is why it is so important to anchor the breakthrough realization that This Relationship Is Oneness. Spiritual vision is restored . . . the capacity to recognize that everything and everyone are part of the universal Love/Intelligence, the One Life. Thus, we are all *one* . . . all woven together at the deepest level . . . all aspects of God, the divine Spirit. Wilber speaks to this healing perspective: "In unity consciousness, in no-boundary awareness, the sense of self expands to totally include everything once thought to be 'not self.' Growth fundamentally means an enlarging and expanding of one's horizons, a growth of one's boundaries, outwardly in perspective and inwardly in depth."

Eventually we grow to realize that the real world is a universe of no boundaries, of absolute oneness . . . everything interconnected and interdependent. In Buddhism, this is the teaching of "dependent arising" . . . everything arising in life dependent upon everything else with nothing existing in pure autonomy or isolation. Or as the poem and song goes, "No man is an island, No man stands alone!" We find ourselves out of balance when we live as though we're cut off from the whole. Perhaps, if you boil it all down, we don't have a violence problem, a hunger crisis, or environmental breakdowns. All of these are symptoms of the real problem: most of humanity remains asleep to the essential Oneness of all Life!

Ernest Holmes writes that all of humankind's suffering ultimately stems from our entrapment in "the illusion of separation." At the dawning of human awareness, we remembered our shared life with one another and with nature. The indigenous ones still do. As consciousness explored and developed, humans banded together in tribes for better survival. This helped secure early humans for a time, but eventually our awareness began to explore its basis and possibilities within individuality. From one perspective this was inevitable and necessary to the unfolding of consciousness. However, challenges would arise as we began to judge by appearances, agreeing with the reports of the senses that as individuals we seemed to be alone and different in a world of many separate life-forms.

From this limited perception, fear at the personal level increased and spread with viral intensity. The sense of separate selfhood soon morphed into the fearful ego that would magnify the apparent threats and find reasons to wall off the individual from life and others. Much of humanity's early savagery was the result of this raw ego gone amok. Even as human awareness has taken leaps of evolutionary growth beyond this, the egoic sense of separation remains active at deep levels. Though more sophisticated and hopefully more controlled, the ego continues to take on a convenient sense of inferiority and work to defend against risks, embarrassment, intimacy, and, ultimately, love . . . embracing just about any form of protection that would block us from our fellow pilgrims and further ensure personal safety.

The fearful and unsupervised ego is an archaic aspect of our awareness that, all too often, is allowed to find new means to impair us, individually and collectively. The fearful ego finds it difficult to share and threatening to contribute to the well-being of others. The fearful ego feels disenfranchised and estranged, which makes others seem even more dangerous, especially if they are different in one way or another. The fearful ego is often deeply pained and angry. It values benefits for the present over caring for future generations. The fearful ego often opts to lash out or run away, rather than to bond together and cooperate. The fearful ego loves conditionally and only under controlled circumstances with carefully selected others. Magnify these dynamics globally over the centuries and it's no wonder there are so many grievous problems facing humankind.

Each of us fills the roles of both teacher and student. We offer one another great gifts and opportunities for personal awakening. This is especially true in the most difficult relationships, the most painful and apparently divisive ones. These relationships are our greatest teachers! Who would qualify in this capacity in your life right now? Have you realized that the people in your life are not there by accident? Most of the people in our lives we draw in, whether we realize it or not. They arrive to share and evolve with us in a growth journey of one kind or another. Our problem is that we often deflect the lessons offered us by lapsing into the delusion that the challenge is mostly with the other person—not ourselves. Now, the other person surely has a role and responsibility in the state of the relationship and their own lessons to learn. However, we grow most powerfully and masterfully when we readily explore and integrate the realizations and insights about ourselves that the turmoil reflects back to us. There is something there about ourselves to see, own, and transform. Our job is not to change others to our satisfaction or to run their lives. Our main job is to evolve ourselves . . . and to remember that the other person is, still and always, our brother or sister.

I love the story of the cat that was stalking a mother mouse and her five offspring as they went on their morning hunt for food. Like a good cat, it had them all cornered and was about to pounce as the five little mice cowered behind their mother. Then, most unexpectedly, the mother mouse began to bark loudly like a dog. This so shocked the cat that it became frightened, turned tail, and ran away as fast as it could. With that, the mother mouse turned to the little mice and said, matter-of-factly, "Now children, you can see the power in knowing a second language!"

Humanity is being called to learn a second language . . . Oneness. It is a universal, deep-seated language, and we need to practice it no matter what our primary language. Our greatest relationship lesson is to proclaim our shared essence even when we're hurt or afraid . . . and to become masterful at both celebrating uniqueness and honoring Oneness. When we realize that we are so much more than separate organisms, that we are actually Beings of Light, each of us radiating a unique expression of the universal Light, we gain access again to our Source of true Power. All other means of forcing and manipulating pale in comparison to this true Power.

There is an affirmation I love that I offer to students in many of my classes: "Deeply we are One." To use this as a moment-by-moment mantra is enormously powerful. It brings us out of the trance state of separation. Even declaring it silently has the power to open the heart and shift inter-actions. One student reported back that her boss, whom she would pre-viously have described as caustic, cold, and unsupportive, softened before her eyes and listened openly to her suggestion and request as she simply and silently kept giving her awareness and heart to that high truth, "Deeply we are One!"

It is invigorating to carry this same mantra into nature. Much of hu-manity sees nature as inanimate, inferior, and separate from human life. This mind-set has promoted a terrible indifference to the earth and its untold life-forms. The mounting ecological crisis is the rude awakening we have set up for our species as a mirror of this toxic relationship with the earth. We can begin at the individual level to promote healing. In addition to your personal steps of more environmentally sound living, take that mantra, "Deeply we are One," into nature and open yourself to Life Energy dancing in and through the trees, the rocks, the flowers, and creatures. This will renew you at depth as you commune with the Life Essence in everything . . . and also in yourself.

A rabbi asked his pupils, "How can you tell when night has ended and the day has begun?" Many answers came forth. One student replied, "It is when you can see an animal in the distance and tell whether it's a sheep or a dog." Another declared, "It is when you can look at a tree in the distance and tell whether it's a fig or a peach tree." More answers like this followed, until the rabbi held up his hand for silence and said to his beloved pupils: "None of you are correct. It is when you can look upon the face of anyone and see that they are your brother or sister. If you cannot see this, it is still night."

The good news is that we don't have to continue to dwell in darkness or learn our lessons exclusively by means of pain, divisiveness, struggle, and crisis. We can allow Oneness to guide and grow us. First let us attune to our Oneness with God, with the all-originating Spirit. From this place of inspiration, we can open our hearts to others and to all of life, experiencing our Oneness through unconditional Love. Then we shall be equipped to heal the wounds among the people in our lives and those inflicted upon the earth. This practice of realized Oneness will lift us to a greater spiritual mastery and restore us to our destiny to be peacemakers and beneficial presences. We will discover the power of compassion to bridge all divisions, and we will enter into the realization that we are all much more alike than we are different.

When she was sixteen years old, a high school student named Amy Maddox wrote a poem titled "Underneath, We're All the Same." In it, she itemized the many ways another person could seem different from her . . . their religion, food, language, clothes, and skin color. However, her concluding line brings us all back to the essential ways we are the same, the deeper elements of our Oneness:

> But when he laughed, it was how I laughed . . . and when he cried, it was how I cried.

Everywhere you go . . . and in all your interactions, I invite you into the courage and mastery that remembers: This Relationship is Oneness!

– The Experience –

Some experiences to shine more light on our Oneness:

Ditch Digging!

After finishing my undergraduate studies in psychology and religion, I knew I had to earn some serious money to take the next step. I had paid my personal and living expenses over the previous four years of college by playing tenor banjo four nights a week as part of a Dixieland/ragtime duo at a Shakey's Pizza Parlor. But I needed to earn far more to be able to relocate to California for ministerial training. So I took a job with a plumbing company that was part of building officers' housing at a local military air base. I had no idea what I was getting into. On my first day, I was told that I would spend my time in the trenches being dug by backhoes. I would be smoothing out these trenches so that they could receive the sewer pipes that led up to each residence under construction. Now, I'd never done manual labor at this level of intensity. I'd delivered furniture for a furniture store, worked at a foundry organizing and delivering patterns, and jobs like that. But this job was much more demanding. After my first few days I ached everywhere; I ached where I didn't even know I could ache!

But more than that, I was being given the opportunity to address an arrogance I had carried into my young adulthood. Without fully realizing it, I found myself harshly judging my coworkers. The lifestyles of my fellow laborers seemed alien, along with their jokes, their preferences in music, the things they talked about, their opinions of others and the world. All they seemed to focus on was putting in their hours, then gathering at a local bar when the quitting whistle blew. They must have sensed my standoffish attitude because few of them reached out to me. So I ate my lunch alone and talked only sparingly to the backhoe driver I was assigned to support. I was miserable at every level. I was experiencing physical agony aggravated by feeling like I was among a different sort of people that I would never have chosen to associate with and didn't particularly like. I couldn't imagine making it through a whole summer of this.

At the end of the first week at this job, I can't tell you how relieved I was to have the weekend off. I savored every second of those few days, but then Sunday evening arrived and I faced another full week. I hated this prospect but it was too late to find another job. When I arrived for work on Monday morning, I felt resentful and emotionally removed from everyone else. My body was stiff and ached even more as I hopped down into the trenches to begin digging again. My anger grew with every shovelful. When it was lunchtime, I followed my first week's pattern of finding a house-in-process not being used by the other workers. I slumped down against a wall and heaved a heavy, heavy sigh. I wasn't the least bit hungry, because I was at war with myself. I gave serious consideration to quitting.

But then I challenged myself to remember why I was doing this in the first place. I was moving toward the most important dream I'd ever had or ever could imagine for myself: evolving my life and working to uplift humankind. Remembering this vision helped me begin to feel better. But then I had a rude awakening: the way I was behaving and the way I was judging my coworkers was absolutely incongruent with the purpose at the heart of my dream. Radical personal honesty is usually painful and humbling at first, then it is intensely freeing. I felt deeply embarrassed at my smugness and shallowness. I realized that I had created a first-class opportunity to grow up more, spiritually, and to integrate my belief in the Oneness of all people. It was time to get over myself and to reach out . . . to embrace not only the job but also the people around me.

I started that very day. After lunch I spent a few minutes asking the backhoe driver about his family. He seemed surprised yet gratified that I cared. Then for the first time, he asked me about my life and why I was working at this job. Through the remainder of the day we chatted and joked off and on. Already I felt more comfortable and the physical toll on my body didn't seem as significant. The next day, I decided to follow this operator to the place where other workers were having lunch. I began to chat with a few others, especially laborers near my age. Over the next few days I continued to challenge myself to meet and talk to others. By the end of the week, I knew at least a dozen workers well enough to maintain some ongoing conversations.

Going back to that job in the ensuing weeks of the summer was no longer agonizing. It wasn't the most intriguing job I'd ever had, but it was no longer repulsive to me. The days passed much more quickly because I invented a trick. Since my vision was to earn enough money to move to California, I imagined that with every shovelful I was digging my way to the West Coast. And I grew closer and closer to about five of the workers, even hanging out after work several times. I began to know them as caring, yearning, vulnerable beings—just like me. They had their quirks and problems—just like me. They had their dreams and fears—just like me. And they were all beings of Light—just like me.

At the end of the summer, I was choked up my whole last day of work. I had grown a lot. I knew I owed this experience so very much. Moreover, I had come to care for many of these people—some at pretty deep levels. I felt genuinely sad to drive away that day. I knew, however, that this particular summer would be one of those defining times . . . and that I would carry its lesson with me always. The concept of Oneness was now far less theoretical, much more real and heartfelt.

A Human Healing at the Vets

One day my wife, Erica, was at the veterinary clinic with our two small dogs. It is a very popular clinic, always crowded. A woman who was somewhat new to this particular vet was becoming angry at the long wait. She shouted at the girl behind the desk when a man and his dog were seen before her. The girl explained that he had been waiting in his car, but the woman shouted that she'd been there the past four days with her very sick dog. She was frustrated and had to get somewhere else soon. Then another lady got pulled into this energy and began to bristle at the waiting time as well.

When the angry lady sat down, Erica felt moved to say: "Your puppy must really be sick for you to have been here the past four days." Then the tears began to well up for this lady. Erica told her about our miniature pinscher that nearly died the past summer and how she and I had been at that vet every day for more than a week. Erica went on to share that this vet was amazing and had saved our dog's life. Then others in the waiting room chimed in with similar comments about the skill and compassion of the vet. It seemed, then, that a spirit moved in the room. The once-angry lady was different now . . . transformed. She'd been heard, then inspired. She'd been cared for . . . and now all was well. Such is the power of moving past personal boundaries to make the deeper connection. As Eckhart Tolle has said: "To love is to recognize yourself in another."

A Cultural Impasse Is Bridged

In the mid-'90s, I was part of founding a group called the Association for Global New Thought. This organization went on to create many projects and conferences that would express the principles of New Thought, universal spirituality, and connect our aligned churches, centers, and organizations with other groups doing similar work. Our mission was also to promote greater interfaith and interspiritual understanding and connections. One of our projects was the Synthesis Dialogs, held in 1999, 2001, and 2004—three gatherings of acclaimed and respected spiritual leaders, authors, researchers, and spiritually motivated social activists. At the first part of each of these gatherings, the assembled groups would discuss world challenges and opportunities for a higher synthesis of ideas and efforts. Then the second half of each event featured the arrival and involvement of His Holiness, the Dalai Lama. It's probably no surprise that the presence of His Holiness always took the deliberations to a much higher level.

At the beginning of the third of these events, an unusual incident would catalyze and direct the rest of the experience. Leaders from all the major faiths and spiritual paths had been invited to this set of dialogs. Before our first assembly there was an incident: a young rabbi from Israel and a female Muslim reporter living in Canada, both in their thirties, encountered each other on a stairway. Rather than a conversation, their meeting became a loud confrontation. A crowd of attendees gathered. Then members of our leadership group intervened and suggested to these two that they continue this interaction at our first meeting and that their challenge with each other could become the context for our explorations. They agreed and suspended the "conversation" for the moment.

Later that morning, the entire group was assembled, and the rabbi and Muslim reporter were eventually invited to begin a dialog. It resumed in a contentious and angry way. Each of them accused the other's people and leaders of heinous misdeeds. When one was finished, the other seemed able to counter with an equally grievous transgression from the past. This went on and on throughout the rest of the day. When the group reassembled the next day, the dialog was continued and it went on in the same way ... vicious, accusatory, unrelenting, unforgiving. The rest of the group had been coached not to take sides but to create a space of compassionate listening, a space that could invite a breakthrough. But the possibility of a healing seemed remote. The interaction of these two passionate beings perfectly mirrored the eroding state of Jewish and Islamic relations.

Then quite "by chance," one of our facilitators asked each of them to share the nature of the pain they felt for all the hurts and traumas, the pain they felt for conditions in the Middle East. Both individuals shifted from attack mode to their more genuine feelings. Each sharing was extraordinarily moving. But what was most transformative: each sharing was essentially the same. They were shocked to discover that the facets and dimensions of each other's pain were exactly the same. Then a facilitator asked them to articulate their dreams for their people and their children's future. These sharings were equally powerful ... *and* they were also equally parallel. Common ground had emerged. They came together across the bridge of their shared pain and vision.

The session culminated with the two of them sharing a long and sincere embrace, mixed with tears flowing and interspersed with bits of laughter at the unlikeliness of it all. They went on to become almost inseparable throughout the rest of the conference. It seemed they were now empowered to get to know each other with boundaries transcended and in an unprecedented way. This new and enthusiastic relationship became the touchstone for the rest of the conference, with other participants taking risks to draw closer in understanding and caring. I am told the rabbi and Muslim journalist continued to stay in touch and develop their friendship after the dialogs. There is no gap so wide that it cannot be bridged by an open heart.

What Matters Most

I'll never forget something I saw on television years ago. It was during the end days of the United States' involvement in Vietnam. The fighting was over and our troops were withdrawing. Yet there was the problem of the thousands and thousands of children orphaned because of the war. An American ship had docked with stores of food and care packages. A food line had been set up so that the children could be fed, and a film crew was taping the whole event.

The fence bowed as the children were pressing against it, anxious to get some food in their starving bellies. Finally, the gates were opened and they began running frantically toward the food lines at the end of the dock. All of a sudden, however, most of the children veered out of the camera's view toward some other destination. Confused, the cameraman panned over to find out about the distraction. What we saw touched hearts: some nurses standing on the docks had begun dispensing hugs . . . and that became an attraction even greater than food for these starving children.

The truth is, we all hunger for love—to love and be loved. It's our deepest human need *and* our highest spiritual gift. Our lives are fulfilled when we say "Yes" to love . . . for our vision is then clarified . . . *We see only God!*

– The Expression –

To Further Establish a Steadfast Awareness of Oneness in All Your Relationships, I Invite You to Embrace These Practices:

1. "Deeply we are One!"
   Practice affirming this mantra throughout your days. Use it when you're with people. Use it in nature. Use it when you watch the news or read

the news reports. Proclaim it when you are in the presence of people who are difficult or challenging for you. Apply it when you're in the midst of a "ditch digging" type of experience, one you'd just as soon detest.

We have all been acculturated into the mind-set of separation. It is the most deeply embedded perspective in human experience. It begins when we are separated from our mothers at birth, and it continues as we bow to the reports of our senses and agree with the teachings of others immersed in separation consciousness. How important it is, then, to diligently and continually practice the higher truth as we move from relationship to relationship: "Deeply we are One."

Also, consider making journal entries of the times when you notice shifts of one kind or another while immersed in Oneness awareness. All of these are precious and powerful miracles!

2. Always remember the power of realized Oneness and radical experiences of Love.

I offer you the words of Helen Keller. They express the blessings she experienced from the dedication and love of Anne Sullivan, the therapist who freed her awareness. They speak to Love's unequaled healing and transformative power:

> Once I knew the depth where no hope was and darkness lay on the face of all things. Then love came and set my soul free. Once I fretted and beat myself against the wall that shut me in. . . . My life was without a past or future, and death, a consummation devoutly to be wished. But a little word from the fingers of another fell into my hands that clutched at emptiness, and my heart leaped up with the rapture of living. I do not know the meaning of the darkness, but I have learned the overcoming of it.

3. A powerful way to move into the experience and miracle of Oneness is to embrace opportunities to care for and serve others. For instance, I invite you to follow in the footsteps of an incident that occurred at a basketball game. Maurice Cheeks was then coach of a professional basketball team, the Portland Trailblazers. Thirteen-year-old Natalie Gilbert was selected to sing the National Anthem at this nationally televised playoff game. She did fine for the first few lines. Then, somewhere around "the twilight's last gleaming," she forgot the words. She appeared to be on the verge of tears and she desperately looked for her parents. That's when she saw Cheeks walking toward her. The coach put his arm around the girl and began singing with her—and I'm here to tell you he can't carry a tune, but that didn't stop him! And he encouraged the crowd to sing along. Together, they made it all the way through to "the home of the brave." Cheeks said he wasn't even sure *he* knew all the words, but that he just had to help her . . . and he added, "I wish I could help some of my players like that!" They must have been inspired by their coach, because they went on to win the game and end a ten-game postseason losing streak.

An act of caring flowed to him in the moment. The good news is that he was ready and willing. Moments like these swirl around us all the time. You see, we're all in this together . . . and our lights never shine brighter than when the boundaries are relaxed, our hearts are open, and acts of compassion and caring occur. For always . . .

This Relationship Is Oneness!

6. THIS JOURNEY IS SURRENDER

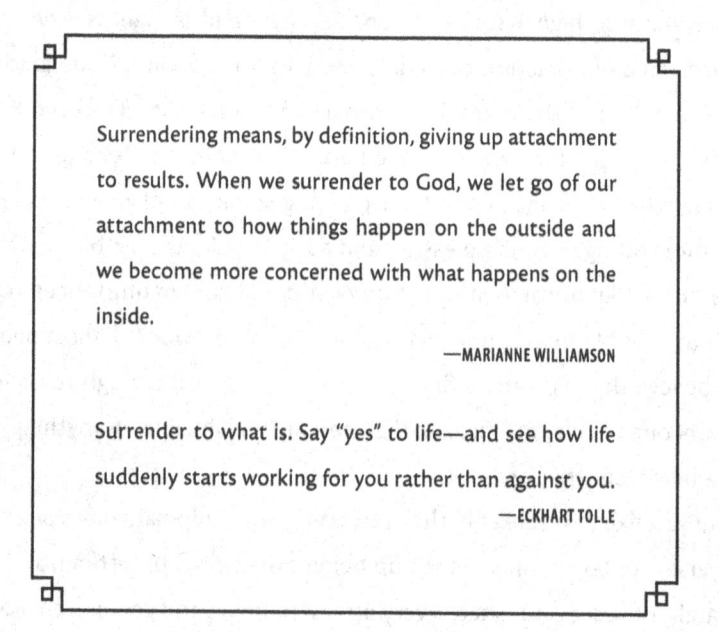

Surrendering means, by definition, giving up attachment to results. When we surrender to God, we let go of our attachment to how things happen on the outside and we become more concerned with what happens on the inside.

—MARIANNE WILLIAMSON

Surrender to what is. Say "yes" to life—and see how life suddenly starts working for you rather than against you.

—ECKHART TOLLE

– The Essence –

It is a common misconception that *mastery* is just a fancy, sophisticated term for forcing, manipulating, dictating, or controlling. You don't have to look very far to find growth seminars, motivational rallies, or leadership events that promote these very approaches—covertly or even overtly. While these programs may offer benefits for enhancing business or personal productivity, they do not necessarily acquaint their participants with the deeper essence of masterful living, especially when considered from the perspectives of spiritual awakening, soul unfoldment, and ideal living . . . and it is mastery at these very levels—when all is said and done—that generates the most profound personal growth, reveals lasting levels of fulfillment, and makes the greatest difference in the world.

Each of our lives is a magnificent journey . . . a journey of progressive awakening into higher states of consciousness and livingness. Few of us were given an instruction manual for how best to be on this life journey, so we've followed the examples of others and, when that didn't work, we made things up along the way. We have tried many different tactics for getting what we want or need, for creating some semblance of security, and for creating as much pleasure and as little pain as possible. Typically these strategies are attempts to lord over people or circumstances: to be their master. No matter how many times this hasn't worked, most people still believe that they must find a way to be powerful enough to control the uncontrollable and master the seemingly invincible. If anything, we are a persistent species!

But just like that seeker in the cave, trying to manipulate one's personal universe—outer or inner—ends up being exhausting, unsettling, and, ultimately, unsuccessful. There's very little well-being and genuine creativity in this aggressive approach to life, no durable fullness, peace, or joy. However, to change or end this style of constraining and coercing is often denounced as giving up. Voices shout, "Don't cop out. Just keep trying, push harder, give it more of your time, do more, feel less, attack it from a different angle. You're the boss, so come on . . . make it happen. Don't you want to be a success?"

Lots of people are afraid to explore a different paradigm for living and creating. But even more people have simply become addicted to this forceful, frenetic, assertive, demanding way of being. Stephen Covey, author of *The Seven Habits of Highly Effective People*, calls this "urgency addiction," and declares that it is life threatening just like the other more publicized addictions such as drug and alcohol dependency. He also shares the haunting insight that the excessive and urgent "fires" burning in most people's lives are fueled by our culture's widespread neglect of practices that could empower centeredness, clarity, and heart. Too often it's quantity over quality, results over relationships, production over processes, and forcing over flowing. It seems so easily forgotten that we are spiritual beings, not just human doings.

Back in that cave story—after trying everything he knew, searching every square inch, pounding against his enclosure—the seeker finally found transcendence when he could do no more. It was then that he stumbled onto one of the most powerful of personal responses . . . surrendering. It's been given a bad rap and touted as a form of weakness. However, I invite you to consider that this just could be the missing key to a life well lived . . . a most powerful opening into life mastery: This Journey Is Surrender! For as Sylvia Robinson declared, "Some think it's holding on that makes one strong; more often, it's letting go."

Another teaching story illustrates the options before us as we consider how to live: Two men were walking together from their village to another one further down the river. It was early morning and dew was still on the leaves and grass. As they walked along the riverbank, they became lost in conversation and, when the bank became steeply sloped, they both lost their footing and slipped into the rushing waters. One of the men began fighting the current fiercely. He struggled against the water, trying to swim upstream or toward the bank. But the force of the water was too much for him and he soon became exhausted. It wasn't long before he was taken under and drowned. Though the other man was quickly separated from his friend, he took a different approach. He relaxed and surrendered to the force of the currents. Lying on his back in the rushing river, he allowed it to take him where it would. Occasionally he'd lay an arm in the water to change his direction and to avoid a rock or log. After a while, the river deposited him safely on a sandy edge. He got up, walked away from the river, and, to his surprise, found himself just outside the village that was his intended destination.

There Is a Form of Surrendering That Is Masterful, and When Fully Understood, It Is What This Life Is All About. Consider These Expressions of Purposeful Surrendering:

- *Rather than "giving up" . . . it is flowing with and opening into.*

- *It is attuning to the wisdom and possibilities that are being obstructed by resistance and forcing. It is clearing a space for intuition and higher guidance to be realized and followed.*

- *It is higher-level allowing . . . allowing something better to emerge.*

- *It is discovering the forces at play, then cooperating and cocreating with them to bring forth results that are often unexpected and of a higher order.*

- *It is nonresistance . . . letting "what is" play out into what can be.*

- *It is releasing hollow certainties and fearful expectations, and having the courage to open to what we don't know we don't know.*

- *It is an absolute faith that something greater and more wonderful than we realize is available to flow into our experience . . . if we are willing to welcome it skillfully . . . and let it be.*

- *It is allowing higher energies to work through us, to use us.*

- *It is not compromising but synthesizing . . . releasing the lesser and inviting the greater.*

The apex of empowered surrendering is to let go of attachments . . . the ones that block, limit, or close us down. There are so many potential attachments, so readily seized . . . attachments to ideas, approaches, relationships, routines, jobs, organizations, roles, expectations, people, behaviors, praise, dreams . . . the list goes on and on. Where we get most obstructed, though, is in our attachment to certainties and outcomes. By getting attached to outcomes, we often reject or block a better way, an unexpected yet better result. Remember, this world is consciousness, and it is taking form through a creative process more powerful and intelligent than we could ever imagine. When we choose to make ideas substantial through our total conviction in them, a Power greater than we are takes over to reveal outcomes and end results that are of a higher order than we could ever have designed by ourselves. When we get welded to an outcome, we block this creative process from leading us into our highest and best.

In the same way, when we get attached to our certainties, we close ourselves down to the revelation of more expansive ideas and realizations. It's not that it's wrong to build our lives around some of what we regard as certainties; it's just that it's best to hold them lightly and stay open to greater and greater realizations about them. You may believe deeply in God, or some ultimate creative Life or Source, call it what you will. It serves to hold fast to this knowing and, at the same time, to stay radically open to realizing more about this infinite Spirit. In this way your spiritual life is buoyed by your faith, yet continually enlarged and vitalized by your openness.

There was a time when most of humankind was certain that the earth was flat. It appeared then that the theory was absolutely correct. Of course, there came a time when that notion had to be surrendered. Even in these current times, we move about on the earth as if it were flat. We just know there's a higher truth about it. Copernicus was willing to go to the front of the line in surrendering the idea that the earth was the center of our solar system. He paid a steep price for it, but also opened the way for orbiting the earth, satellites, stepping onto the moon, and exploring the planets. A higher truth about everything is waiting to be revealed. So why get attached to what seems so certain when history and experience clearly demonstrate that a more advanced or complete understanding will eventually show up? To master this, we have to stay alert to how fervently the ego wants to be right so it can be justified. We open ourselves to dynamic possibilities for growth when we are courageously and humbly willing to surrender our certainties and outcomes.

Letting go is quite often a difficult process. As someone quipped, "It feels like everything I've ever released has had claw marks on it!" I've experienced this along my own path, and I bet you have, too. I've worked with countless individuals whose core struggle was letting go. Oh, they thought it was the other person or the predicament they faced, but inevitably we journeyed to that place where it became clear . . . the actual opportunity at hand was, in some way or another, to sincerely release, let go, surrender. These were the transformative moments when something greater than either of us saturated the instant with waves of grace and clarity. The healing was at work because it was finally being permitted . . . through surrendering. Even when we masterfully work with an idea to move it to that substantial place of true faith, then we must let it go . . . commend it to the higher workings of the Law, the universal creative process. So many invitations to the masterful process of surrendering!

The wisdom of surrendering does not replace the necessity for action and effort. There is usually an important role for our personal efforts in support of an idea or project. The quality of the action is different, though. Where before our efforts were imbued with struggle and the intention to force results no matter what, a new way of being in action is available. We take action without attachment to the outcomes. We want good or productive outcomes; we just surrender our picture of how that needs to look and stay open. We also have the opportunity to bring a higher quality of consciousness to our doingness. As I was writing this book, I kept a small handwritten sticky note attached to the top of my computer screen with an important reminder: "Love the process!" Where in your life would it be freeing and empowering to "love the process" rather than resist the effort, resent the time and energy involved? Imagine how the quality of the end result will be changed with this shift of awareness and intent. Efforts energized and informed by surrender activate miracles.

Beyond each person's unique path of unfoldment, I believe that we all chose to come to this earth so that we might discover our inherent greatness of wisdom and heart, learn spiritual principles, comprehend existing forces, and allow ourselves to be "instruments" for love, peace, and creative unfoldment. To become an instrument of something more than the urges and fears of the worldly ego, we must learn to surrender. It is a necessary emptying prior to a heartfelt opening. At a symposium in the early 1990s, I heard the great flautist and teacher Al Huang declare between musical pieces, "We must all let go and open. The universe can't play a stuffed flute!" Many people have jammed their minds full of so much that isn't true. They're clogged up. Our most dynamic growth is by way of *un*-learning, rather than learning. It will not be new information that transforms our world; it will be new inspiration, cooperation, and unification. As Ernest Holmes points out, "Making the great surrender to Spirit does not mean losing anything worthwhile, but getting rid of those things which deny the Presence and Power of the Spirit."

On several occasions I've been a member of problem-solving groups that were charged with creating solutions and better approaches. In almost every case, the group arrived at a point of frustration where nothing was happening. We were either bogged down in the problems or oversaturated with ideas that fell way short of a great answer. This was usually after many hours of deliberating, debating, and consternating. We had become worn down by the struggle. In none of these groups did we ever make any progress . . . until we found a way to surrender. In the giving up of intimidating problems and insufficient ideas, there were those times when we fell into a spacious and dynamic openness. Then a brilliance greater than any of us began to flow by means of us. The results were almost always something we would never have expected at the outset.

Repeating Emerson from earlier, we really do "lie in the lap of immense intelligence, which makes us receivers of its truth and organs of its activity." But this only happens when we are willing to practice the high art of surrender.

Where would it be most freeing and empowering for you to let go . . . to practice enlightened surrendering? Is there any area in your life in which this would *not* be an opening into mastery and unimagined blessings? Claw marks or not, I invite you to take a deep breath . . . and let go!

– The Experience –

The following are powerful illustrations of the dynamics and miracles involved in spiritual surrendering.

A Radically Different Direction!

As a youth, Bob embraced the dream of having a military career and attending West Point. He had numerous physical challenges, however: he couldn't pass the eye test, he was underweight, he had flat feet, and, to top it off, he had a heart murmur. But Bob was passionate and determined. He practiced picking up marbles with his toes to develop his feet, along with eye exercises to train his eyes. Then he began drinking a pint of cream a day and working out in the weight room. The heart murmur vanished and he passed the physical that allowed him to attend Virginia Military Institute for a year and then to enter West Point. His dream of a life of military service was happening!

Bob graduated from West Point and through rigorous training became an Army Ranger and Paratrooper. After a six-month stint setting up Ranger training in Vietnam, he was based in Hawaii. One day, he and some buddies decided to see a movie, *The Longest Day*, which is about the D-day invasion during World War II. When Bob got to the ticket counter, something came over him. He couldn't bring himself to see the movie, so he told his friends to go in without him. He sat on the curb outside the theater, and something deeply buried within him bubbled to the surface. He became aware that he did not want to pursue a military career, after all. He became profoundly aware that war is not the way to peace, and a military career wasn't the highest direction for his life.

Fueled by this epiphany—and despite the tremendous efforts he had undertaken to get this far—he nonetheless seized this guidance that his path *had* to be different, and he left the service as soon as he could.

Once he was out of the army, he was often overcome with doubts. He went through a period of grieving for the decision he'd made. He had no idea what to do with his life, and was often tempted to return to the military path, but something within him wouldn't allow this. Eventually, Bob went to work for IBM, learning business and leadership skills that are key to his success as a business consultant today. While he was working there, he met a woman who was hired the very day he was and she introduced him to metaphysics. He began studying the Seth materials, *A Course in*

Miracles, and then in the late 1970s he found the church I serve, and resonated with our teachings.

It took Bob quite a while to recognize the perfection of this path, but now he sees that there *is* a Higher Guidance and that he had managed to trust it enough for the blessings and true steps of his soul unfoldment to emerge. Bob is very successful at all levels and has become a sensitive and visionary spiritual facilitator.

Surrendering . . . to Become a Receiver

Another experience continues to light my heart: Betsy was a wonderful person. She was thoroughly involved in our spiritual community and volunteered in at least six areas. She was a great light, spreading joy wherever she went and in whatever she did. As a result she was greatly loved. Then came the diagnosis: a rapidly spreading form of cancer. She went over her options with her husband, sought spiritual counseling, and then made the decision to go ahead with the recommended radiation and chemotherapy treatments. As she walked this path for the next several months, she maintained her upbeat optimism. The therapies weakened her body but could not dim her light.

I got a call from her husband that Betsy had been readmitted to the hospital and had asked to see me as soon as possible. I was at her bedside within a few hours. She wanted to talk. She was clinging to her faith, but she was fragile and fearful.

"I want to continue to live what I know to be true. But I'm feeling so weak. I thought my faith would carry me through this, but now I don't know. I don't want to fail my husband and children, my friends, or you. I'm just finding it hard to stay strong."

We both gave way to some tears. Sometimes our moments of vulnerability are openings into real power.

Truthfully, I had no idea what to say, so I remember just agreeing with myself to stay clear of overthinking and to let the words flow from my heart. First I remember telling her that there was no way in the world that she could ever fail me. She was an inspiration and an angel in my life, and I knew I spoke for many others as well. I reassured her that her life and her example during this illness were gifts to us all and especially to her husband and children. With my every word, I sent her waves of love. I know I said a lot more—after all, I am a minister—but what I know is that the words were meant to be carriers of love. I learned that by surrendering the need to solve the problem or have impressive ideas, I could become a vehicle for what was really being sought: Love. Realizing that she was getting tired, I prayed with Betsy, then said good-bye.

Several days later I got a call from her husband. Betsy was improving. She had told him that my visit helped immensely and was a great blessing. I was elated with this news, yet very clear that whatever helped her had shown up when I surrendered and got out of the way.

Over the next three months, Betsy continued to improve. Doctors were hinting that it could be classified under the "miracle" category. Then I had another memorable visit with Betsy, this time in the family room of her home. After sharing some of the latest news, I asked Betsy what she felt was the key to her turnaround. She told me that after my visit with her in the hospital, she slept for a few hours. It was in the wee hours of the morning that she awakened. It was so quiet and she said it seemed like a moment full of energy. She told me that she "had a talk with God" right then . . . and I remember what she said because it so moved me that I wrote it down as soon as I could. In that moment of inner communion, she told me that she declared, "I don't want to die, God, but I'm willing to let go if that is best for me. But what you need to know is I can't fight all this anymore. I'm exhausted and I surrender. I'm ready to let the highest and best be done. I know you love me, and I sure love you. Into your hands I place the care and keeping of my soul. Thank you for taking care of this from now on."

She said she felt better that very next day and continued to get stronger and more vital. She concluded that the lesson for her was that throughout her life she had always strived to give more than 100 percent in everything she did, as a wife and mother, and in her involvements in the church and community. She had always been the strong one for everyone around her when they felt weak. She always put on a happy face and tried to uplift others. But as she lay there in that hospital, she realized that she had forgotten the power of admitting her own needs, the importance of letting go so she could receive. She had always been the great giver; now she was learning how to surrender and become a great receiver. She stated that receiving the love I shared with her started it off. Then her "little chat" with God took her the rest of the way into divine surrender. Betsy surprised me by concluding, "Once I surrendered totally . . . well, I just couldn't lose. I would either be taken on my greater journey into God's Life and Love, or I would be strengthened and healed. I'd be fine either way. Now, don't get me wrong. I'm glad it's turning out this way, and I feel a peace I've never felt before, now that I know what I know."

Betsy lived ten more rich, full years before moving into her soul's expanded journey. She taught me, however, that our ultimate journey is surrender!

– The Expression –

1. The first practice I offer is based on an experience attributed to one of the finest opera singers, the great Caruso. On the night of one of his biggest and most important concerts, this master singer was unusually

nervous. He wanted to do well and win over this American audience. Caruso was pacing back and forth backstage . . . and was overheard to be quietly proclaiming over and over:

"Little me, move over . . . Big me, take over!"

This is a great affirmation to use throughout your life to facilitate a shift from your human initiating to spiritual surrendering and trusting. Great things emerge in this way!

2. Something to contemplate and pray upon: What is it in my ways of being and living that God can no longer use on my soul's journey?

To listen deeply and to open to realizations can bring you into a level of personal honesty and openness that is so beneficial and powerful. It is moving to a level of radical willingness to realize and yield the lesser baggage that can congest our lives and slow our progress. It is a supreme way to let go of past pain and stifling control strategies. This can lead to a level of sincerity and spiritual maturity that lays the groundwork for unimaginable growth and opportunities.

3. I also invite you to contemplate two powerful statements: First, from Ramana Maharshi:

> It is not enough that one surrenders oneself. Surrender is to give oneself up to the original cause of one's being. Do not delude yourself by imagining such a Source to be some God outside you. One's Source is within oneself. Give yourself up to it. That means that you should seek the Source and merge in It.

This great reminder encourages us to not allow the practice of surrendering to cause us to lapse into duality . . . into separation thinking. Instead, we are surrendering a sense of division from our Source and from all of Life. We are surrendering any sense of the absence of the Good of God for us, right here and right now. We are surrendering lesser means and misguided perceptions. In all our surrendering, we are entering into a more conscious and dynamic experience of our Oneness . . . with Source, with Love, with all beings and all creation, with transformative Ideas, with the Highest and Best ways and means, with Peace and Joy in this moment. Surrendering is an opening into Oneness and our access to partnering with Spirit.

And then there are the words of Rumi:

> *I have spent my days stringing and unstringing my instrument . . . while the song I came to sing remains unsung.*

Where in your life is it time to surrender the excuses and the holding back? Are you caught up in endless rehearsing and preparing . . . "stringing and unstringing" your instrument? A powerful function of spiritual surrendering is to let go of the paralyzing fears and the hesitancy to honor and express the gifts we are here to share. Surrender . . . and start singing the song you came here to sing!

7. THIS LIFE IS JOY

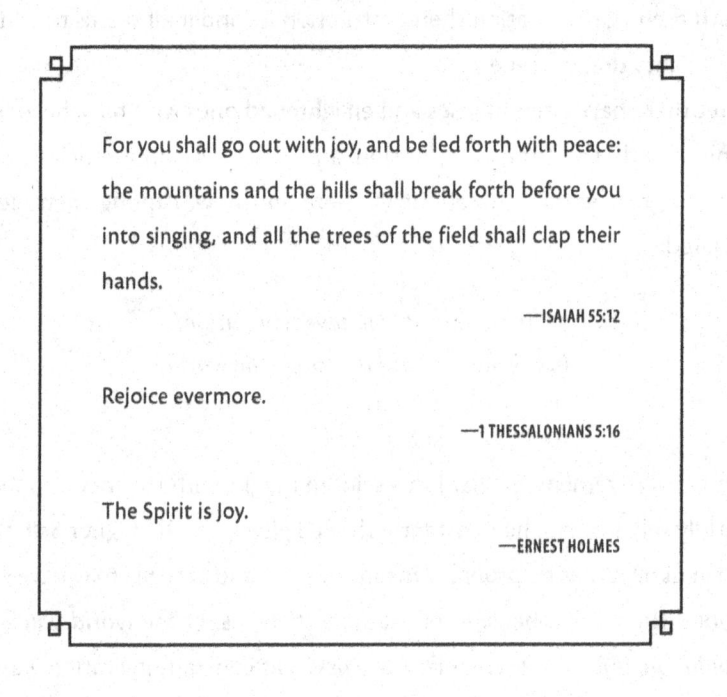

For you shall go out with joy, and be led forth with peace: the mountains and the hills shall break forth before you into singing, and all the trees of the field shall clap their hands.

—ISAIAH 55:12

Rejoice evermore.

—1 THESSALONIANS 5:16

The Spirit is Joy.

—ERNEST HOLMES

– The Essence –

Are you in touch with the fountain of Joy within you? Can you sense this Joy bubbling up everywhere, trying to proclaim itself once more to a weary world? Do you remember the secret power hidden in this Joy . . . and are you ready to dance with it again?

In many quarters there is widespread agreement that the human condition on this planet is difficult, if not deplorable. Age after age, century after century, year after year, humankind continues to play out themes of struggle, limitation, alienation, impoverishment, violence, and heartlessness. Various political and religious systems have attempted to change this recurring drama, but with little lasting success. Then add to this the natural processes of change inherent in all life systems: birth then death, youth then aging, creation then destruction . . . and it all seems to add up to a mighty dreary scene.

Yet there have been mystics and enlightened ones who have been very familiar with the human condition and who have, nonetheless, proclaimed great good news about life here and now. Among them, Jesus declared:

> *"In the world you have tribulation;*
> *but behold, I have overcome the world."*
> —JOHN 16:33

It helps to remember that Jesus seldom taught with the focus upon his worldly self. Instead, he constantly shone light upon the higher Self, the I Am in us all. What he probably meant to say—and actually may have said, beyond the comprehension of listeners then—is, *In the world you have tribulation; but I Am overcomes the world.* His constant invitation was for each of us to discover and re-present the I Am truth of our being. In this way we, too, overcome the world. Further, that great one said:

> *"Ask and you shall receive, that your joy may be full."*
> —JOHN 16:22

There is also the great biblical affirmation

> *"This is the day the Lord has made; I will rejoice and be glad in it."*
> —PSALM 118:24

THIS LIFE IS JOY

This realization of spiritual Joy also flows through the mystical currents of other great faith paths. In the Lotus Sutra of Buddhism, the Divine declares:

> *"I appear in the world like unto this great cloud, to pour enrichment on all parched living beings, to free them from their misery, to attain the joy of peace, joy of the present world, and joy of nirvana."*

IN THE KORAN:

> *"For those who believe, and whose hearts find satisfaction in the remembrance of God . . . is inward joy and a beautiful place of return."*

FROM *THE HEART OF HINDUISM*:

> *"The Infinite is the source of joy . . . Ask to know the Infinite!"*

AND FROM THE SANSKRIT:

> *"Thou art God, and God enjoys being God!"*

From a modern perspective, Ernest Holmes adds the following:

> *I believe in a religion of happiness and joy. There is too much depression and sorrow in the world. These things were never meant to be and have no real place in the world of reality. Religion should be like the morning sun sending forth its rays of light; it should be like the falling dew covering the land with fragrance and sweetness; like the cool of evening and repose of night. It should be a spontaneous song of joy and not a funeral*

*dirge. From the fullness of a joyous heart the mouth should
speak.*

What if there is a larger truth about life . . . beyond the drama that re-
peats itself over and over at the surface levels of human experience? Yes,
it is painful, burdensome, cruel, and seemingly hopeless at the level of
circumstances and conditions, and none of us is immune to the impact
of it all. As caring, feeling beings, it would be a greater tragedy if we had
no significant feelings about all the suffering, but instead just hid ourselves in an abundance of distractions. Yet is this all there is, or is our
problem that we have just lost track of other dimensions of life?

As children we innately communed with something more about life. Of
course we were innocent then and, if fortunate, were sheltered for a time
from the more difficult levels of experience. It is the saddest thing when
any child is wrenched by painful experiences out of the bliss that is the
province of early youth. For in the early stages of life there is more obvious
access to the flow of an expansive vibrancy and joy. It is the glorious pro-
nouncement of aliveness you can also see in colts or kittens or puppies. Is
this to be written off simply as naïveté and inexperience . . . or is it our
true foundation for life . . . an immersion in the deep dance of Spirit that
we sacrifice later on? I believe we gave up something precious and vital
back then . . . and I also know that we can reclaim it. What a wonderful
opening into life mastery when we discover the following again:

This Life Is Joy!

There is a mighty rushing river of deep Joy at the center of all life. Oh
yes, there is also a roller-coaster ride of pleasure and pain at the surface of
human experience. Yet transcending this is a Joy that is the very efferves-
cence of Life, Itself. Deep Joy is an eternal quality of the Spirit. When we

remember that Life is Consciousness, then it makes more sense that the pain or changes we endure at the material or worldly level of experience are just as temporary as everything else at that level. What endures—that which is ultimately real—is God, Spirit, the Infinite . . . and the nature of this all-originating One is Love, Light, Truth, Wholeness, Peace . . . and Joy!

To have lost track of the Joy of Spirit is a great tragedy, though a repairable one. This Joy is so much more than the fleeting pleasures most try to get by on in their daily rounds of life. In this Joy is power, the power to endure, to continue on. In this Joy is creativity, for Joy is the mighty dance of possibility. In this Joy is aliveness that nothing has the power to dampen. In this Joy is vision, a vision of the greater magnificence of Life beyond the squalor created in human affairs. In this Joy is oneness and community, for Joy unites all in its commitment to exalting creation. In this Joy is the heart of prayer, for Joy is the peak realization that "it is well with my soul," no matter what.

Pleasure . . . or Joy?

There is a great difference between pleasure and Joy. So many people have lost track of inner Joy and are resigned to settling for and maximizing the pleasures of human experience, and this is a significant challenge. Pleasures are fleeting; they come and go as the by-product of desirable experiences. If there is no taproot into Joy, then people become addicted to their pleasure sources and seek to maintain them, sometimes at any cost. When there is no pleasure source or experience at hand, all that is left is some degree of pleasure's opposite: pain. If the pain persists, then the next step is to find ways to numb it. Thoreau must have recognized this when he wrote that most people lead lives of quiet desperation. Because of this sad cycle, we have a society that, to a great degree, is frantically focused on generating pleasure experiences—especially by means of rampant consumerism—alternating with anesthetizing the increasing pain levels that emerge when pleasure becomes more and more difficult to manipulate. Added to this are other destructive side effects: increased abuse, addiction, crime, destruction of the environment, and weakening of the social fabric, just to name a few.

It can be startling to get in touch with the destructive wake that ripples forth because of our estrangement from deep and pure Joy. It is even more sobering to recognize that many business and social structures are highly committed to keeping the majority of people distanced from anything other than the usual pleasure/pain syndrome. As long as this syndrome prevails, it is easy to sell people the next feel-good elixir, the next panacea. With Joy comes true empowerment, inner peace, renewed creativity, and natural independence. Knowing this, the majority of businesses and organizations work hard and spend billions of dollars to keep people inwardly disempowered and dependent on their products, services, or support. It's about selling the next bit of relief and gratification . . . keeping the populace under their thumb through guilt, fear, and the dampening of the spirit . . . keeping a lid on the inner wellspring of wholeness and fullness that Joy automatically taps.

Tenzin Palmo, one of the first Westerners to be ordained as a Tibetan Buddhist nun, asks, "How many people are genuinely happy? I don't mean happy because they've just met the man or woman of their dreams, or because they've got a new car, or a new house, or the job they've always wanted. I'm talking about being inwardly happy. I'm talking about having a wellspring of inner joy and peace. . . . How many people do you know like that?"

Whatever your answer, I invite you to dedicate yourself to owning and expressing this genuine happiness, this deep Joy of Life. This is our original and optimal state of being. It is our essence and our natural equilibrium. Joy emerges when we cultivate a deep sense of flourishing and fulfillment . . . not because something gratifying has come into our experience, but because it is deeply natural. It is who we really are. Practice proclaiming this with every ounce of your being:

"I Am the Joy of the Spirit!"

Keep doing and being this, and your life will change! You'll make different and more life-affirming choices that are extensions of lasting Joy instead of temporary pleasure. You'll notice a surge of creativity. This Joy practice will further open your heart to life and to others. Your compassion will soar as you behold the natural pain on life's path, as well as the unnecessary pain produced by pain/pleasure addictions. You'll care because you know there is something so much deeper and richer that awaits any person's call. You'll also experience a deeper strength, an equilibrium that is solid and strong, and an indestructible foundation for living.

When the Children of Israel were in a particular phase of their Babylonian captivity, they endured great hardships and suffering. This went on for years, and it's amazing that they retained their spiritual and cultural identity, as well as their stamina to carry on. This may have been their secret: After toiling for many hours each and every day, the Israelites would quietly sneak down to the river's edge. There they had hidden musical instruments—their harps and lyres—in the willows and rushes next to the river. Then they would spend hours singing and dancing to the music their hearts created, renewing themselves in this Joy that nothing can dampen or destroy. They were in physical captivity yet they were spiritually free. So, I ask:

Do You Have "A Harp in the Willows"?

Reconnecting with inner Joy doesn't mean that your life experience will always be easy. It doesn't mean that changes or hardships will pass you by. It doesn't mean that there will be no more betrayal or loss. It doesn't mean that you will cease feeling pain or grief. What it does mean is that beneath all of this—and whatever else occurs on your path—the healing balm of spiritual Joy will comfort you, the inner strength of spiritual Joy will uphold you, and the inner peace of spiritual Joy will inspire you. I have had this experience, especially in my times of loss and the natural grieving that followed. Despite the pain, I still sensed this Joy and I knew with certainty that it was all part of the tapestry of Life's magnificence.

It's important to cry our tears when we lose dear ones; to grieve when a project, business, or dream falls away; to mourn when tragedies afflict our communities or world. Our honoring of these dimensions of pain is different from the pleasure/pain syndrome. The natural pain that accompanies changes or loss is a pure and beautiful part of who we are. In losing a loved one, we grieve because we have first loved. Our tears also express love. What is so important about simultaneously sensing spiritual Joy is we realize that though we are feeling pain or grieving, at the same time we are not without hope. There is a buoyancy that keeps us afloat no matter what pulls us down. Joy links us to the eternal verities of Life, Itself. Joy supports the flowing of the pain, until it passes . . . and the Joy remains.

How beautiful it is to know that there is a Joy that the changing tides of experience cannot squash! In his book *Lessons at the Halfway Point*, Michael Levine tells of a day when he went outside into 100-degree temperatures and rain forest–like humidity. He passed his eighty-three-year-old neighbor, who was leaning on his cane. Michael asked him, "How're you doing?" And the wise old man proclaimed, "Best day yet!"

What a great lesson. Ours is often a complaint-oriented society, so we learn well how to major in complaining and minor in appreciating. Sure, there are plenty of annoyances in our modern lives. But it's the unhappy people who scream the most and try to inflict their joylessness on others. It's as though these folks back up the garbage truck of their toxic emotions and dump as much of this trash as they can, wherever they can. Have you been "garbage trucked" like this lately?

Along with each person's unique soul agenda, I believe we all came to this planet with a shared mission: to be happy. Happy people are caring people. Happy people are less likely to lash out or inflict injury. Happy people refrain from manipulating others. Happy people are more likely to feel a reverence for all life-forms, for all of creation. Happy people gush with creativity and often come up with great advances for the good of all. Happy people create great celebrations. Abraham, through the channeling of inspirational speaker and author Esther Hicks, declares:

> Life is supposed to be fun. No one is taking score of any kind, and if you will stop taking score so much, you will feel a whole lot better—and as you feel a whole lot better, more of the things that you want right now will flow to you. You will never be in a place where all of the things that you are wanting will be satisfied right now, or then you could be complete—and you never could be. You are right on track, right on schedule. Everything is unfolding perfectly. All is really well. Have fun. Have fun. Have fun!

If you needed permission, there it is! Also, happy people spread the healing balm of laughter. Philosopher, author, and human potential movement leader Jean Houston writes, "At the height of laughter, the universe is flung into a kaleidoscope of new possibilities." Bottom line: happy people are keepers of the treasure map to the fountain of inner and eternal Joy.

Lots of people are simply out of practice at experiencing and proclaiming their Joy. There is no better time to sense what your inner child already knows . . . lasting spiritual Joy is your divine birthright! No matter whatever happens, remember, This Life Is Joy!

As Ernest Holmes so wisely advises, "Let us waste no further time looking for the key to happiness. Already the door is open and whosoever will may enter."

– The Experience –

With great love, I offer these vignettes to further inspire your reunion with Joy.

A New Prayer

I heard of a lady who was always praying for things to make her happy . . . for this or that to happen, for this relationship to work out, for this or that to happen with her kids, for more money or opportunities—always praying for these things! Then one day she had a startling realization: She was never praying to *be* happy . . . simply and directly to *be* happy. She had been praying for things and situations to make her happy, but whenever she'd get them—if she did—she was seldom any happier than she had been. So she asked herself, "Am I willing to *be* happy . . . happy from the inside out?" So, she created a new affirmation for herself:

"God, I am willing to be happy!"

His Holiness

It has been such a profound privilege to be with His Holiness, the Dalai Lama, on three occasions for extensive four-day sessions. His very essence conveys his message of compassion and kindness . . . his very presence offers the deepest of lessons. His spiritual leadership has been uniquely influential in our time. I have been in awe of his inward buoyancy, especially when his life path is considered. The Chinese invaded Tibet in 1950. His Holiness fled to India in 1959. Since then, he has worked unendingly to free his country. He has borne the agony of a systematic genocide of his people at the hands of the Chinese, along with the devastating destruction of many of the sacred and cultural artifacts and temples of Tibetan Buddhism. And yet, he continues to inspire much of the world. One thing in particular illustrates his deep, spiritual grounding. Most often when His Holiness enters a room, he is giggling. This is not a superficial thing. It is the genuine outpouring of his inner knowing, of his rigorous spiritual practice. With all the burdens he shoulders, his spirit remains unencumbered. He exudes the reality of spiritual Joy.

We Eat Now!

A strong facilitator of the experience of inward Joy is mindfulness. Increasingly popularized by Eastern spirituality and meditative practices, mindfulness is being fully present in the moment . . . with whatever or whomever is present in the moment. Rather than the mind flitting frenetically from thought to thought . . . rather than attention jumping from subject to subject like monkeys leaping from tree to tree . . . mindfulness is centering oneself totally in the present moment, being fully with whatever is going on, taking in the gifts and qualities of each and every moment. It is the antithesis to the shallowness of multitasking. Practices of mindfulness can restore inner peace; enhance mental, emotional, and physical functioning; and retrieve a sense of the eloquence and fullness of each moment's experience.

At one of our gatherings with His Holiness, the Dalai Lama, our convening group had arranged for a luncheon exclusively with His Holiness, his small entourage, and us. When the morning session concluded that day, my colleagues and I assembled in a special room arranged for the luncheon. The long tables were arranged in a square so all could see one another. I took a seat at one of the corners. Soon His Holiness arrived and, to my delight, he chose the seat on the other edge of my corner—right next to me. I rejoiced at this prospect. I had always wanted to spend a bit more personal time with him. I began to consider some topics and questions for our impending chat. After a blessing, the meal began to be served family style. I began talking with His Holiness and he acknowledged me cordially as the food was served. I continued to set the stage for an in-depth conversation. Our plates were full, so we began to eat and I continued to talk. Then—most graciously, gently, and lovingly—His Holiness reached over, placed his hand on my forearm, and said quietly, "We eat now."

In my exuberance and enthusiasm, I had missed the point of the moment. The primary activity was nourishment . . . and being quietly and fully in each other's presence. I realized that there would be a different setting for a conversation in a magazine interview I would later conduct with him. The focus for the moment was to be fully in that place, fully present to the qualities and tastes of the food, fully present to the equally nourishing energies pervading the room. As I shifted into this mindfulness, I felt a rush of Joy . . . the realization that this was every bit as great a gift . . . eating silently with this beautiful soul and with all the other beautiful souls in the room. I loved the meal, loved simply being and being with him, and, furthermore, I loved being "out of my head." I share this lesson with you: Our indestructible inner Joy is very often reclaimed when we are "out of our minds"!

Unparalleled Strength!

Thor Heyerdahl was the Norwegian adventurer who crossed the Pacific in 1947 on his little raft, the *Kon-Tiki*, when for three months, he and his companions saw no land at all, mostly giant waves towering over their heads and crashing onto their raft. They were drifting the midocean currents to demonstrate the theory that early South Americans could have reached Polynesia that way. But for Heyerdahl, this journey was an even greater breakthrough. As a child he went through several experiences that seeded in him a tremendous fear of water.

He carried this fear into his adulthood. During World War II, he joined the Free Norwegian Forces training soldiers in guerrilla warfare in his occupied country. During this time, he found himself on a portage trip on a rampaging river with two fellow soldiers. The racing tides capsized his boat, and Heyerdahl and his crew were swept into currents that were carrying them toward some huge falls just two hundred yards away. His friends found safety clinging to the rocky shore but Heyerdahl, with his heavy winter uniform and thick army boots, was dragged beneath the surface with nothing to grab on to. At that moment, he started to pray with all he had in him:

> With that prayer came a sudden burst of will. I would fight. I would not yield. As my prayer grew surer, warmth seemed to flood my frozen body. I began to swim with long, rhythmic strokes, while my feet in their water-logged boots began a rhythmic kicking. As I continued to swim, the warmth turned into a kind of joy, an awareness that something greater than myself was present within me. . . . Though exhausted, I fought against the current. My companion was stretching out his hand. I battled the last few inches. Finally I felt his fingertips.

And so years later after the war, I was able to set out on the Kon-Tiki *across the Pacific. I had learned for myself that there is an invisible world of caring all around and inside us—different from our world, unimaginable by us, but as close as a cry from the heart.*

Full Out . . . All Day!

Finally I share with you a memorable day from the early 1990s. My younger son, Bobby, was excited that he was about to turn ten. I asked him what he wanted for his birthday and he proclaimed: "I want you to take me and my friend Trevor to Magic Mountain. And I want us to arrive right when it opens, and I want us to stay all the way 'til it closes!" A chill went through me. Magic Mountain is a huge amusement park located in Ventura County. Bobby knew this park well because we had lived for a year in Simi Valley, just south of this park. He'd always wanted to go, but we never accomplished it while living close by. We ended up moving to Orange County and I thought his interest in going to Magic Mountain had waned. I stood corrected and agreed to this gift along with all his specifications.

On the appointed Saturday, Bobby and I got up in the morning while it was still dark, gobbled down a bit of breakfast, and headed excitedly northward to Simi Valley to pick up his friend Trevor. After about a ninety-minute drive we arrived, picked up an equally excited Trevor, and headed about thirty minutes farther north to Magic Mountain. I bought tickets and we stood at the entry gates for about another twenty minutes. Finally the gates opened and the boys took off into the park like flashes of light. They were so giddy with excitement, they could hardly decide what to do first. They chose a ride and loved it. Then ran off to another. I tried to keep up. Ride . . . after ride . . . after ride . . . after ride. There were no prolonged snack breaks, just gulping down some sodas, devouring some candy, then back to the rides. Near lunchtime I finally coaxed them into a twenty-minute pizza break. I was already exhausted, but they were just getting started.

It was more of the same in the afternoon. I noticed that they'd been avoiding some of the scarier rides, romancing the possibility but backing off. As the afternoon ensued, they began to take some risks—a roller coaster, then a big people holder that all of a sudden fell about thirty feet downward, then a huge twirling drum that had a floor that descended, leaving the people plastered to the sides. They approached each of these gambles with an excited fear and departed from them with joyous boldness. Then they tore off to their next adventure. I remembered this as a lesson for me . . . that life is about leaning into the fears that restrict us from discovery, and advancement . . . and joy.

The day seemed to go on and on. The boys were relentless—never stopping—taking it all in, every ounce and speck of it. Occasionally I'd go on a ride with them, but I also honored the camaraderie they were having together. I noticed that the sun was beginning to edge closer to the horizon . . . and then I heard some of the loveliest words I think I'd ever heard: "The park is closing. Please gather your belongings and make your way to the gates. Thank you." No, I thought, thank *you*! We started toward the gates. By this time, the boys were pretty much played out. I gave a few piggyback rides to top things off. I'd met Bobby's criteria: a full day there from the time the gates opened to the time they closed. When we pulled out of the parking lot, I glanced at the backseat to find that both boys were already asleep. I drove Trevor back to his house, then headed onto the freeway for the long commute south. It was dark now and Bobby was still passed out in the backseat. I, too, was exhausted. My feet and back hurt. My eyes were stinging . . . but the day had been a lot of fun.

When we got home, Bobby resisted waking up, so I carried him upstairs to his room. I deposited him on his bed, pulled off his sneakers, and threw his quilt over him. He was out . . . in some other land. I went to the door and reached for the light switch . . . but was moved to pause. I looked back at Bobby snoring away. I was struck by a certain quality about him as he lay there . . . the lingering echo of a dream day fulfilled . . . the aura from living it absolutely completely, nothing held back . . . the peacefulness of Spirit from all the sheer abandonment to playing, risking, bragging, tasting, running, jumping . . . celebrating the panorama of it all. He'd had a DAY . . . and he was fully present, even omnipresent in it. A few tears welled up and I thought to myself, *I remember that! I remember living that intensely and fully . . . no reservations, no pretenses, giving everything within me to it all! Unbridled enthusiasm and immersion in the joy of it all! I want more of that back in my life!*

I turned off the light . . . fully aware that Bobby wasn't the only one who'd been given a really great gift of a day. I'd received a renewed understanding that Life is a banquet feast. Sadly we often just collect crumbs instead of tasting and enjoying it all. Join me in granting more of the outrageous wishes of the child within you. They'll lead us back to a festival of deep, unwavering, precious . . . Joy.

– The Expression –

1. Use this great Bible phrase as a mantra: "This is the day the Lord has made; I will rejoice and be glad in it!"

   Use this to start your days . . . but go one step further. Instead of this is the "day," insert the word *moment*: "This is the *moment* the Lord has made; I will rejoice and be glad in it!"

   Allow this to lead you into a sense of mindfulness as you fully embrace and take in each moment. Decline to fight with whatever fills the moment. Decline to demand anything from the moment. Simply be present with it . . . present with the joy *you* bring to the moment. Remember, Joy is the gift in you that you bring to your life.

By doing this you will find greater and greater access to the mystic essence of life. You will be able to fully relate to William Blake's words:

> *To see a world in a grain of sand*
> *And a heaven in a wildflower*
> *Hold infinity in the palm of your hand*
> *And eternity in an hour.*

2. When troubling or painful experiences come your way, honor your genuine feelings and emotional responses. And explore your capacity to also summon a sense of the deep Joy that abides within you no matter what is going on. This deep Joy can caress and support you even in those times of immense grieving.

   Remember this Chinese proverb:

   > *You cannot prevent the "birds of sorrow" from flying over your head. But you can prevent them from building nests in your hair.*

3. Schedule some specific and nonnegotiable "willow time" into each week. These will be the times, no matter what's going on in your life, when you let it all go and abandon yourself to some fun, some play, some dancing for your Spirit. These will be your times to allow your Being to transcend the problems, challenges, duties, drudgeries . . . all the stuff of the human experience. It will be your times for genuine freedom and "in-JOY-ment!" You'll be amazed how renewing these times will be for you. After a while, you'll feel their echo amid your day-

to-day, moment-to-moment activities. They'll be the cause of that sly little smile that leaves your faces less and less.

Bottom line: Life Is Good!

4. A spark that always ignites the realization of deep and eternal Joy is caring for and serving others. Seek out opportunities to generate acts of grace, compassion, generosity, and kindness. Your heart will reverberate with Joy and you will induct yourself ever more fully into the ineffable, mysterious, and magical experience of that infinite, omnipresent Spirit . . . God.

SEVEN PILLARS OF TRUTH
A SPIRITUAL PRACTICE

I invite you to amplify the impact of the seven chapters in Part Two by focusing on one of the chapter titles during each day of each week. This is a simple yet extremely powerful spiritual practice. During each day of the week, remind yourself frequently of that day's title, using it as a mantra or affirmation. Allow this remembrance to create a shift . . . a shift of your energies, awareness, and behaviors into the essence of that chapter's message. You might choose to carry a card bearing that title/mantra, or set a soft watch or phone alarm as a reminder. Be creative and find ways that work best for you. Eventually, you'll memorize this process, and it will take on greater and greater meaning and results. It will enhance the quality and vibration of your consciousness, and guide you into more effective, openhearted, abundant, and joyous living.

Here's a suggested format:

Sunday: *This Instant Is Love*
Monday: *This Being Is Light*
Tuesday: *This World Is Consciousness*
Wednesday: *This Idea Is Substance*
Thursday: *This Relationship Is Oneness*
Friday: *This Journey Is Surrender*
Saturday: *This Life Is Joy*

PART THREE

Nine Portals of Transformation

*Breakthrough Realizations and
Strategies for Some of Life's
Greatest Challenges*

8. THIS FEAR IS FRIEND

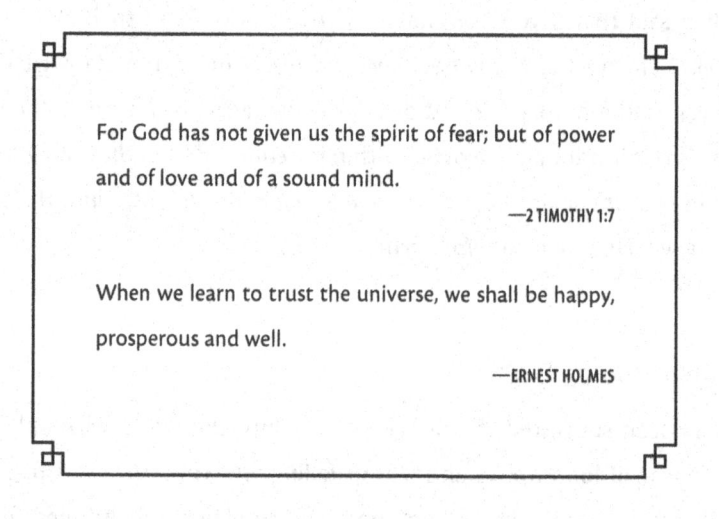

For God has not given us the spirit of fear; but of power and of love and of a sound mind.

—2 TIMOTHY 1:7

When we learn to trust the universe, we shall be happy, prosperous and well.

—ERNEST HOLMES

– The Essence –

Fear gets a bad rap. Most of the time, it is loathed and despised. Often-times as soon as it shows up, it gets hidden away and denied. For to admit it to others—or oneself—is sufficient cause for feeling weak and ashamed. Despite being so obnoxious, some people are in the habit of having it around nearly all the time. Whenever it is present, it is seen as a torturer or a robber, and this amplifies the discomfort because fear seems so cruel and offensive. Isn't it odd that we have such a poor relationship with something every one of us experiences at various times throughout our lives?

There is an opening into life mastery within this thing called fear. It brings us to a rigorous yet fruitful practice. It shows up when we shift our relationship with fear and discover that, in truth, it is friend not foe. It is a guest that knocks on the door of our awareness bearing some very valuable gifts. It is high time we stopped treating fear so shabbily and explored what this friendship is meant to provide.

It is said that if you boil down all your emotions to their most basic level, there are really only two: love and fear. Among the many gifts fear brings us, the most profound one is the invitation to return to the Love that is this instant and all of life within it. *Fear is a friend that shows up to tell us that it's time to open our hearts again and to enter into the Spirit Divine which is, now and forevermore . . . Love.*

Understanding Fear

It has been suggested that a baby comes into the world with only two fears: fear of loud noises and fear of falling. But then the fears begin to multiply and accumulate: fear of the dark, fear of being abandoned, fear of starting school, fear of pain, fear of disappointing loved ones, fear of being unpopular. Then come the fear of things we've neglected and fear of the mistakes we've made. In adulthood another tier of fears emerges: fear of not getting a job or mate, fear of losing a job or mate, fear for our children, fear of change, fear of people or ideas that are different, fear of not fulfilling dreams or succeeding as well as others, fear of losing ones we love. Eventually there's fear of old age and, of course, the granddaddy of them all, fear of death. *Fear* in so many forms! A few are essential for safety or survival. Yet we make most of them unnecessary blocks to happiness, fulfillment, and more abundant living.

Having fear doesn't make us terrible; it makes us human. Fears are a natural part of our journey into spiritual empowerment. As we stretch and seek to grow, our traveling buddy—fear—shows up just in time to remind us that what we're up to is new, different, significant, or challenging. This adds a kind of exhilaration, if we'd let it . . . like when you decided to ride your bike without training wheels for the first time, or to climb that ladder and dive off the high dive. It was scary, but in a juicy way! By encountering and transcending fear in these ways, we came out on the other side with a much greater belief in ourselves.

But the time arrives when most of us stop having that kind of healthy relationship with fear. Instead, we embrace a lot of erroneous beliefs that magnify the power and impact of fear, and *this* is when it takes over and steers the vessel of our lives into lack, limitation, and excessive difficulty. We need to delve into our subconscious beliefs if we're to shift the role of fear in our lives.

There Are Three Common Beliefs That Distort Our Relationship with Fear

1. "My needs may not always be met."

This is the belief that you may not be taken care of, that the Love and Givingness of your Source, the One Life, may not always include you. Many harbor this fear especially when they doubt their worth in the divine scheme of things. Does this live within you and haunt you?

I heard of a man who was on the verge of losing his marriage. Nearly all he ever did was work. He had two jobs and also did odd jobs for people when he found spare moments. He was never around for his wife and kids, and he was threatening his own health and well-being. Finally he went into counseling and at one point, when he was trying to defend himself, he shouted: "Nobody will ever see me having to hunt for food in garbage cans!" Then it came out that when he was a child, there was a feebleminded old man who used to go through garbage cans around town, and this frightened him a lot. His father compounded it by declaring, "If you don't look out, you'll grow up and have to dig around in garbage cans to get enough to eat!" This became a deep-seated fear that unconsciously drove him in his adult life to over-work, and while he had plenty of money, he was deeply impoverished emotionally.

2. **"My problems are bigger than me . . . so my fears are stop signs."**

This is such a common assumption based on a belief that we may have been abandoned. Dr. Ernest Holmes wrote, "There is a Power for Good in the Universe, greater than we are, and we can use it." But many im-agine that they are alone and their access to power is meager. It is then that problems and challenges begin to look like huge ogres looming over us. "Instant paralysis" then becomes the new and habitual re-sponse to fear! I ask you, has fear become a "stop sign" for you . . . when it could become a "green light"?

3. **"It's better to think small and play not to lose."**

For some it can seem too dangerous to play to win. This assumes that trusting is foolish and that risks are our enemies, so don't even go for the win. Believing this, we develop a stifling lifestyle of excessive caution and deep comfort zones. Maybe at some point someone said, "You bet-ter not get bigger than 'ur britches!" So we complied and decided not to dream too much or too big. That way we wouldn't be disappointed, and if we slipped, it wouldn't be too long a fall. Or maybe you did fall down in some undertaking and then decided not to allow that to hap-pen again.

A farmer was sitting on his porch, rocking, when a stranger came along and asked, "How's your cotton coming?" "Ain't got none," the farmer answered. "Didn't plant none. 'Fraid of the boll weevil." So this visitor asked, "Well, how's your corn?" "Didn't plant none. 'Fraid o' drouth." "How about your potatoes?" inquired the passerby. "Ain't got none. Scairt o' tater bugs." Really confused now, the stranger asked, "Well, what *did* you plant?" "Nothin'," answered the farmer. "I just played it safe!" Avoid risking in order to avoid losing: that's the way of life for so many. But this also forfeits the harvest!

The Search for Security

I remember working with a man who started our session by stating, "I'm fighting depression." I first invited him to stop "fighting." Instead I offered, "Let's unlock the message in all this." So we began exploring as he began to share more and more openly. Eventually we uncovered some things that happened in his youth that hurt him a lot. When he recounted these events, he remembered the very moment when he decided "Life's not safe . . . Hide yourself!" This lodged in his subconscious. He began to realize that the rest of his life, from that moment on, had been about one form or another of hiding. It had greatly stifled his personal expression. It's been said that the opposite of some forms of depression is *expression*. Impelled by his empowering realizations, this man reembraced a greater and more genuine expressiveness in his life, and over about a six-month period he found that he was freed from the depression.

Fear, in its myriad forms, is usually based on the search for security. Our human tendency is to seek safety and security in people, things, and conditions, and yet all of these are fleeting and subject to change or loss. Fearing this change or loss, we cling to the objects of our security and avoid doing anything that might "upset the apple cart." To further bolster a false sense of security many decide, at one point or another, to hide themselves . . . or at least certain aspects of themselves.

Yet the truth is—and it can seem harsh—there is never certainty, security, or permanency in the outer world of people, things, and circumstances. Security can only be found within, and refusing to accept this is what drives us to try to fabricate and then protect myths of security. The result is we often stagnate in comfort zones . . . and become even more fearful. Emerson puts it bluntly but ever so honestly: "People wish to be settled. It is only as they are unsettled that there is any hope for them."

It is also important to realize that fear draws its life and power from our notions of the past and future. Fear increases and can become debilitating when we drag memories from the past or worries about the future into the present moment. These are the lifeblood of fear. It's as though we infect the present moment with unhealed energy from the past or with unsubstantiated concerns for the future . . . which is why a popular acronym for FEAR is "false expectations appearing real." And when this is operating in our lives, another acronym also applies: "forget everything and run!" Then it's just a step away to "feeling empty and ridiculous!"

The emotion of fear depends on thought for its energy and direction. When Life calls us to take some significant step, our thinking gives the energy and impetus to fear . . . thoughts like these: *I'm not good enough . . . capable enough . . . attractive enough . . . smart enough . . . loved enough . . . powerful enough . . . creative enough.* Thoughts like, *There's not enough . . . I might not be taken care of or provided for . . . I might not be able to recover from setbacks . . . I might be humiliated and not loved.* Thoughts like these provide the fuel for the engine of fear. However, consider this: pure awareness in the present moment is free of fear.

Fearful experiences also provide us with the opportunity to face what we *really* believe. I love the story of the little boy—six or seven—who got his first two-wheeler bike. He rolled it to the top of a hill and prepared to ride it down, risking life and limb. All the while, a retired preacher sat rocking on his porch watching it all. The little guy hopped on, started rolling down the hill, wobbling all the way . . . faster . . . before he crashed and scraped his elbow. The boy jumped up and yelled, "I'll be damned!"

He gave it a second try and was just as wobbly before crashing again. This time he tore his pants, and again he yelled: "I'll be damned!"

The boy walked his bike up the hill and prepared for a third attempt. The old preacher called out, "Say young" un, if you'll shout out 'Praise God,' no matter what happens, things will turn out a whole lot better!" So, the boy hopped on his bike and cruised down the hill . . . and actually made it to the bottom this time without crashing. He leaped off the bike excitedly and yelled, "Praise God!" At that very moment, his elbow healed up and his pants were miraculously mended. Seeing all this, the preacher leaped right out of his rocking chair and shouted, "I'll be damned!" Fear shows us what we really believe, especially when we're facing the new or unknown.

Fear is seldom stronger or more persistent than in times of uncertainty.

The Entry Mat

A wonderful friend told me about an incident that involved her granddaughter. This beautiful little girl had just learned to walk and was navigating all over the place to her own delight and to the cheers of her parents and grandparents. At one point, the little girl wobbled into the home's foyer and it was there that she came upon something new: the thick entryway mat in front of the door. She stood there at the edge of this mat and became confused and frightened. She wasn't about to step up onto that contraption. So, faced with this challenge from something so unknown, the little girl began to cry with everything in her. Hearing the screams, her grandmother rushed over to her and sized up the situation. It was more than an odd floor mat in her granddaughter's way. The little girl was having one of her first experiences of something we all encounter over and over in our lives: fear of the unknown.

She comforted her granddaughter for a moment, then stood up and stepped right onto the mat. She held out her hand and encouraged her precious little one to join her. The girl paused, still skeptical about that mat, but, after all, it was her grandma. So she went ahead and placed her little hand into her grandmother's and gingerly stepped onto the mat. For a few moments, nothing happened. *Then* the little girl let out a squeal of delight and began to giggle nonstop. After that, you couldn't keep her off that mat!

What is the "entry mat" in your life right now? What are the steps before *you* that you fear to take? When it's time to grow, or some opportunity calls, how readily and enthusiastically do you step forth into the unknown? It's normal when facing life's uncertainties to feel fear, but how do you deal with it? Is it a friend and partner on the journey . . . or an impediment that blocks your progress?

When faced with some significant step in life, we have a choice: to become intimidated, overwhelmed, and paralyzed by fear *or* to utilize that step as an opportunity to develop a greater trust in the Source of our very being. Ernest Holmes writes, "There is a power within us which is greater than any condition we can ever contact. It knows no obstruction, no obstacle. It transcends all because it is the final fact of creation, the Almighty indwelling our own souls."

There's more to the story about the granddaughter and the entry mat. Not long after the grandmother involved shared this story with me, she received a diagnosis of breast cancer. Of course, the fear welled up immediately and powerfully. It even caused her to question her spiritual awareness and connection to the Divine. At one point as we talked, I said to her, "This cancer is *your* entry mat. And the Great Presence has extended Its hand to you. You can step forward into that Love and forge a deeper trusting than you've ever known. Could that be your gift here?" The tears of realization flowed and, in a very beautiful way, I sensed that she was already "on that mat" soaking up the Love that is always offered. It was about a two-year journey, but this wonderful lady is now cancer-free. She is also now in the ministry with a special focus on healing. The crowning glory of all advancement is sharing the gifts from our journey with those facing their own challenges and uncertainties.

A New Relationship with Fear

Through spiritual understanding you can move to an opening that has the power to shift your relationship with fear forever. Begin by moving yourself into this Now moment. Move yourself out of the swirl of your thoughts and into your quiet Center . . . pure Awareness in and as you. Then energize the Truth that you are a spiritual being—a being of Light. Realize that you can change and direct your thinking. Immerse yourself in a growing sense of the loving and powerful being God created you to be. Involve yourself in a vibrant consciousness of the full Presence and Power of God, with and within you—your real and lasting security.

After you spend precious moments cultivating this awareness, a semblance of fear may remain, but it will no longer have the power to intimidate you or hold you back. You are empowered to take your next step. Eleanor Roosevelt put it so well: "You gain strength and courage and confidence by every experience in which you really stop and look fear in the face. You're able to say to yourself, 'I've lived through this. I can take the next thing that comes along.' You must do the thing you cannot do."

With a greater understanding of fear, I invite you to realize that it is here to serve as a signal . . . a reminder to get reenergized in the truth . . . and to step into a greater experience of Love. From this, a higher trusting emerges. Then fear becomes more of an excitement energy . . . something of a good friend or companion on the journey of becoming. Our real journey is always into a greater embodiment of the Love and Presence of God and a greater knowing of the Truth of our inner spiritual Light. It is the unfolding of spiritual maturity . . . an undeniable faith in who we are, in That which supports us, and in all that we are designed and destined to become.

Remember, "Perfect love casts out fear." That Love is here for you now . . . and always. May we arrive at the place where we can wholeheartedly proclaim, "Thank you, fear, for my homecomings!"

– The Experience –

A God Job!

I'll never forget my first night in Portland, Oregon, in the mid-'70s. I had just moved there from California to launch forth on my ministerial path . . . the very start of a journey that seemed so vague and imposing. I remember pulling over in my car when Portland's skyline came into view. The first major wave of panic washed over me. I didn't know a thing about this city, and the only people I knew were those I'd met when interviewing for the position. After a few minutes, I took a deep breath, put the car in gear, and drove into town.

I drove around in an area that had been recommended to me and found a "For Rent" sign on an apartment complex. They had one available unit, so I took it. Then I carried all my life's belongings—they all fit into my car—into that small apartment. When that was finished, I wasn't sure what to do next. Another surge of fear welled up in me. So, I put a few books and a legal pad into my briefcase and headed over to the church office. The church I was to serve was tiny—twenty-five dedicated people. They had no assets, only a rented office in a Masonic Temple where we would be meeting on Sundays in a small auditorium that was also rented week to week. They had mailed me a key to this office. When I unlocked the door, the next wave of panic hit. There was only one thing in the room: a Steelcase desk. There was no chair and there was nothing in the desk. No phone had been installed yet. There was nothing on the walls, either. I sat my briefcase on the desk and opened it. But I wasn't sure what to do. Eventually I took out the books, sat them on one corner of the desk . . . but then what? I knew I'd have to present my first Sunday message in five days, but I also knew I was in no position to be very creative in that moment.

I left and got some dinner. The fear and loneliness were increasing with every minute. After all, I was only twenty-four years old! What business did I have launching out into such a career? I wondered. Waves of doubt and self-criticism poured over me. When I returned to the apartment, there wasn't much to do. I got things organized as best I could. I would use a sleeping bag for a few weeks, until I could arrange for some rented furniture. I read for a while, but couldn't stay focused. Then I tried to go to sleep, but it didn't work. I just lay there for several hours trying to keep my wits about me. Honestly, I felt miserable and questioned what I could do.

Then I experienced one of those moments when, despite myself, a greater Guidance went to work. I was moved to reach for a book given to me by my cherished mentor, Dr. Fred Vogt. He was such a force of love and encouragement in my life. He thought of me as the son he'd never had, and publicly proclaimed me to be his "son in the ministry." On the inside front page of this book, Fred had inscribed these words: *Remember Jeremiah . . . and just BE!*

I figured he wasn't talking about Jeremiah the bullfrog, made famous in the 1970s hit song. Instead, the story of Jeremiah from the Bible began to come back to me. I remembered that Jeremiah was called by God into spiritual leadership when he, too, was quite young. Jeremiah was also bound up with fear and misgivings at this outrageous calling. He was struggling and cried out to be relieved of this assignment . . . or at least to get some help. Here's how Jeremiah relates that God responded: "Then the word of the Lord came to me, saying . . . Before I formed you in the womb I knew you; and before you were born I consecrated you; I ordained you a prophet to the nations."

Then Jeremiah said—and boy, could I relate—"Ah, Lord God! Behold, I cannot speak: for I am a youth." But God replied to Jeremiah, "Do not say, 'I am only a youth'; for to all whom I send you, you shall go, and whatever I command you, you shall speak. Do not be afraid of them, for I am with you to deliver you."

Then there was a beautiful culmination. A direct blessing was given to Jeremiah: "Then God put forth his hand, and touched my mouth. And the Lord said to me, 'Behold, I have put my words in your mouth'" (Jeremiah 1:4-9).

Now I understood why Fred had invited me to always remember Jeremiah. It was to remind me not to focus on my age or my inexperience, but to remember why I was embarking upon this path in the first place. He was telling me to stay in touch with my vision, to shine forth the Light of Spirit however I could. Furthermore, it was an insistent reminder to not lose sight of the fact that Spirit is fully available to place Its inspiration "in my mouth" and to guide me in all the steps I would have to take. If it was going to work, I was going to have to let it be "a God Job!"

Recounting Jeremiah's story was the perfect opening into life mastery. It flooded me with warmth as it also brought forth a few tears. I lay there in that dark, unfurnished apartment . . . on the brink of more than I could ever know. But somehow the unknown was no longer a fearsome dragon. It was simply a path yet to be revealed, a story yet to be written. In that moment I was clear that I would allow the story to be coauthored by the guiding Light of Spirit and empowered by the healing essence of Love. And when all was said and done, it would be good. My eyes closed and I slept well.

I invite you to cherish the lessons of Jeremiah as you move forward beyond the boundaries suggested by your fears. Remember that before you came into form on this planet, you were known in the Mind/Heart of God . . . and you have been permanently consecrated as an original blessing. You, too, have been ordained to be here, called to express the Love and Light of God in your own unique way . . . and to provide the Divine with a once-in-a-universe opportunity to reveal Its secrets through the glory of your experience. You and I are never alone; we only dwell in self-imagined isolation. The spark of the Indwelling Beloved forever remains sheltered in your heart. Fan it into a flame, and go forth to do mighty, even outrageous works. But remember . . . let it be a God Job!

From Fear to Family

In 1993 my wife, Erica, volunteered for a program that had established several homes for pregnant unwed teens. The program had been inspired during one of the classes I taught at my church. Erica became like a Big Sister for a girl I'll call Nicole. She was twenty, pregnant, and her family had thrown her out of the house. They were very strict and religiously conservative. Nicole's boyfriend, the young father, was confused and frightened. When he was sixteen, his father was serving as a policeman and was killed on duty. So when this young man learned that he'd fathered a child, he panicked and left town soon after the baby's birth. Nicole had nowhere to go, found the shelter for unwed teens, and moved in.

Erica and Nicole began meeting at least weekly . . . lunch, phone calls, little opportunities for Erica to share her love. Nicole was filled with so much fear. She spoke of being afraid of becoming a mom like her own mother. Erica coached her to take the good things her mom imparted then add her own good things. Nicole would ask things like, "Will I ever get a man? . . . How will I support myself and my baby? . . . Will I always be dependent? . . . What will I tell my baby? . . . Have I messed up both of our lives? . . . Will I ever be an accepted part of my family again?" So many fears.

On Mother's Day, a month before the birth of her baby, Nicole was allowed to be with her family at their church. At one point, the minister asked all mothers to stand to be recognized and to receive a flower and gift. Nicole was too ashamed to stand. Then a friend, also pregnant, stood and a lady behind Nicole nudged her shoulder and encouraged her to stand. So, she stood. Then she saw the glares and anger pouring forth from her parents. She felt awful, went back to her room at the shelter, and cried and cried. The House Mother knocked on her door and told her she'd gotten mail the day before. An envelope was slid under the door. It was a Mother's Day card from Erica. In it Erica praised her, told her the baby was lucky, and that she would be a fabulous mother. Erica wrote that she was proud of her and that everything would work out fine. That card changed everything for Nicole.

Nicole gave birth to a beautiful girl. A little over a year later, the baby's father moved back to town and Nicole "freaked out." She called Erica, overflowing with fear and resistance because he wanted to meet with her. Erica responded by encouraging her to go ahead and meet with him. Nicole reacted angrily: "Why are you taking his side? You never say anything bad about him." Erica went on: "Just meet in a public place. Give him an hour." Reluctantly, Nicole agreed. As they sat down in a restaurant, her former boyfriend asked Nicole to tell him everything . . . to say everything she had been wanting to say to him. So she laid it on him . . . unloaded full bore. When she was finished, he mirrored it all back to her so she'd know he really understood. Then he surprised her and said, "I'd like to start dating again." Nicole paused . . . then sheepishly said, "Okay."

They were married six months later. Erica and I hosted the reception at our house. Nicole and her husband have had two more beautiful daughters, have created a wonderful family, and have experienced more joy than either of them thought was possible. It might not have been so wonderful if fear had been allowed to chart the course.

Sliding into the Unknown

Sir Ernest Shackleton envisioned an Antarctic expedition. In 1914 he placed an advertisement to seek recruits that read, "Men wanted for hazardous journey. Small wages, bitter cold, long months of complete darkness. Constant danger. Safe return doubtful. Honor and recognition in case of success."

The ad fielded a crew of twenty-eight adventurers! After all, there are so many unknowns in this life, and always insufficient evidence, so our journeys require great courage.

The expedition encountered horrendous experiences. At one point their ship, *Endurance*, became trapped in ice and they had no way to contact the outside world for help. The crew had to spend the winter on the ship hoping the ice would break in the spring. Instead, however, the ice crushed the ship. So they set up camp on an ice floe. Days turned into five months. The ice began breaking up so they had to get into their three lifeboats and sail for seven days battling the elements. Shackleton steered toward Elephant Island to save his crew and stepped onto land for the first time in 497 days. However, this isolated island offered no hope of rescue.

Shackleton and five other crew members then took the largest lifeboat and set off across eight hundred miles of the roughest seas on earth to try to get to some whaling stations on South Georgia Island. They were at sea for seventeen days but landed on the opposite coast of the island. Now they would have to walk across treacherous mountains and glaciers. After thirty-six hours of trudging on the unmapped island, it was near nightfall. They were atop a steep, icy ridge. Shackleton knew they had to be close, but if they didn't do something bold, they'd die at that altitude during the night. So he tied the crew to himself with a long rope . . . then leaped off the ridge. Together they all slid down the steep incline in pitch darkness . . . and, surprisingly, came to rest safely.

Shackleton thought he could see lights. They hiked a mile, found their destination, and knocked on the door of the Stromness Whaling Station. Can you imagine staffing such a whale station in Antarctica and hearing a knock on your door late at night? Over the next several days, rescue teams were sent to get the rest of Shackleton's crew. Not a single life was lost. Another lesson in befriending fears: When sliding into the unknown, it's best to be tied tightly together. The Lone Wolf approach won't work very well.

– The Expression –

Practicing These Three Steps Will Help Make Fear a Friend for You . . . and a "Green Light"!

1. LINK UP!

First, link up with your Source. There is nothing more powerful than our conscious connection with God, with the Spirit . . . that infinite, in-dwelling Source of our lives and of all Good. This is the step of remembering the provision of God for all of us . . . no matter who we are . . . what we've ever done . . . or what we now face . . . all of us, all the time!

It's Up to Each of Us to Link Up with the Indwelling Presence, So That Its Power and Provision Can Flow Through and to Us. Here's a Good Approach:

- *Admit there's fear. Don't lie about it. Unmask it and reveal it.*

- *Call the Presence and Power of God into your consciousness.*

- *Allow your sense of the divine Presence to energize a greater experience of Love . . . until you can love yourself fully, and even love the fear, itself!*

Next, link up with a group of true friends or supporters. Another approach is to get involved in some form of spiritual community. You have to create your own "Faithbook Network"! Or you might think of this as your "God Squad." Jesus did this by assembling his disciples and followers. He knew that the field of high awareness that would be developed over time would be invaluable to him as he encountered the difficulties and suffering of his day. Followers of Buddhism are encouraged to anchor themselves in the three pillars of "the Buddha, the Dharma, and the Sangha." The Buddha represents enlightened awareness, and the Dharma is one's core purpose in life. Then there's the Sangha . . . spiritual community. Fear yields its grip of limitation when you link up with abundant Love . . . both within you and gathered all around you.

2. LOOK UP!

"I will lift up mine eyes unto the hills from whence cometh my help" (Psalm 121:1). Too often our heads are down, our hearts closed, our feet stumbling.

- Look up to the goal and allow your innate balance and stability to emerge.

- Look up for options. Robert Louis Stevenson was a great poet and writing gave him great joy. But he had many physical challenges. During one of his bouts with a pulmonary disease, he was coughing so intensely that he could barely speak and was bedridden for weeks. His wife came in and saw all the medicine bottles around him; she asked him how he was doing. . . . And he said: "I will never let a bank of medicine bottles keep me from seeing the horizon!"

- Look up for purpose, for purpose breeds passion, and passion is fully equipped to overwhelm fear.

3. LEAP UP!

The time arrives when we must act in spite of fears! Decide to become a person who won't be stopped . . . even if it's uncomfortable. Inspirational writer Charles Newcomb declares, "We fear to trust our wings. We plume and feather them, but dare not throw our weight upon them. We cling too often to the perch!" And Emerson adds, simply, "Do the thing and you will have the power!" Abraham Maslow, in *The Farther Reaches of Human Nature*, writes about "leap up" choices:

> *Life is a process of choices, one after another. At each point there is a progression choice and a regression choice. There may be a movement toward defense, toward safety, toward being afraid; but over on the other side, there is the growth choice. To make the growth choice instead of the fear choice a dozen times a day is to move a dozen times a day toward self-actualization. Self-actualization is an ongoing process.*

Joshua became the leader of the Israelites after Moses died. The Children of Israel had been wandering for forty years, searching for the Promised Land. When Moses led them close to the Land of Canaan, they became afraid because they were told that the inhabitants were giants, and very strong. They hesitated. But after Moses died, Joshua took command and notified the Children of Israel that they would pass over into the Promised Land in three days—the kind of promptness of action that results from inner knowing and empowerment. And they did, indeed, go into Canaan! The Promised Land is a symbol of spiritual realization. The name "Joshua" is identical with "Jesus," which comes from "Jehovah," meaning "I AM that I AM." Through inspired action we become spiritual warriors and move into our natural inheritance of the Good of God!

9. THIS PROBLEM IS POSSIBILITY

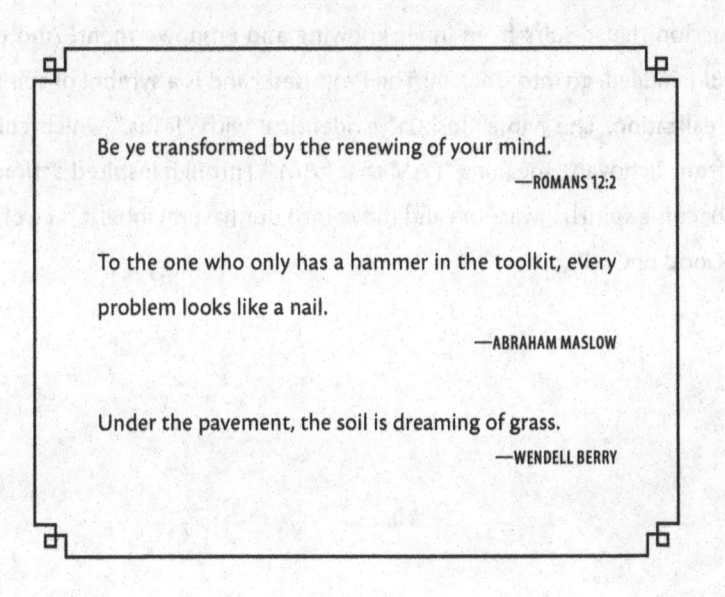

Be ye transformed by the renewing of your mind.

—ROMANS 12:2

To the one who only has a hammer in the toolkit, every problem looks like a nail.

—ABRAHAM MASLOW

Under the pavement, the soil is dreaming of grass.

—WENDELL BERRY

– The Essence –

Most everyone would admit to having one or several problems in their life at any given time. It just seems to be part of the journey, part of being human. What problems in your life are of most concern to you right now? Moreover, what is your relationship to these problems? That is a much more important question to consider. Our relationship with problems determines so much: the length of time we'll have to deal with them, the angst or pain we'll endure while they're in our life, and the quality of the eventual outcome . . . just to mention several.

When an unexpected or difficult life experience makes its entrance, it's pretty typical to quickly anoint it "a problem." That very designation, however, is often the most challenging aspect of the situation. This is because most people are "wired" to feel significantly inferior to problems, whatever the nature of them might be. Thus these experiences are expected to become some combination of complicated, grueling, wrenching, domineering, convoluted, drawn-out, expensive, exhausting, haunting, and maybe even humiliating. It's interesting that the root words for *problem* actually mean "to drive forward." For most people, however, their actual experience is not "to drive forward" but "to sink under" or "be run over."

What is your attitude toward problems? Some people look at their problems as a kind of punishment, unjustified at that, e.g., "I've always tried to do the right thing . . . and now this! It isn't fair." Some are resigned to problems as inevitable: "Well, that's the way my life always is. Guess I'll just grin and bear it." Then there are those who take problems personally: "I just knew it. That's the kind of thing that's always happening to me!" Any semblance of attitudes like these welds problems in place and things go downhill from there.

There is a point at which problems cease being passing experiences. Instead they are embraced and owned. That's when it becomes "my problem," almost like a member of the family. We start hanging on to it emotionally, intellectually, and verbally. When this happens, we're a little like the bear and the bean pot. There once was a bear who grabbed a bean pot that was hanging over a campfire. When it burned him, he hugged it all the tighter, thinking to squeeze it to death somehow—and of course the more he hugged it to him, the more it hurt him. That's what happens to us when we think we're attacking our problems fervently in order to solve them. It's unsettling to discover that we're actually holding them in place by the attention and emotion with which we are energizing them.

155

The more we dwell on the problem, fixate on it—over and over—and identify with it emotionally, we're actually accepting it, anchoring it in our lives, no matter what we say about trying to get rid of it. We are keeping it alive in our consciousness and imbuing it with an undeserved power.

There is an opening into life mastery that can change all this and move our lives forward, even when the difficult and unexpected emerges—especially then. It is to put the picture of every problem into a new frame: This Problem Is Possibility. This will require us to reconstitute our definition of *problem* and reformat our relationship with it, but it makes all the difference. No one can completely insulate his life from hardship, change, adversity, or the unforeseen. What we can do, however, is enhance and fortify our awareness so that these experiences build us up and enrich our lives, rather than robbing and tearing us down.

Locked inside every problem are possibilities hankering to get out. Every problem is an opportunity of some sort. Just like the two sides of a coin are always present, always a complement to each other, so is a problem always united with its eventual solution. The solution is the other side of the coin that is the problem. It is powerful to begin this way, by declaring, "My problems have their solutions already built into them. These problems come bearing gifts of great possibilities. I shift my focus from worrying about the problem to welcoming the possibilities."

In the midst of a problem, things can look mighty chaotic and purposeless. We judge by these appearances . . . things look dire . . . our confidence fades. We have to learn another perspective. Take the example of a Persian rug. On the backside is a jumbled, confusing mess. There's no rhyme, reason, or pattern to it. This is precisely how many feel in the midst of a problem. However, turn the rug over and it's another story. We feast our eyes on the beauty, the symmetry, the complementary colors. Both sides are a part of the total rug; both are necessary for its magnificence. Initially problems show us only the backside. Our job is to believe in and champion the front side.

Do you remember the opening story of the cave in Part One? The seeker battled against the enclosure until he was totally exhausted. He was bruised and battered, and the saddest thing was that his assault was getting him nowhere. Finally he realized that his problem wasn't so much the cave but his manner of dealing with it. This led to his discovery of a different way, the way of becoming and transcending. There is so much wisdom to glean from this story that will enhance our dealings with problems. If we are convinced that the problem is the problem, then we'll probably lash out against it, attack it, try to crash through it, causing a lot of damage in the process. There is an opening into life mastery, however, when we're ready for it. When we choose the opening, we can stop fighting and begin growing.

In the midst of a problem, stop worrying and fighting. Remember that there is a possibility in your midst. It is seeking an avenue to flow into realization and manifestation. That avenue is your awareness. From a place of heightened awareness you can choose to use your mind in a new way. Instead of reacting and attacking, you can choose to fashion beliefs, acceptances, and intentions that will serve as the clearing or space to bring forth the possibilities and solutions. This inner creativity magnetizes the possibilities and aligns you with that universal creative Power that materializes them into actualities.

What we believe becomes an open invitation . . . for manifestation. In the midst of a problem, believe in the possibilities inherent within the problem . . . even if you have no idea, initially, what they are. You are disengaging your vital energies from an attack on the problem, and making yourself available to guidance, inspiration, innovation, and serendipity. You are moving from reactivity to higher-order creativity. This doesn't mean that you do nothing or cease any and all action steps that might be necessary or appropriate to the situation. You do what you have to do at the level of the immediate needs, but you don't get stuck at that level. More important, you take inner action to free your vast creative resources as a being of Light to become a conduit for miracles of greater Good.

If you create a receptivity for something great out of a problem, both you and the universe will be compelled to bring forth its fulfillment. By cultivating a receptivity for higher-order possibilities, you create a powerful drawing activity—a magnetism to bring about the answers or the Good you desire. What you believe becomes an image that produces a tangible form or experience. Your thinking changes reality by shaping your truths. I remind you of the findings in the field of quantum physics called the "observer phenomenon." Quantum experiments revealed that those observing the experiment had the power to affect and even determine the results of the experiment according to their individual expectations. What this teaches us is that we don't really see things as they are; we see things as *we* are. In the midst of a problem you can use this to your advantage. Expect possibilities and solutions, and you actually become the vessel or conduit for creating them.

In the early 1970s, Joseph Chilton Pearce published a best-selling book called *The Crack in the Cosmic Egg*. It is profound and still very relevant. In this classic work, Pearce helps us understand that our consciousness, and its belief systems and values, are like eggs . . . closed systems that guide us and serve us to find meaning in life. But they can also suffocate us and become stifling, unless we find a way beyond them. But we don't want to shatter it all and start over, because the current egg does have some value. Instead, what we need to do is find a "crack" in the egg—a little opening that keeps the system intact while opening to the beyond, to the more, to our greater yet-to-be. Pearce also suggests that science thinks in terms of "empty categories"—unformed possibilities—and seeks to find openings into them. In all of this, we are realizing that we build a "new truth" by thinking in terms of a new category . . . a bold, unformed possibility. As we activate a sense of higher reality in our minds, we become the vessels, the system to support a concept, and this invites the thing or experience into our life. So our prophetic imagining is like bait that draws the big fish to us—toward that bigger category and the answer that we are anticipating.

This calls us to rise above conditions and circumstances—especially those we'd label as problems—to cultivate new categories and to think into them, to imagine into them . . . always expecting that something more than we can know in the moment is preparing to emerge into our experience. American poet, potter, and writer M. C. Richards puts it this way: "The imagination equips us to perceive reality when it is not fully materialized." Go beyond the reports of the economy and imagine new categories or dimensions of prosperity. Go beyond the hurtful words and think into new categories of love. Leap beyond the diagnosis and energize new dimensions of health and wholeness. In this way you are calling forth your preferred future, the possibility within the problem.

William Blake wrote of a man who didn't believe in miracles and thereby made it certain that he'd never take part in one. If you don't believe in miracles—in the revealing of something greater than you could ever imagine—then you remove that dimension of greater possibility from your life's menu. Such a stance is a hardening of the heart . . . a closing of the egg . . . a rejecting of alternate or expanded realities. Remember, *where your mind goes, power flows*. Every thing, every experience begins with a thought. Embracing a possibility—a bold new thought—is the activity of producing the energy that brings about the fulfillment or manifestation. The empty vessels of your belief create a space that the universe is invited to fill.

As we embrace and apply this opening into life mastery—This Problem Is Possibility—in our personal lives, a momentum builds, and it soon becomes apparent that this is the way most great human advances have taken place. At some point, a dreamer—or a group of dreamers—disentangled their imaginations and creativity from the problem at hand and began to think in greater terms, expanded dimensions or categories. This became the conception point for birthing a breakthrough, often historic in scope. Among the many who've walked this path, I have met two great souls whose visionary leadership is particularly inspiring. The first is His Holiness, the Dalai Lama. From the opportunities I've had to work with this awakened soul, I have witnessed and experienced not only his profound compassion for all beings, but also his vision of a higher way of bringing forth change and human progress. His life has been devoted to presenting an enlightened response to the genocide and terrible destruction of the Tibetan culture at the hands of the Chinese government. His message has always been consistent: This is an opportunity for all of us to dissolve hatred and vengeance, to take leaps forward in compassion. The greatest enemy, he instructs, is actually an inner one: the instinct for revenge—vengeful egotism—that exists within all of us. His Holiness has invited every person to join him in a stand against the endless cycle of violence upon this planet, and from this justice eventually is sure to prevail. If we join him in this call, we will have done something very special.

I have encountered another great soul whose path demonstrates, at the collective level, that within any problem are many great possibilities. His name is A. T. Ariyaratne, better known as "Ari." When I met this silver-haired man, I was taken with his immediate warmth and openness. Though slight in stature, he is a spiritual giant. Earlier in his life, he was a science teacher living on the island of Sri Lanka. In 1958 he organized a group of his students as part of a two-week holiday work camp at a remote, poverty-stricken village made up of the lowest caste. He did this so that the students might, in his words, "understand and experience the true state of affairs that prevailed in the rural and poor areas, and develop a love for their people, utilizing the education they received to find ways of building a more just and happy life for them."

He discovered that the most urgent need was for latrines and he came up with a plan to build them. This caused a major uproar. The very idea of upper-class students building latrines for lower-class peasants aroused enormous anger in the nearby high-caste neighborhoods. Several times the work was sabotaged, but by the end of the two weeks, the students and villagers had formed a powerful bond of friendship and accomplishment. This inspired Ari and his followers. Within a short time, more camps and work teams were formed, and his vision emerged for a grassroots movement now called Sarvodaya, meaning World Awakening. Ari resigned from his job as a science teacher and devoted his life to this work.

The Sarvodaya movement has hundreds of coordinating centers throughout Sri Lanka and has implemented programs in education, health care, transportation, agriculture, and energy technologies such as windmills and methane generators that convert human wastes into cooking gas. The movement serves 3,500 communities and has many millions of members involved in the practice of loving service. Sarvodaya was instrumental in the rebuilding of Sri Lanka after the tragic tsunami that hit the island in 2004. Ari is one of the most revered men in Sri Lanka and is respected around the world. At the national and global levels, Ari Ariyaratne is a shining example of revealing powerful possibilities despite gigantic problems.

Problems are usually very difficult and seldom tantalizing. However, if we can embrace them as openings into something greater, we move ourselves into a power position and a creative relationship with them. We no longer have to cower or retreat. We can become proactive, opening ourselves to an as-yet-unknown possibility. Recently I heard someone proclaim, "Each problem I run from, pursues me. Each problem I welcome, transforms me." Make sure you're available to the transforming! Someone once asked Eleanor Roosevelt if her husband, Franklin, had not suffered from polio, would he still have become president of the United States. Mrs. Roosevelt replied, "Yes, but not the same kind of president." She was implying that he gained strength, insights, and many important character qualities from his affliction—a problem that made him more, not less.

There is something else that I invite you to remember: the universe is always conspiring for your highest and best. It might not always look that way. However, if you can eventually move through the shock, upset, and sadness that represent the most common initial reactions to most problems, you are ready to cooperate with the intention of your Source, the One Spirit, to evolve and advance you through all your worldly experiences. You will be ready to proclaim with great sincerity and heart: "My highest and best is unfolding for me—right now. I expect my unexpected Good, now and always."

– The Experience –

There are so many other inspiring examples of the transformation of problems into possibilities. The first one I offer is from my own life experience.

My Ministry Began in 1976 in Portland, Oregon

As I shared previously, I led a very small church in Portland and, much to my surprise (since I was so young and new to the ministry), it grew to about 150 members. Then the rented facility we were using for Sunday services changed its policies and no longer allowed Sunday rentals. A committee began searching for another place to meet and stumbled onto an old Christian Science church that was for sale. We hadn't really imagined buying a church and it needed a lot of repairs, but this seemed like a fabulous community-building project.

We entered into a contract to purchase the building and were allowed to move into it for ninety days, at the conclusion of which an $80,000 payment would be required of us. This would be a very challenging down payment to meet since we had no building fund, but the subsequent monthly payments would be easily within our budget. We got busy, enthusiastically raising funds any way we could imagine. Excitement grew as we began to meet in an actual church building for the first time and as we announced the building fund totals each Sunday. One week before the end of the ninety-day grace period, however, we had raised only $60,000—not bad for such a small group, but not enough.

It was Saturday night. The next morning I would be making the painful announcement that we were $20,000 short of our goal and would have to abandon the sale and move out. I couldn't sleep. Had I failed them? How could I cushion the blow and turn this into a positive? In the wee hours of the morning, I came to the realization that it was time to let this go, to surrender my self-doubt as well as my attachments to that church building and to our fund-raising goal. It was in that tearful moment that higher understanding emerged for me. Raising the money wasn't the important thing at all. What we had become as a community—our courage, enthusiasm, the palpable love—was a huge victory. We had bonded and grown dynamically in consciousness. We would find another place to meet and continue to grow and evolve. My heart was so full as I shared these realizations with the congregation that next day. There was a standing ovation along with lots of hugs and tears of joy.

The next Tuesday, I took some boxes with me so I could begin cleaning out my office. A crew of volunteers would be removing our other equipment the next day. As I unlocked my office, I noticed an envelope had been slid under the door. I opened it and, to my amazement, inside was a cashier's check for $20,000! Neither the check nor its envelope had any identifying information. To this day I have no idea who contributed that final $20,000—the gift that allowed us to purchase a church and continue to grow. All I do know is that miracles occur not only through the passion and power of spiritual community but also through the conviction that no problem is without its wondrous and perfect solution. When I moved past a sense of defeat, I was able to perceive a higher truth: that our project had already blessed and evolved us so beautifully. Even if we had not ultimately purchased that building, the experience had already created "a building"—a building-up of greater community and heart. Purchasing the building was frosting on the cake. I learned that attachment to predetermined outcomes can become a blinder to more expansive, meaningful, beneficial, or healing possibilities.

She Lost It All in the Fire

Elisabeth Kübler-Ross, the acclaimed author of *On Death and Dying*, so loved her farm and the home she'd lived in for many years. But then it was gone in a horrible fire . . . everything, without exception, was lost. There was even speculation of foul play. Eventually, Elisabeth found a higher ground amid this loss, writing:

> *At moments like this, we stand at a fork in the road. If we take the fork most commonly traveled, we collapse, we give up, feeling hopeless and defeated. . . . It takes, after all, very little effort*

to feel victimized. We can, however, take the other fork. We can view the unhappy experience as an opportunity for a new beginning. We can keep our perspective, look for the growth opportunities, and find an inner reservoir of strength. By simply deciding to see the possibilities rather than the pain, I was able to come through the loss of my home with more strength and contentment than I had before the fire. No longer tied to my house, I decided to move to Arizona, to be closer to my son. I love my new surroundings as much as I did my previous environment. Looking back, I see that I was too attached to my old environment to make the move on my own. In a sense, I needed the tragedy to push me onward.

Though Elisabeth passed in to the greater dimensions of life in 2004, she leaves not only a great legacy through her professional work but also a glowing example that This Problem Is Possibility!

Shaving the Pills

In July 2004, I attended a writers' workshop in Santa Fe presented by Bill O'Hanlon. During this workshop, he shared a moving illustration of problems being converted into possibilities. He'd been in email contact with a church secretary who had gotten off heroin through the power of her spiritual path. Later she had an operation and got hooked on the pain pills. She couldn't admit this because she was so often called to testify about getting clean with God's help. And she couldn't afford to go to therapists that Bill was recommending because her small salary as a secretary went to covering her basic needs and buying the pain pills on the street.

Then she reread one of Bill's books, *Do One Thing Different*. Inspired, she created her own program: she shaved a tiny bit off one of her pills—she was taking twenty-seven every day—so that day she took twenty-six and eleven-twelfths of a pill. And each day she continued to shave a little more. After a while she was down to twenty-six pills a day. It took her nine months, but she did something every day and finally got clean again. Then she told everyone the truth, admitted this leg of her journey, and became an even greater force for inspiration and healing. She now lives a happy life.

A Strange Sight!

A friend of mine, Frosty Woolridge, is a great adventurer, author, and proponent of global population control. Every year he bicycles across vast areas of the planet. During this particular year, he was pedaling across the United States, from coast to coast. On a two-lane road in the New Mexico desert, he saw a strange sight: a man walking with what he thought at first was a dog. But as he got closer, Frosty saw that it was a man with no legs who was grasping two rubber pads and walking on his hands!

This man, Bob Wieland, explained that his goal was to cross America by walking all the way on his hands. His friend traveled a short distance ahead in a van, and often came back and walked with him. They had started in San Francisco nineteen months prior and had traveled 980 miles so far. Bob further explained that he had lost both legs in combat. Frosty asked, "Why are you doing it?" Bob replied, "There's a lot of adventure out here on the road. I suppose I could sit back and get fat watching TV for the next fifty years, but I want to do something with my life. I want to make a difference. I have to make do with what I have left."

Two years later it was broadcast on National Public Radio: Bob Wieland reached the Atlantic Ocean, succeeding in his quest to walk on his hands from coast to coast across America—3,300 miles of hardship across mountains, deserts, and through storms, taking nearly three years! No legs? No problem!

She Was Gangly and Plain . . .

By anyone's standards, and she had a strange-sounding voice. Her family was able to marry her off to her fifth cousin and it was assumed she'd be no asset to his public-service career. And yet, she was determined to make her mark. She had a personal vision and would not let it go. She became distinguished among women and all leaders . . . and when she used her voice people listened. She became an ambassador, a woman of letters, an incredible leader.

I quoted her earlier in this chapter: Anna Eleanor Roosevelt. Possibility!

– The Expression –

When You're Ready to Let Problems Reveal Their Possibilities, Do These Things:

1. Create some perspective.

Write down what you think the problem is. Then ask yourself, *Is this really the problem or is it just the symptom of the problem?* You may think your problem is that you don't have any friends; but that may turn out to be a symptom. Your problem could actually be low self-worth, a poor self-image. You may think your problem is depression. It may be that you are actually blocking your genuine self-expression. When you can zero in on the essence of the problem, then the fires of real opportunity will start to burn.

You may also find a greater perspective by looking at the bigger picture of life's ups and downs. Sometimes things seem really huge at first.

Some perspective tames them down a lot. Acclaimed author Robert Fulghum shines light on this:

> One of the best coping mechanisms is to know the difference between an inconvenience and a problem. If you break your neck, if you have nothing to eat, if your house is on fire—then you've got a problem. Everything else is an inconvenience. Life is lumpy. A lump in the oatmeal, a lump in the throat, and a lump in the breast are NOT the same kind of lump. One needs to learn the difference.

2. Take on only your own!

Let go of problems that are not yours to handle. It's not your problem to see to it that two other people get along with each other as you'd like. Your responsibility is to hold the high vision for their healing and growth. So many times people create problems for themselves by taking on other people's issues. If you do this a lot, what is the greater possibility that beckons for your own life's advancement?

3. Move into the space of possibility.

As pesky as problems are, they don't have to rule your every thought and demolish your creative openness. Breathe deeply—many times. Know that you are a being of Light capable of masterfully working with a vast creative process, for remember This World Is Consciousness. Cultivate an ever-growing sense that you are totally available to greater possibilities in this situation than you could ever know. Sense that they're pressing against you. Don't try to figure it all out; just be sensitive to your guidance and to moments of inspiration. Use the exercise of Affirmative Prayer explained in Chapter 4. Don't be surprised if things begin to move and unexpected developments begin to pop up. You've put out the welcome mat for them. They'll be there!

And remember these words from the late, great metaphysician, Eric Butterworth: "There is a Divine Mind counterpart to every human problem."

4. Move.

When the guidance is clear, there will be times for inspired action. Do not act if, in your honest assessment, you're trying to force things or make things happen. However, as you keep focusing on an acceptance of your highest and best, you will get creative ideas for supportive action. Know that there is something creative that you can do each day to support your unfoldment, and be alert to spot what it is. Remember these words from metaphysician and author Gene Emmet Clark: "Think, say and do only what reflects your conviction that the accomplishment of your goal is certain, knowing that it will be done unto you as you believe."

10. THIS JUDGMENT IS YEARNING

Do not judge, or you too will be judged. For in the same way you judge others, you will be judged, and with the measure you use, it will be measured to you. Why do you look at the speck of sawdust in your brother's eye and pay no attention to the plank in your own eye? . . . First take the plank out of your own eye, and then you will see clearly to remove the speck from your brother's eye.

—MATTHEW 7:1-3

Before one commits oneself to a judgment, one must at least attempt to see whence the reaction came.

—BRUGH JOY

Knowledge is received only in those moments in which every judgment, every criticism coming from ourselves, is silent.

—RUDOLF STEINER

– The Essence –

In the quote that begins this chapter, Jesus is adamant about one of the most common blockages to entering the kingdom of Heaven—the kingdom or experience of omnipresent Love—and that is judgment. This is the life-limiting habit of forming harsh, belittling, limiting, pessimistic, or uncaring opinions of people or situations. It is life limiting because all of our energized thoughts or conclusions come back to us clothed in some form or experience, so we are unwittingly "doing a number" on ourselves by means of our hurtful judgments. It is also life limiting because the most significant and fulfilling growth occurs when we free ourselves up and surrender to the impulse within the Higher Self for advancement and becoming. Spiteful, negative judgments bog us down in the turmoil of the ego's littleness and, however juicy or justified these assessments may seem, they cast us into a dark, stuck, no-growth place.

In speaking of judgments, it is important to make the distinction between judging and discerning. It is necessary and important to discern that which is most caring, wise, and life enhancing. Our ability to discern empowers us to make higher-level choices based on our accumulated experiences and wisdom. By discerning that an action is careless, unkind, shallow, or irresponsible, we can choose differently and save ourselves from having to clean up the fallout we otherwise would have generated. By discerning that an individual is up to no good or of questionable integrity, we can make a higher-level choice and do this individual some good by not allowing him to play out his intentions in the arena of our life. By discerning the skills or gifts of our children, we can make choices on their behalf that enhance the expression of their brilliance, instead of forcing them down a path that serves mostly to satisfy parental needs, longings, or opinions. By discerning the ego's fears, strategies, or needs, we gain the wherewithal to open our hearts and enter into the healing and upliftment of our consciousness. The gift of discernment is the gift of clear seeing, recognizing forces and factors involved, so that from keen understanding and insight, we are empowered to make optimal choices.

It is far more common, however, to become entangled in a web of harsh and hurtful judgments. Most everyone stoops to making them. The bigger problem is that we are apt to fade into a trancelike acceptance that our judgments are actual reality when they are, in truth, merely a story we have composed. But we tend to become more and more adamant about our judgments once they're in place and inflate them so that the story becomes juicier and more satisfying. It's like the case of the elderly spinster who died and left explicit instructions for her memorial, including the demand that there be *no* male pallbearers. She wrote: "They wouldn't take me out when I was alive ... I don't want them taking me out when I'm dead!"

Negative judgments are the mainstay of a fearful ego. What better way to deflect self-realization and the risks of vulnerability than to slap criticisms and put-downs on people or situations! This also intensifies the feelings of self-righteousness, and the ego dearly loves to feel that it is right. Although the judgment syndrome is extremely tantalizing, the saddest thing about it is that it sabotages personal honesty and the healing it can bring about. Our judgments mask us from ourselves by making us negative experts on people and things. This is suggested in a cute poem. Though I don't know its author, I do know that there's a nugget of truth in it.

Judge Not

I was shocked, confused, bewildered
As I entered Heaven's door;
Not by the beauty of it all,
Nor the lights or its décor.
But it was the folks in Heaven
Who made me sputter and gasp—
The thieves, the liars, the sinners,
the alcoholics and the trash.
There stood the kid from seventh grade
Who swiped my lunch money twice;
Next to him was my old neighbor
Who never said anything nice.
Herb, who I always thought
Was rotting in hell,
Was sitting pretty on cloud nine,
Looking incredibly well.
I nudged Saint Peter, "What's the deal?
I would love to hear your take.
How'd all these sinners get up here?
God must've made a mistake.
And why's everyone so quiet,
So somber—give me a clue."
"Hush, child," he said, "they're all in shock.
No one thought they'd be seeing you!"

—AUTHOR UNKNOWN

A significant aspect of the spiritual journey is understanding the ego's penchant for judging in hurtful and limiting ways. Fortified by these insights, we can practice transcending the dark cave of a negative judgment by regularly reminding ourselves that . . . This Judgment Is Yearning. To realize the yearning involved brings us to an opening into life mastery that is supremely healing and freeing.

There are several incidents from the life and ministry of Jesus that can help us take this step. The first is the incident reported in the eighth chapter of the book of John. A woman had been "taken in the very act" of adultery. An angry crowd had gathered, encouraged by the Pharisees—a sect of the Jewish people obsessed with asserting the minutia of Mosaic law. The law would require that both parties found in adultery be put to death by stoning. However, since women were regularly considered second-class citizens, in this case only the woman was being condemned. The Pharisees presented the woman to Jesus as a way to trap him. He could agree that she be stoned to death; this would probably cause a riot outside the city gates, infuriating the Roman authorities, and he would be accused of insurrection. Or, he could disagree with the stoning and would thereby be guilty of disregarding the law. The Pharisees believed Jesus would be in trouble no matter what he did.

That great teacher of spiritual Light, however, transcended this either/ or situation by invoking a higher dimension of Truth, transcending the laws by extending divine Love. He bent down and wrote something in the dirt with his finger. What he wrote was never disclosed, but the crowd of vengeful accusers shrank away at the sight of it. Then Jesus said, "He that is without sin among you, let him first cast a stone at her." One by one the crowd dispersed, leaving only Jesus and this woman. He said to her: "Woman, where are your accusers? Has no man condemned you?" And she replied, "No man, Lord." And he concluded, "Neither do I condemn thee: go, and sin no more."

This expression of higher Wisdom and Love demonstrates the power of

Spirit to neutralize all errors. He was affirming the integrity and power of the soul to override the errors of worldly mistakes. The Pharisees and the angry crowd symbolize the forces and strategies of the ego, which are intent on judging, condemning, and being right. Jesus represents the I Am Presence in each of us, the spiritual Light of the Divine. When we lift up our awareness into this place of consciousness, we are able to recognize the path of spiritual awakening every person is wending and the eternal presence of healing Love. From this space, a transforming compassion emerges that dissolves the lesser hostilities and judgments.

This glorious example of enlightened Love seems to contradict the theological fearmongers who have patched together a picture of a vengeful God and a coming day of judgment. Instead, we are offered a path for the experiencing and practicing of unconditional Love, for this is the very essence of the Divine, of God. Realizing this, we are all challenged to take stock of our condemning and hurtful judgments, and to realize how they limit us and keep us smaller than we are designed to be. We can each be an emissary of healing Love, but first we must understand more about the lure of our judgments.

The second illustration from Jesus' life comes from the beginnings of his ministry as he was casting about to find his disciples, his core of dedicated followers. He found Philip and invited him to become a disciple. Philip was so excited about this that he went to Nathaniel and told him about the Love he'd felt and the support role he was being allowed to play. Nathaniel asked, "Where is this Jesus from?" Philip told him, "Nazareth." Then Nathaniel's judging tendencies surfaced, and he proclaimed, "Has anything good ever come out of Nazareth?" Such an odd thing to say, but it has much to teach us.

At that time, Nazareth was a despised place. Jesus was born in that simple, unpretentious place—and, let's face it, probably a smelly and dirty place. He also grew up in a rigid religious climate that was not very nurturing. Still he emerged to bring the long-awaited message to humankind that each person is more than their upbringing, more than their past or present experiences, and more than the naysayers in their midst might proclaim. What this tells us is that the Divine is fully capable of emerging from the despised or the unloved.

Can anything good ever come out of the despised, the unsophisticated, the lowly, or disappointing aspects of your life? What human judgment has sized up your life as unworthy of containing the Divine? And have you given in to these judgments? "I'm too [this or that] . . . I'm not [good enough in so many ways] . . . With the mistakes I've made [how could I be lovable?] . . . With all my weaknesses [how could I succeed?]." Here's the point in all of this: we judge others so readily because of our own continuing self-judgment. We have identified with the "Nazareth" in us, instead of the Christ in us. Then the fearful ego looks upon situations and others through this lens of unworthiness and chooses harsh and limiting judgments to appease its own sense of guilt and inadequacy. However, the Authentic Self—the Inner Christ, the Buddha Nature, the Atman Essence—resides at the center of each of us, awaiting the opportunity to heal our lives and our world.

This Judgment Is Yearning . . . yearning for what? In our judging we are secretly yearning for *assurance*. Imagine: feeling a deep sense of assurance . . . that you are loved, that you are freed of the past and empowered in the present, that you are strong and joyous, that you are creative and secure. Your tendency to move into a space of harsh or limiting judgment would be neutralized, and you would have instant access to a vast array of more powerful options for how you might speak, feel, and act. Nothing in you would derive a sense of gratification from lowering or limiting another, or for demeaning a situation. Your heart would guide you to shining your Light and offering your gifts.

Isn't this profound assurance what we all so deeply desire? However, when we give the reins of our inner life to the ego, it seeks a kind of assurance that is better termed *security*. It achieves this first by propping itself above others, above situations and then by negative interference, increased estrangement, and hurtful judgments. This is the ego's way of attaining security. There is always, however, that creative moment of choice. *We always get to choose between ego security and spiritual assurance.* The problem is that we have opted so often for ego security that this has become, for much of humankind, a deeply etched pattern. To move into life mastery through this opening, we must "set a high watch" upon our habit of instantaneous judging—projecting our inadequacies onto others—and allow this to signal us that it's time for the more conscious and compassionate choice: spiritual assurance.

Think of it this way: *It's time for us to download a "Spiritual Assurance APP!"* Apps give instant access to an Internet site or program, along with a lot of great resources at the touch of a "button." Since there's an app for just about anything, why not an app that could move us out of the painful, stuck place of judgments—an app for spiritual assurance? You won't find this on the Internet—you'll have to open to your "inner-net," your immersion in the infinite Wisdom network of divine Mind. In fact, you can have it right now . . . by memorizing this APP as an acronym for "acceptance . . . purpose . . . and peace." This is exactly what spiritual assurance gives us whenever we're willing to receive it.

ACCEPTANCE: Opening to greater acceptance, you are allowing yourself to love and be loved. First focus on accepting yourself, and then you will have no need to deny another. Love is always what each of us most deeply desires to transform and heal our lives. When you open your heart and allow this Love to function in you, it heals the fears and naturally radiates from you.

PURPOSE: To move beyond hurtful judging does not necessarily require being passive. By entering into spiritual assurance and acceptance, the fog of fear and separation dissolves. This allows you to open to higher imagination and creativity. A sense of inspired purpose will then generate actions and behaviors that seek to uplift, inspire, and reveal greater Light. This is learning to live proactively as a "beneficial presence."

PEACE: A life built around the practice of nonjudgment becomes a life that epitomizes nonviolence. However, you will only become a peacemaker by first establishing inner peace. By knowing of a certainty that you are whole, loved, and supplied—now and forevermore—you can relax. There is nothing left to prove, for nothing is missing. You remember how to initiate cocreation and how to access all that you need. All that's left is to share your gifts from this place of peaceful knowing. This peace cannot be fabricated by acquiring wealth or power. This peace—the peace that surpasses human understanding—is the result of full-orbed spiritual assurance. Claim it now! Nothing stands in the way.

In 1988 I met the late, great singer and activist John Denver, when he sang at our ministry. Soon afterward, he invited me to officiate at his wedding to his second wife, Cassandra Delaney. Erica and I just happened to have arranged for our own honeymoon in Aspen that very week. We extended our stay there so we could participate in his wedding. At the rehearsal dinner, I remember sharing with John my immense regard for his music—especially the choice he had made to direct the messages in many of his songs to the themes that resounded in his heart . . . especially ecology and world peace. I said that I imagined that this choice of direction had made a major impact on his career. He laughed a bit and shared that channeling his passions for human advancement into his music had made him the brunt of a great deal of judgment. Much of his audience shared his feelings and vision, yet there were those who were more interested in "Country Roads," so to speak. And his recording and distribution company, RCA Records, had chosen not to renew his contract, even though he was their best-selling artist ever. He concluded that it had all been worth it because he knew he was making a difference and there was no way he could not include his core beliefs in the expression of his art. I was greatly moved by this sharing. It serves as a lesson that there may be times when we must move forward along the lines of our highest vision despite the judgments that may be coming our way. John Denver's choice of direction is a beautiful example of moving forward on the basis of acceptance, purpose, and peace. It is a wonderful way to live.

One of my favorite John Denver songs is "The Gift You Are." Spiritual Assurance reveals each of us as God's great gift to Life. You will be giving your soul's gift each time you recognize the yearning within the temptation to judge . . . and fulfill that yearning with great spiritual assurance.

– The Experience –

What a Troublemaker!

In the mid-1980s, I found myself on an important committee created by the spiritual movement with which our ministry in Denver is affiliated. We had important work to do but I, and others on the committee, were convinced that one of our colleague ministers was the great stumbling block to our progress. As we held our meetings I found that he irritated me more and more. I thoroughly and comprehensively judged him: arrogant, uncooperative, hardheaded, accusatory, unkind, belligerent. He was also generating rumors and misconceptions outside of the committee. Others agreed with this assessment. Have you noticed that you are always able to find agreement for your judgments? (We're all on this healing path together!)

Now, if you want your judgments to remain unaltered, do not stay current with your prayer work! As I prayed about this situation, I steadily began to feel a gnawing realization that perhaps I was the one who first needed healing. Gradually I began to take stock of my thoughts about this man and my reactions toward him, spoken and unspoken. When I really looked at this objectively, what I saw wasn't pretty, wasn't the ways of being to which I had dedicated my life. Furthermore, I noticed that at each meeting I chose to sit absolutely as far away from this "troublemaker" as I could . . . the very opposite corner of that long set of conference tables. I was reinforcing separation, inwardly and outwardly. Something had to change.

So for the next meeting, I arrived early. Soon my colleague/teacher arrived as well. When he chose his seat, I proceeded to sit right next to him. This shocked him and felt very uncomfortable to me, but nonetheless I stayed there. After a few moments, I turned to him and said something to this effect: "You know, I'd like to understand your views on our project better. Could you summarize them for me?" Though he seemed quite surprised, he obliged and launched into a rundown of his concerns. I just listened, though I had to bite my tongue a lot. Others noticed this unusual conversation and gathered around to listen as well. When he finished, I thanked him and told him that I understood him better. During the rest of this meeting, he objected and interjected less than usual. Things moved along a bit better.

The most important thing about that day, however, was a permanent shift in my relationship with this colleague. During the remaining life of that committee, most of my angst about him seemed to have been washed away. I still didn't agree with his views, but the emotionality in me had disappeared. In the years following that experience, this colleague and I continued to grow closer until a genuine friendship emerged. My earlier judgments of him had blocked my ability back then to behold his deep dedication to the ministry and to the gift of our teaching in the world. I hadn't been able to connect with his personhood, his sense of humor, his love of his family—all the elements of his wonderful life. As the years continued to pass, we became very close friends, and we shared and rejoiced with all the developments in each other's families. I attended his retirement party and honored him. I cried when he "slipped the leash" and passed over into the greater Good of God. He was a powerful teacher for me. I'm just grateful that I followed Spirit's guidance and opened my life and heart to him.

And Then There Have Been the Spiritual Activists

Before completing this chapter, let us remember and honor those whose discernment perceived and proclaimed injustices and who found ways of nonviolence to seek change. Mohandas K. "Mahatma" Gandhi saw the pain of the British tyranny and dedicated his life to freeing his people. Beginning with the Great Salt March and concluding with his assassination, he led peaceful efforts that would eventually bring one of the largest empires ever to its knees.

Then there is the shining example of Martin Luther King, Jr., who followed in Gandhi's footsteps and lent his inspiration and gave his life for equality and social change in the United States. I am also remembering William Lloyd Garrison, who more than two hundred years ago was willing to proclaim that slavery was a monstrous crime against God and humanity, and he dreamed that he could help end it. The odds were certainly against him, especially back then. Prominent statesmen insisted that the good of the country relied on the continuance of slavery. Even the general assembly of a church had stated that slavery was ordained by God. People jeered and laughed, but year after year Garrison continued in his quest. He played his role in the great quest—not by harsh and insensitive judgments, but by championing a vision whose time had come.

So many examples for our guidance: There were the many women who championed the women's suffrage movement in the United States during the late nineteenth and early twentieth centuries, such as Susan B. Anthony, Elizabeth Cady Stanton, Margaret Fuller, and Frances Wright, to name a few. We are blessed by the leadership of Mother Teresa, H. H. Dalai Lama, Caesar Chavez . . . all showing us that discerning injustice and taking compassionate, nonviolent action is the best way to dissolve ignorance and the toxins of heartless judgment. This is the path of one who chooses to be a beneficial presence.

– The Expression –

1. Set the "High Watch"!

Remember that judging is a deeply ingrained habit for most of us. With compassion for yourself, and a sense of loftier purpose, stay alert for those moments when a limiting or hurtful judgment or condemnation is forming. The intense emotions involved will be the greatest clue. Remind yourself, This Judgment Is Yearning! And remember that the real yearning is after *spiritual assurance*. You might be tempted to settle for some ego security, but it won't improve the situation and, in the end result, it will not make you happy. Take a deep breath, disengage from the situation, and explore the gifts you'll receive through the assurance that is Acceptance . . . Purpose . . . and Peace! Use your spiritual app!

And remember this wisdom from Ernest Holmes: "If one sees unloveliness in others, it is because unloveliness is a strong element in himself. The light he throws on others is generated in his own soul and he sees them as he chooses to see them."

2. Balance Your Perceptions

Fulke Greville wrote: "There is an unfortunate disposition in man to attend much more to the faults of his companions which offend him, than to their perfections which please him."

Balance your perceptions by focusing on the strengths and wonders of the other people with whom you interact—even if they are difficult to perceive amid current behaviors. Remember, "Judge not by appearances." It helps to remember that there is much more to you than your weak or misguided moments might reveal. This is true for all people. Hold this perspective and you won't be so easily lured into the quicksand of harsh judgment.

3. Practice Peacemaking

The poem I wrote that was shared at the end of Chapter 1 seems very relevant to this topic as well. I invite you to reread it and use it to take stock of your own wounds . . . your desire to be lifted up . . . the tendencies to make others wrong . . . and the opportunity to always live the openhearted life. May you heed the call to the inner healing that leads to great and lasting assurance.

4. Discern Needs

Discern needs in your community or spheres of influence. As a person of discernment, follow your heart into modes of service, of making a difference. Remember, what this world needs is an enlightened citizenry that is sensitive, proactive, and compassionate, rather than judgmental, critical, or apathetic.

11. THIS CONFLICT IS FORGIVENESS

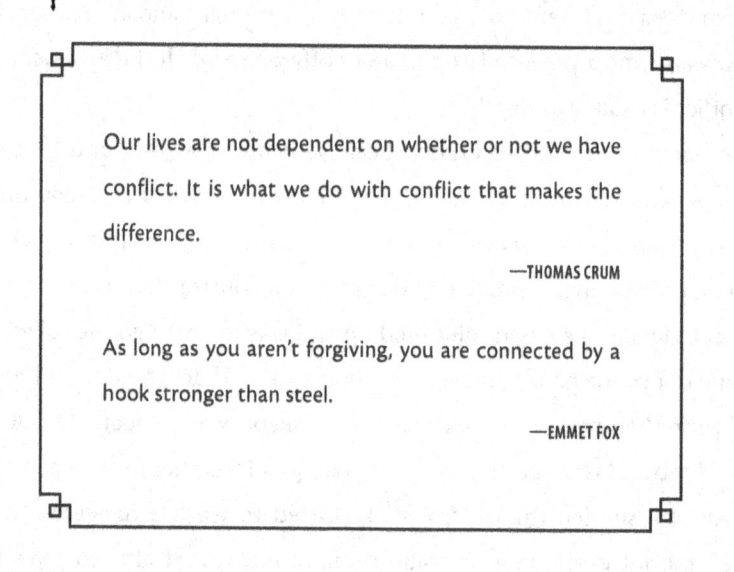

> Our lives are not dependent on whether or not we have conflict. It is what we do with conflict that makes the difference.
>
> —THOMAS CRUM

> As long as you aren't forgiving, you are connected by a hook stronger than steel.
>
> —EMMET FOX

– The Essence –

The clash of human uniqueness and ignorance has produced strife throughout our history as a species. This has made conflict among people and groups inevitable, especially considering the diversity of cultures, traditions, ideologies, aspirations, idiosyncrasies, needs, and hardships. When conflict emerges in personal experience, it is usually regarded as so unpleasant and unacceptable that the typical response is to try to squelch it by any means available. If that doesn't work, the next best thing is to avoid it or deny it. Few opt for the radical approach of embracing and exploring the conflict.

Conflict, in its essence, is not negative. It only becomes destructive if it is needlessly escalated or ignored. As with many of life's most trying situations, conflict often comes bearing gifts and offering opportunities. Admitting and examining conflict can bring unaddressed issues to the surface to be considered in open and healthy ways. It can also bring people and teams closer, and even lead to breakthroughs and innovation. But always the most powerful opportunity offered through the experience of conflict is healing at depth.

A certain man was so excited because winter was over and he could fly his beloved classic airplane again. He drove out to the hangar on an early spring day, threw open the doors, and there was his prized plane. It was an older single-engine plane that had a control stick rather than a wheel. He had the engine all tuned up and was ready to go. He rolled the plane out of the hangar, revved up the engine, and delighted at its beautiful purr, then taxied to the runway. His takeoff was perfect. He enjoyed the climb and rejoiced that he finally had good weather for flying.

All of a sudden the control stick started to wobble dangerously. He checked out everything he could think of but wasn't able to solve this dilemma. *I've never experienced this before!* he thought. The control stick continued to wobble. Then it came to him: *What if something crawled into the tail section? And what if it's chewing on the control cord that runs from the control stick to the flaps and rudder! Whoa, if this is what's going on and the lines get severed, I'll lose control of the plane and probably crash. I could be in deep trouble here.*

Then, in a flash of inspiration, he pulled that control stick back as far as he could, sending his plane into a steep climb. He climbed and climbed until the engine began to sputter and he began to get dizzy. Just then he noticed that the wobbling in the control stick ceased. So he leveled off, carefully brought his plane around, and came in for a soft landing. He taxied over to the hangar and shut down the engine. He got out and removed a little panel on the side of the tail section, looked inside, and, sure enough, there were three rats in the tail section, each one suffocated during his high-altitude climb. And sure enough, one of the control lines was gnawed nearly in half. He'd just barely made it back down safely!

I love the moral to this story: if you want to stop the rats from chewing at your control cords, you've got to climb higher! If there's anything that chews on the "control cords" of our lives, it's ignored or unresolved conflicts and the wounds they so often inflict. A key opening into life mastery beckons to the one who is ready to climb higher from the lift provided by conflict. This opening is imbued with unequaled power. It is understanding and surrendering to the power of forgiving.

There was a time in Jesus' ministry when they brought before him a man paralyzed from the palsy. Jesus looked at this man—I would imagine that this awakened being peered through his own vibrant heart right into the very soul of that man—and he knew what he needed to say: "Son, your sins are forgiven you," and in that moment the man was able to stand up and walk away. Now there were scribes nearby who were real troublemakers. They kept meticulous track of the codes and the laws, and demanded that they be rigidly applied. These scribes were incensed at what had just happened and suggested that Jesus had blasphemed, for it was written that only God can forgive. Jesus responded that it was easier and more effective for him to forgive the man than to tell him to take up his bed and walk. What the Great Teacher was trying to get across is that if he could get someone to let go of his guilt and move into a space of forgiveness, this would heal nearly everything. Amid conflict, inner or outer, the tendency is to struggle with surface elements; forgiving goes right to the core of it all.

In another instance, it is written that Jesus said that it is given to the

Son of Man to heal and to forgive. Anytime Jesus spoke about the Son of Man he was speaking from the higher consciousness of the True Self, the I Am . . . in him and in all of us. I believe that Jesus' primary mission on this earth was to reveal and exemplify the higher Self, to show us the possible human, and to activate the Christ Essence seeded in us all. He demonstrated how we can live and how we can heal when we have awakened to our spiritual Beingness . . . when we shift into a cocreative relationship with the Divine. So by saying that it is given to the Son of Man to forgive, he was saying that the highest consciousness in you—the Christ Self in you—is equipped to forgive; your lesser self, the worldly ego self, has trouble with this . . . but your higher Self is given the spiritual wherewithal to forgive. Jesus would also enjoin us to forgive not seven times, but seventy times seven. In biblical numerology this symbolizes forgiving endlessly; we are called to cultivate a life anchored in healing Love and forgiveness . . . not just occasionally, but all of the time.

None of us can move through this life without accumulating an abundance of opportunities to forgive. This is because we are all learning and growing, thus our reach very often exceeds our grasp. Much of the time, we learn by trial and error. Vast amounts of conflict inevitably emerge. Forgiveness is the best way to clean up the residue from our mutual discovery processes in this life. This is why it is so important to seize the opportunities to engage the power of forgiving. We can all get bruised and wounded as we interact with others along the path of life. More than any other process, forgiving initiates the healing process and activates the limitless potential of Creative Consciousness within us all. With every act of genuine forgiving, we free ourselves from the illusion of separation and open into a greater dimension of life mastery.

On the other hand, unhealed wounds cause us to become stuck; they eventually take our lives into a downward spiral. Unhealed wounds perpetuate pain and actually attract or "call in" more wounding. Unhealed wounds fester and create toxins that impair all levels of expression, especially within the physical body. Unhealed wounds become "a ball and chain" that drags down any possible progress and keeps a lid on creativity. Unhealed wounds become the greatest possible prison.

Whether a wounding is the result of unresolved conflict or the infliction of an injury, one thing over all others fuels resistance to the healing: the ego takes it all personally. In any hurtful experience, something is said or done that is perceived as harmful, hateful, or injurious. There is an unpleasant, cruel, or painful incident, to be sure. However, the ego goes one step further by arriving at a powerfully debilitating conclusion. The ego proclaims to itself: *I have been diminished! I have been lessened because of this experience.* Long after all restitution and repairs have been made to address or redress the original harm or injury, the tendency of the ego is to continue to foster the sense of diminishment. It is then that resentment and bitterness become the only recourse for the ego that believes it has been belittled. The strategy from this point on is to continually increase the intensity of the resentment as a way to try to lessen the pain. But this never works. So all that is left is for the ego to accustom itself to carrying the immense burden of its relentless fear and pain.

There is a sobering realization that is the catch-22 in all of this: in most cases, the ego feels weak and inadequate *before* any trouble, conflict, or injury. Hurtful experiences only amplify the unworthiness already seeded within the ego. So when the ego concludes that it has been diminished, this is not, in truth, something that has actually been inflicted or imposed on it by another, however unacceptable or painful the interaction may have been. The perception of diminishment is a confirmation and an extension of the deepest foundational conviction of the ego. It is the fearful ego's very nature. So this is why the ego is reluctant to let go of resentments and bitterness. To do so would be to call into question the deepest core principles that support the ego's existence. For so many people, the ego is pain and hurt waiting to happen, and this is something that the ego, itself, cannot heal.

As the seeker in the cave eventually brought himself to the realization that his freedom emerged through expansion, by becoming more, so also is true healing an experience of transcendence. Forgiveness not only introduces the "fresh air and antiseptic" that can facilitate the healing of circumstances, it actually takes us into a larger, more expansive dimension of ourselves. In this dimension, we realize that we are born of God and cannot be diminished by anything or anyone in the world, thus there is no benefit to remaining attached to pain, guilt, or a sense of unworthiness. In this higher dimension of Being, we realize that there is really nothing to heal, only wholeness and magnificence to reveal. In this higher dimension of being, we move ourselves beyond the convulsive grasp of a fearful ego by bathing ourselves in compassion and, like the prodigal child, reuniting ourselves with the wholeness and fullness of divine Love . . . in us, around us, and for us. Through forgiveness we rise up anew into the fuller expression of our true spiritual nature as an embodiment of divine Love and Light.

Empowering Forgiveness

It is a precious and powerful moment when we sense the quickening of Truth and move our awareness back into its innate healing mode. The foundation for all forgiveness is Love. I remind you again of one of the most beautiful and empowering biblical statements: "Perfect love casts out fear" (1 John 4:18). However, the first application of this Love is not toward the other person or persons you may have been resisting or resenting. The first step is to throw open your heart and to allow the Love of God to fill you, heal you, renew you. Feel the fear dissolving in the healing balm of Love. In this Love, passionately embrace the feeling that you are enough, that you have never been inconsequential or flawed. All that was a lie! Allow Divine Love to soothe you, caress you at depth. Next, practice loving yourself and feeling solid and strong in this love. The sense of being offended will begin to dissolve and you will find yourself emerging out of the trance of unworthiness as you expand beyond fear and resentment. Then I invite you to ask deeply, *How shall I go forth to express the greatness of my loving and healing nature?*

These words from Ernest Holmes can also be really helpful: "We are to know that passing events cannot hinder the onward march of the soul. The temporal imperfection of the human cannot dim the eternal integrity of the Divine."

The Three *Ws*

The lofty spiritual practice of forgiveness can be bolstered by these three Ws:

First . . . *Willingness*. This is a primary requirement on the path of Forgiving. Remember, lack of forgiveness and resentment causes toxins, actual poisons at the inner and the outer levels. They poison the mind and emotions and also generate toxins in the physical body. Then the venom moves out vibrationally and begins to affect and infect everything in our life—our relationships, our creativity . . . everything is downgraded and weakened because of anger and resentment. It just doesn't serve us, though the ego thinks it is finally getting its due. Someone has said that resentment is like taking poison and waiting for the other guy to die! It just doesn't help us a bit.

There have been times in my life when I've had to bring myself to the point of surrendering into a willingness to cooperate with the healing and uplifting energies and intention of the Spirit. But first I had to clarify some things about forgiving. First of all, I had to learn what forgiveness *is not*. It is not forgetting. Despite that old trite phrase—*Forgive and forget!*—you really can't forget. Everything we have ever experienced is recorded and stored at deep levels of the mind. We may not recall it all, but we don't really forget anything; a part of you remembers it all.

Forgiving is not condoning. It is not rationalizing that the conflict or hurt was no big deal, or that what someone did was acceptable. Whatever happened may have been hurtful; it may have been misguided, vicious, or unkind. Losses may actually have been experienced due to another's actions. So forgiving is not condoning what happened. It is changing your relationship with what happened even though it may have been a hurtful or damaging experience.

Nor is forgiveness getting on your "high horse" and self-righteously absolving someone of something . . . as though you are superior. It's not declaring, *I am going to finally forgive you . . . you worm of the dust. Now get out of my life, be gone!* Though the ego loves to try to feel and act superior, genuine forgiveness is not found in this delusion.

It is critically important to realize that forgiveness is not entering into martyrdom, either. It's not saying, *Oh, I forgive. Now you can come back into my life and wreak havoc all over again. Do whatever you want all over again because I'm forgiving.* No! Many of the lessons in hurtful incidents challenge us to consider how to take better care of ourselves, how to have effective boundaries, how to love ourselves and others fully enough to refuse to allow demeaning or hurtful behaviors.

Finally, forgiving is seldom a quick fix. It is seldom a onetime experience, especially when it involves the more significant events of our lives. Instead, forgiving is like peeling back the layers of an onion. We bring our hearts to that healing moment of forgiving and make whatever inroads or progress we can. Each engagement of the practice of forgiveness is a blessing; however, forgiving is often done layer by layer, until we realize a sense of fulfillment, of authentic freedom. A good gauge of this is the genuine sense that you now no longer hold on to the wish that the hurtful experience had never happened. You have woven it successfully into the tapestry of your soul's evolution. It's not that you have finally arrived at a once-and-for-all completion. Instead, you have transformed your relationship with the experience, you have grown because of it and have fully established it as a gift upon your path. If vestiges of pain emerge in the future, this is simply an opportunity for further remembrance and blessing.

What then is forgiveness? Forgiveness is one of the highest expressions of self-love. It is loving yourself enough to move out of that stuck place, to get out of that quicksand. It is taking all of the energy devoted to fear and resentment, and channeling it into something that is constructive, life giving, and uplifting. Forgiveness is freeing yourself to get back to the higher agenda of your life—no longer tethered to the past. If you insist on staying tethered to the past, you're never going to go forward. The rats are going to chew at your control cords and you're going to be grounded, or in the worst case, you'll crash. And the people around you who are hearing you moan about your plight will become fewer and fewer because people really want to get on with their lives. They will not for long want to support you in staying stuck.

Yes, there are times for grieving, for acknowledging the pain we may feel because of the actions of others. There are times when we have a right to be upset. And there comes a time when we must go forward, when we must free ourselves so that our soul agenda can continue to fulfill itself in this lifetime. We must bring ourselves to that dynamic place of heartfelt willingness. In your affirmative prayers, don't forget to ask for help in forgiving, for help to move to that place of true willingness. It's not always easy, yet it's always freeing. It can be some of the deepest inner work we ever do, yet I believe there's that Presence throughout this Universe that leaps for joy when we are ready to seek help, ready to be brought to the place of willingness to forgive and let go. Even if a part of you believes that the forgiving just can't be done, there is a higher Love that can lead you forth into your freedom. Give your heart to this positive acceptance: *I'm open and willing to allow the Power of Forgiveness into my life.*

I met Hugh Prather, a wonderful author and spiritual teacher, when he presented a seminar at our spiritual center in Denver. At this event, I remember him saying that our lives are like one of those old slide projectors with the carousels on top that hold the slides. Every experience in our lives is a slide that gets projected . . . and Life's constant question is, *Can you forgive this?* If we say "No," then the slide remains in the carousel to eventually get projected onto our experience again. On the other hand, if we say "Yes," that slide is removed from the carousel, and we are done with it. Slide after slide, experience after experience, we are asked, *Can you forgive this?* Forgiveness is the willingness to say "Yes." And then forgiveness is moving on!

The second *W* is *Wisdom*. Call upon the greater Wisdom within you when you're ready to forgive. There's a part of you that knows more about you than you know in your conscious awareness. The ego stays fixated on the "lesser story" of who did what to whom. However, there's an inner Wisdom that knows that anything that ever goes on in your life can be transmuted at the soul level into something beneficial and glorious. It is this soul wisdom and power that can transform any experience into "gold," into precious ingredients that will ultimately inspire, ennoble, and free you. I invite you to consult with this Wisdom within and ask, *What is my soul's possibility in this? How can that part of me that is indestructible, that cannot be diminished, use this experience to evolve, grow, and spread its wings?* Listen deeply to this Wisdom and you'll progressively receive inspiration from on high. You'll feel yourself expanding further and further beyond the former limitation and pain. Who knows how this healing will lead and direct you as you open to a guidance greater than your surface awareness, to that Something deep and rich within you—that is always conspiring for your growth and transformation!

The third *W* stands for *Within*. When you say, "I forgive you," you're really not saying it to that person; you're saying it to the picture you are holding of them. You're saying it to the emotional field that coalesced around whatever happened. You're working within yourself. Forgiving is not something you do to "them" out there, or to the world; it is a holy act, a sacred shift within yourself. As you let go of the venom and emotional toxins, as your Wisdom opens you to the "larger story" of what is evolving in your life, everything will align within you to become a conduit for divine and healing Love.

The most powerful form of forgiving is self-forgiveness. As we move along our life path, we oftentimes discover that we've had blinders on. We come into a realization of the blind spots that prompted our own mistakes, our shallow intentions, our acts of unkindness. Certain theologies contend that the Ultimate Source and Love of this Universe is keeping score, keeping meticulous track of every person's misdeeds and errors. However, I invite you to explore whether that ideology is consistent with the higher truth that God is Love—a Love so vast, so wise, so inclusive, so healing, that we can scarcely comprehend It. Perhaps the notion of a judgmental God is a reflection of the ego's persistent sense of unworthiness and fear. The Love that created you from its own heart, that same Love that has sustained you at every level and blessed you in countless ways . . . how could it ever really lose hope in you? How could it ever desire to condemn or abandon you . . . much less relegate you to some torturous hell?

The fail-safe for our actions on this earth plane is that "it all comes back to us" through the law of Cause and Effect, that karmic Law of reciprocity. Ultimately, then, we inflict upon ourselves the consequences of our unenlightened motivations and actions. There is no need for divine judgment to correct humanity. We reap what we sow, and this is one of the cornerstone lessons at this level of human expression. Some object to this concept, suggesting that they've known of people who have hurt others and seemingly gotten away with it, maybe even prospered from it. However, we should remember that we do not always comprehend how this inexorable Law works things out in someone's experience. It is also written that a person may sow in one field but reap in another. We can be sure that everyone is reaping what they have sown; the reaping, however, may not be in a "field" or area of the other's life that we are able to perceive or understand. The great good news is that our awakening into accountability for our thoughts and actions, coupled with the opening of our hearts, can lead us to an experience of grace, whereby we have fulfilled the learning that completes the lessons at play in our experience. Thus we no longer have to experience the reaping. The purpose of experiencing the effects of the causes we set in motion is not to punish us, but to evolve our awareness, to expand us into greater expressions of Love and Light. When this is fulfilled, we are released.

As we explore the nature of spiritual maturity, it is incumbent on us to let go of those beliefs about God that project human littleness upon Divine Greatness. If God is infinite Love, then that Love has no capacity to condemn you. It only seeks to cultivate you, to encourage your blossoming into all that It has created you to be. What's really in the way, then?

Self-condemnation and that penchant for feeling unworthy, not enough. In the Bible, it speaks of "grieving the Spirit." I believe we grieve the Spirit when we cling to hurtful, judgmental, and demeaning ideas about ourselves. Everyone is in the process of learning and growing by means of experiences and relationships. What does God, or the Universe, require of us? To awaken, to realize the creative impact of our thoughts and actions, to open our hearts, to learn and grow, and ultimately . . . to forgive—both others and ourselves. May we "grieve the Spirit" no longer. May we fulfill the Spirit through self-forgiveness. Then we shall be fully empowered to forgive others "seventy times seven," all along our path. May you give yourself this gift . . . within . . . now.

Three *Ws* . . . www.forgiveness! Surf your "inner-net" and you'll find that this site opens you to a progressively greater, more fulfilling, and freer life. Conflict is inevitable! Resentment is optional. Suffering is optional. Violence is optional. Belittling is optional. Self-sabotage is optional. Rejection is optional. Hatred is optional. Unhappiness is optional. We all have the spiritual wherewithal to claim more magnificent and life-affirming options for ourselves and for the community of humankind. It is a fine art we must learn now, before it's too late. As Tom Crum, in *The Magic of Conflict*, puts it, "Seeing conflict as an opportunity to create art from our very being is a challenge for the artist in all of us."

When conflict arises within you or around you, remember that your opening into life mastery will appear when you realize that This Conflict Is Forgiveness. All conflicts are forgiveness opportunities in disguise. The master sees conflict as a creative portal. Though difficult, every conflict is a mighty and wondrous opportunity to bring forth the very best in you. It is the sacred opportunity to let contention lead to invention, to the breakthroughs that opened and joined hearts always bring forth. Marianne Williamson, in her book *Enchanted Love*, writes:

Forgiveness gives us new eyes, and with that, the capacity to give new life. . . . It releases us to be who we are capable of being. What all of us need, at bottom, is the same: to be free of the past, free to start over, free to feel that we're good and decent people, and free to feel that there's something good and true and beautiful we can contribute to this world. Our learning how to see others that way is the greatest contribution we can make to their lives. And the person who makes us feel this way is a gift beyond rubies or gold.

– The Experience –

The Betrayal Is Healed

In Chapter 1, "This Instant Is Love," I told you of my experience with the woman who abruptly ended our relationship just when I thought we were about to announce our engagement. This betrayal eventually led me to a pinnacle experience . . . the opening of my heart. Since then every aspect of my life has been so very different, so very much better. My greatest joy is the heart-opening practices that keep me anchored in Divine Love.

There is an epilogue to this story. About two years after "the breakup," I was shocked to receive a call from this former girlfriend. I had not heard from her since our parting. She said that she felt it might be time for us to have a conversation. Maybe she sensed that I had done an enormous amount of inner work and that my heart was in a different place. I do know that when we open our hearts, the vibration ripples out and those who are sensitive to this will know something has shifted. I agreed to meet with her.

We had a two-hour lunch. We talked about our three years together.

She talked about how difficult it was for her to walk away, and that she didn't believe that she could talk it through with me. She shared that she felt it was the only way she could make a clean break of it, the only way she could intervene on the path we were walking, a path that would have led us both into a lot of difficulties and pain. She explained that she felt weak to make the case that our relationship was not well grounded, and that she didn't feel she could resist my pleading to give the relationship another chance. So she did things the only way she felt she could.

I listened. I understood. I shared how deeply I grieved and how angry I became. Then I shared the transformational path that I discovered and all the gifts it had brought to me. I underscored how difficult it was to walk this path, but that the difficulty was in my own resistance, not her actions. We then expressed that having been together had vaulted both of us into a better place and this, after all, is one of the greatest gifts of loving relationships. We laughed a bit. We saw things so very clearly . . . as though we were on a high peak looking down on a path we'd wended together.

We realized that we had brought an immense amount of love energy into each other's lives, and that we had, indeed, been angels for each other. We cried just a little, for just a moment. I forgave her. She forgave me. We forgave ourselves. We said good-bye. We walked away. We were complete.

A Mother's Day Healing

One of the great joys I have found in spiritual service is the privilege of partaking, even at a distance, in the sacred unfoldment of people's lives. Keeping the author's identity confidential, I want to share with you a letter I received that moved me deeply:

Dear Dr. Roger,

   I was born fourth of six children to a very unhappy woman. My birth did not bring her any joy, nor did my life, although I was always a good kid, by kid standards. She was usually depressed, always tired, and always irritated. She knew how to yell but not how to hug. I grew up without ever hearing once the words, "I love you." She never took any interest in me, nor did she have any time for me. I craved her love, so what I perceived as her rejection became the core of who I became. I suffered from severe and debilitating depressions and always felt worthless. These feelings fueled self-destructive behaviors in me so painful I can't even think about them.

She went on to share that she eventually had a daughter and felt instant love for her. However, her love for her own child made her even more angry at her mother who had never offered her this same love. Then her mother was diagnosed with cancer and died soon thereafter. She struggled with guilt feelings because she didn't feel a sense of loss. Her issues with her mother remained stubborn, cold, hard, and deep inside.

Then a Mother's Day came along, and she thought, *I don't miss my mother at all. Good.* But with this, she realized pointedly how angry she still was feeling. She tried to work on all of this. She talked with her father and siblings to gain insights into her mother. She even flew to her home state to visit her mother's grave. While there, she went to the hospital where she'd been born and to the house where she'd lived. These steps took her farther down the path, but she still felt wounded and didn't know how to finish the process.

She concluded her letter:

As is so often the case, sometimes we just need to surrender. One day I was sitting in your church during a service, and the lights were dimmed. I felt all the loving energy I always feel when I'm there. Although the message that day did not have anything to do with forgiveness, I was suddenly flooded with it. I felt such raw love for my mother, and the understanding that she had done the best that she could do. I felt how desperately she had needed love and how that had bound her up, and how she hadn't understood that it was always there for her. I had not understood it either. I sent all of my love to my mother's spirit. I instantly felt her love flow into me then. I was overcome with emotion and healing. That was eight years ago and I have never again felt any anger at her, nor any pity at my childhood, nor any of the negative feelings I had dragged along behind me. I only feel love. To know love, I must surrender to forgiveness.

To her beautiful sharing, I would add, it is never too late to allow a deep and lasting forgiveness. Forgiveness, like Love, transcends all apparent separation . . . and in our eternal Oneness, a choice to let go and to love can be felt and honored across dimensions . . . and even returned.

Lincoln's Approach to Conflict

There was an incident in which Abraham Lincoln was being criticized by a lady for speaking kindly of his enemies: "You should be destroying your enemies!" she said.

President Lincoln then replied, "Madam . . . do I not destroy my enemy when I make them my friend?"

Ari and Choppe

In Chapter 9, I introduced you to a glorious soul, Ari Ariyaratne, founder of the Sarvodaya movement in Sri Lanka. There is another incident in his life that is revealing and powerful. After launching his nationwide movement, Ari learned of an assassination plot on his life. A notorious underworld killer named Choppe had been hired to kill Ari at a Buddhist center where Ari was scheduled to speak. Immediately upon learning of this plan, Ari—in the dead of night and on the eve of his speech—went to Choppe's house. He stood before this man who'd expressed so much darkness throughout his life and said, "Choppe, I am Ariyaratne whom you are planning to kill tomorrow." The gangster seemed shocked. "Please do not desecrate that sacred Buddhist seat of learning with the blood of a beggar like me. Kill me here instantly."

Choppe gazed into the eyes of that brave science teacher turned reformer and mystic, and declared, "I cannot kill you." From that moment on, Choppe was changed and became a great admirer and supporter of Ariyaratne.

– The Expression –

There Are Many Ways to Invite and Engage the Healing Power of Forgiveness. Remember That Your Willingness, Wisdom, and Inner Focus Will Lead You to Your Own Perfect Means. Here Are Some Suggestions That Can Support This Journey:

1. Bring It into the Light.

Bring any wounds from your past into the light of day. Wounds only heal when they are cleansed and brought into the air. It is the same with our inner wounds. Own them, share them . . . hide them no longer.

2. Write About Your Experiences.

Focus especially on how these experiences are really about your soul potential to grow and reveal more of who you really are. When you're ready to begin releasing and shifting your sense of conflict, write down a brief description of the incident and bury it in a pot you'd use to grow a plant. Practice letting it go, and reminding yourself that you are releasing the anger and pain, while also receiving a sense of the gifts and opportunities this experience is bringing you. After seven weeks, un-earth it and see if you're ready to let it go permanently. If so, bury the piece of paper again and plant something green or flowering in the soil to remind you of the greater expression of life that has come from this experience.

3. Nurture Your Inner Child.

Close your eyes, relax . . . and imagine yourself as a child. Then bring that child onto your lap. Caress the hair and reassure this child. Now tell him or her the Truth about them . . . that nothing can diminish them, ultimately . . . that others' actions do not define them, and that they are loved and loving. Decide together that it's time to let go of fear and sadness . . . and that it's time to go out and play again!

4. Carry This Truth in Your Heart: *The God in me can let it be!*

5. Take the Lead.

Take the lead as an advocate of forgiving . . . especially amid the con-flicts that congest and limit too much of life. Remember this declaration from Robert Muller, former assistant secretary general of the United Nations, and a mystic in his own right:

Decide to forgive

For resentment is negative
   Resentment is poisonous
   Resentment diminishes
and devours the self.
Be the first to forgive
   To smile and take the first step
   And you will see happiness bloom
   On the face of your human
brother or sister
Be always the first
   Do not wait for others to forgive

For by forgiving
   You become the master of fate
   The fashioner of life
   A doer of miracles

To forgive is the highest
most beautiful form of love
In return you will receive
untold peace and happiness

12. THIS DISEASE IS DISCOVERY

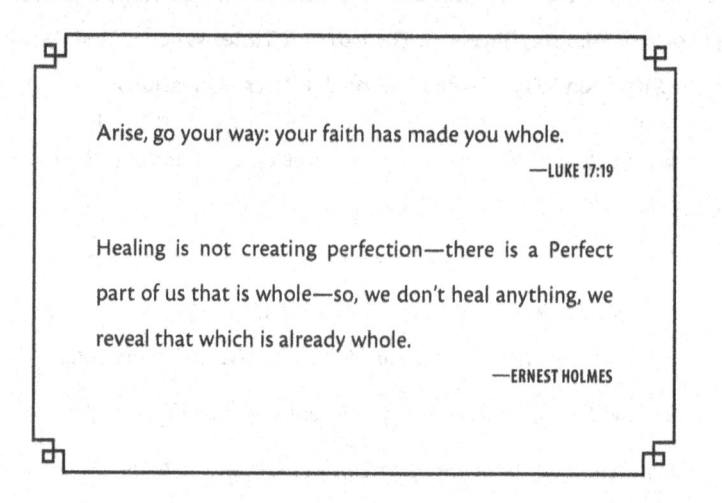

> Arise, go your way: your faith has made you whole.
>
> —LUKE 17:19

> Healing is not creating perfection—there is a Perfect part of us that is whole—so, we don't heal anything, we reveal that which is already whole.
>
> —ERNEST HOLMES

– The Essence –

The experience of disease is one of the most challenging and difficult aspects of human experience. The term is most often used to indicate disorders of the physical body; however, disorders or "diseased states" can afflict any area—the mental, emotional, and psychological dimensions, relationships, vocations and careers, finances—just about any facet of human expression. At one level the goal seems obvious: change what's going on and make it better, reestablish basic wellness and harmony. This is a natural and understandable desire, and there is an abundance of helpers, professionals—even entire industries—that seek to fulfill this objective. When afflicted, we are usually quite satisfied to bandage up the condition, resolve the obvious trouble, and be done with it. Even in spiritual disciplines, the most common approach is to simply try to "pray it away." In any situation where a speedy elimination of the problem is produced, a healing is typically pronounced.

I Invite You to Reflect on Times in Your Life When You Have Experienced Some Form of Disease, Illness, or Disorder . . . Times When It Was Assumed That the Situation Was "Healed." Consider These Questions:

- *Is it healing if there has been a surface cure yet nothing else has changed?*

- *Is it healing if there is no clearer understanding or inner growth?*

- *Is it healing if the "taproot" remains and the condition emerges again, though the situation or players involved might be altered?*

- *Is it healing if, in all honesty, a deeper wound still festers?*

- *Is it healing if there are opportunities left on the table . . . especially ones that could have led to greater compassion, wisdom, clarity of purpose, or aliveness?*

- *Is it healing if there is no gratitude for the ordeal and the gifts it offers?*

- *Is it healing if the experience fosters no greater sense of higher Life Forces and our ability to align with them to reveal Wholeness at all levels . . . if there has been no expansion into greater life mastery?*

A cure is seldom true healing. Cures most often deal with surface conditions, effects, symptoms. Healings resolve things at the causal level. For instance, a marriage may be "sick." The couple is at each other's throats most of the time. A solution would be for each of the persons to find new hobbies to occupy them and to develop strategies to avoid each other as much as possible, thereby creating an atmosphere of greater peace in the home. The situation seems to be cured. The relationship is still sick, however, and waits for genuine healing. Another example: a cure would be to whack off a weed at the surface of the soil. The unsightly situation is cured. A healing would be to extract the entire root . . . *and* to plant something lovely in its place. A cure is seldom true healing. Healing is revealing the reality of Spirit and the activity of Truth.

In disease and disorder experiences, something is usually striving to get our attention. There is a higher purpose at hand. Beyond simply changing the condition, whatever it may be, there are treasures to be gained by delving into the meanings and messages within the situation. We are being called to radical inner questing. By agreeing to this larger adventure, we seal a sacred covenant with Spirit, with Love/Intelligence, that invokes experiences, opportunities, and insights that often lead to profound blessings and healings at depth. For in so very many cases, disease and disorder are clever disguises for transformational launchpads on the soul's expansive journey. Yes, embracing this requires courage, but even more so, the resolution to not just live at the surface of our lives. It is the heart's willingness to let disease be a further opening into life mastery. It is understanding that . . . This Disease Is Discovery.

There's a cute story about Ethel and Myrtle, two adorable, elderly ladies. One day they decided to attend an exhibit they'd read about. They were excited as they got in the car and headed to the museum. As they drove along, Myrtle noticed that they ran a red light. She chalked that up to Ethel's absentmindedness. Soon, however, they ran a stop sign . . . then another red light. Myrtle turned to her friend and said, "Ethel, do you realize that you've been running red lights and stop signs!" Ethel was shocked. "Oh Lord!" she cried. "Am I driving?"

We, too, can forget that we are, indeed, in the driver's seat of our life.

This forgetfulness is especially common during the experience of disease. Something alien seems to be going on in the body or situation that needs to be stopped or removed. The problem seems to take on a life larger than our own and it's definitely in the driver's seat, especially if there's a great deal of pain involved. As this expands, there is usually a distancing from any personal connection or participation. Outer, worldly remedies or procedures are initiated, and the patient's role is mostly to endure—sometimes both the disease and the remedies.

It's helpful to remember the opening revealed in Chapter 3, "This World Is Consciousness." Fundamentally, everything is consciousness. Everything is the energy and intelligence of the ultimate, universal Source, the Spirit, God. As creative centers in this divine Mind, we are equipped to participate in the revealing and manifesting of higher Ideas. It is not possible, however, to step into this role while we still believe that Reality is primarily material and worldly. This is what usually happens with the experience of diseases and disorders. We slip back into focusing and fixating on the materiality and power that the disease or problem seems to wield. The pain, difficulty, or danger involved make it more challenging to remember that the disease or disorder is not ultimate Reality, but an experience we're having. And the experience we're having is equally an opportunity we are offered . . . an opportunity for higher-level discoveries.

Discovery #1: Awareness Messages

This leads us to understanding one of the higher-level purposes of disease or disorder: they alert us that something in our awareness—some idea, feeling, judgment, conclusion, or way of being—is obstructing or interfering with the natural wholeness inherent within the physical body or the body of our experience. After all, the physical body is fundamentally spiritual—Light, Energy, Intelligence. The materiality of the body is a by-product of its ultimate spiritual Essence. A template of perfection is the core intelligence in every substance, cell, fluid, system, organ, or function of the body. We can, however, "jam the frequencies" of this essential bodily intelligence and harmony in so many ways: feelings of prolonged fear, shame, agitation, discouragement, sadness, stress, anger, resentment, and hatred . . . these are particularly toxic.

These feelings often energize a whole host of debilitating self-concepts: *I'm not worth much . . . I don't matter . . . I'm a failure . . . I'm not meeting expectations . . . I'm not loved or supported . . . I always have to struggle . . . Nothing turns out well for me . . . I'm always misunderstood . . . I'm not safe . . . I'm not attractive . . . I'm not creative . . . I am a victim . . . I can't do what I have to do . . . My body is weak or unacceptable . . . I'm trapped in something unacceptable . . . My work is more important than my body or my relationships . . .* and the possibilities go on and on. These feelings and thoughts are further aggravated by traumatic life experiences that are allowed to go unresolved.

There are also ways of being that are debilitating and disruptive to innate wholeness: addictions and dependencies (including workaholism); continual forcing and manipulating; carelessness with food, exercise, and rest offered the body; judgmental habits; perfectionism; and this list also goes on and on. Sometimes the challenge is a deeply engrained belief that the body is inherently fragile and imperfect, rather than vibrant and beautiful. It's like the simple inscription on the headstone of the hypochondriac: "See!"

There are so many factors in awareness that can hinder and distort the expression of the intelligence and grace within the body. The diseases or disorders that result, though often mild at first, are symptoms of this deeper turmoil . . . wake-up calls inviting us to understand how we are being, what we are doing, and the impact of all this. If we focus superficially on removing or curing the physical symptoms, but neglect to address the underlying factors in our awareness, the interference becomes more damaging and "taps on the shoulder" grow into "whacks from the cosmic two-by-four!"

In understanding the impact of our thoughts, feelings, and ways of being on the physical body or the body of our experience, there is a danger: it is the tendency to go on an inner witch hunt for what we have done wrong, to assume a sense of guilt for the disease or disorder. (Most of us in this culture are, after all, well trained in heaping guilt upon ourselves!) People can be heard wondering, "What did I do to bring this on? Where did I go wrong?" This is seldom very helpful and can actually add to our problems.

Instead of Becoming Preoccupied with What We May Have "Done Wrong" or with Scrutinizing How Some Condition Came to Be, a Better Approach Is to Ask the Following:

- *What are the messages and opportunities in this situation for me?*

- *What is it time to release . . . and what is it time to embrace?*

- *How can I express more love, peace, and joy throughout my life?*

- *What is highest and best for me, for all involved, and for this situation?*

- *How could this situation become a transformational launchpad for me?*

Contemplating questions like these with deep sincerity and openness can introduce insights and possibilities for change that are the most beneficial and truly healing.

There is a wellspring of healing energy already within the physical body. Our job, in Emerson's words, is to "get our bloated nothingness out of the way of the divine circuits." When we get rid of the interferences in awareness . . . when we remove the toxic mental/emotional frequencies and poisonous practices . . . when we create an energetic frequency of peace, love, and well-being throughout our lives . . . then the quantum phenomenon that is the body can naturally reveal its balance and perfect operation . . . its Light. As the quote from the work of Ernest Holmes at the opening of this chapter suggests, healing is revealing. It is not dissolving disease or creating superior states in the body. Healing is revealing the inherent wisdom, perfection, and power throughout the body that is fully capable of dissolving illness and producing superior states.

Understanding this, there are no "healers," there are only facilitators of healing, those who are adept at revealing the inherent wholeness of body, mind, emotions, and spirit. Even those in the medical professions do not actually create healings by means of their therapies and procedures. Instead those therapies and procedures interact with the healing forces already resident in every aspect of the body. The Power that heals a cut on a finger is not the medication or bandage applied. It is the mysterious, miraculous force of healing Light . . . in the body and throughout this Universe. Let us remember: enhancements within the inner life initiated by the one experiencing some disease, illness, or disorder are every bit as important and powerful in the healing process as the treatments of medical professionals.

Discovery #2: Body Messages

Our physical bodies are "the temple of the Living Spirit." They are intricate and glorious masterpieces. Our bodies also have an enormous job to fulfill. However, they are often unappreciated and under-supported.

There is also a vast wisdom and storehouse of information within the body, but it is most often ignored. After all, how common is it to be taught how to perceive the voice of the body and to establish communication with it?

Therefore, the appearance of disease can also be the body's cry for help. Usually the body gives us some advance signals, warning signs that greater pain or illness will emerge if we refuse to listen to and heed the body's requests. Though we are ultimately not our bodies, they are still a manifestation of our Spirit and our vehicle for earthly experience. So it is important to actually "be in our bodies" rather than to float through our lives oblivious to them.

Imagine a more conscious relationship with your body. Imagine taking time each day to listen to the innate wisdom and deep requests of this physical miracle, learning your body's language, wants, and needs. Imagine being so attuned to your body that you innately sense what foods your body most wants, when it's important to eat, and how much to sleep. Imagine responding readily and lovingly to your body's longing for movement and exercise. Imagine the power of consciously dissolving inner toxins. Imagine a new lifestyle of nurturing your body in all the ways you are guided, along with loving and blessing your body-temple every day. Having imagined all this, imagine also the enormous gifts of vitality, strength, resilience, powerful brain functioning, and longevity that will be returned to you. Greater body consciousness returns amazing dividends. We no longer have to demand that the body get our attention through diseaselike wake-up calls!

Discovery #3: Soul Messages

Disease will, at times, serve as a messenger of the soul. By soul, I mean the spiritual You, the Higher Self, the I Am of you. Your soul is the God Self, your authentic and eternal Beingness. This dimension of your true Essence has an agenda far more elaborate than the dreams you most passionately cherish at this time . . . and a mission far greater than this lifetime could ever complete. Duane Elgin, in *The Living Universe*, shines great light on the service provided by our bodies and our experiences: "We are spiritual beings having a bodily experience. Our bodies are biodegradable vehicles for acquiring soul-growing experiences. Every experience plants its feeling-knowing resonance in our soul."

There are many ways that the soul inserts itself into our worldly experience. There are the defining moments and unmistakable wake-up calls. There are those peak experiences of inspiration and attunement wherein we sense the higher path we are walking amid the lower-level demands of this lifetime. And . . . there are those experiences that can "drop us to our knees"—the times when our personal, human resources and powers are obviously feeble in handling the situation. Sometimes disease is one of these experiences.

Soul messages ultimately bear good news . . . always messages of spiritual empowerment and unfoldment. Disease experiences are often a way the Soul offers precious gifts . . . gifts that can bring radical changes and quantum leaps. Sometimes disease is a way the soul "gets a word in edgewise," since most of us don't listen or respond well to our inner depths. Something has to get our attention. Yet know this: as difficult as they may seem at the time, soul messages sent by means of disease offer unparalleled Grace and Goodness.

Sometimes Disease or Illness Is a Soul Message . . .

- *To love more, play more, share more . . . and work less*
- *To let go of haunting regrets and guilt . . . and to live anew*

- *To finally say "Yes" to change, to some new chapter, or some bold leap*

- *To slow down and explore your heart's gratitude*

- *To lean into pain and to discover that inner strength, peace, and joy remain*

- *To say the things you've always wanted to say . . . mostly, "I love you"*

- *To know, once and for all, that fear is not your master, but your friend*

- *To cherish the simplicity and fullness of the moment*

- *To experience divine AWE—"amazement with everything"*

- *To fully embrace a shift or lesson that this lifetime is really about*

- *To transcend roles, status, and power so you can remember who you really are*

- *To let Spirit introduce you to ever-deeper Love and higher Light*

And . . . Sometimes Disease or Illness Is a Soul Message

- *That it's the perfect time to let go of the body that has served you so well . . . that you might move into the greater dimensions and joys of Infinite Life and Love already prepared for your Immortal Spirit . . . that it is your soul's Graduation Day!*

These are just a sampling of Soul Messages placed in that curious wrapping we call disease. As with most life experiences, there comes a time when we realize that labeling some of them positive and others negative is a kindergarten approach. There are light and shadow sides to everything, and every experience transcends the labels we place on it. This is so very true of the experiences we classify as "disease." When we finally quit making it a cave we must fight to get free from, we can then make it a catalyst for discovery of the highest order. What we learn will be soul stirring; what we will become will be authentic and radiant. As the wonderful physician/psychotherapist Rachel Naomi Remen has written, "Healing may not be so much about getting better, as about letting go of everything that isn't you—all of the expectations, all of the beliefs—and becoming who you are."

Limitless Healing Potential

Please know this: No matter what the disease or situation, there is always a divine and boundless capacity for healing. It is never by personal initiating, however, that a healing is accomplished. Instead, it is by believing, attuning, and surrendering to Innate Perfection, thereby revealing Spirit's Wholeness of Being as that which you are. Healing energy abounds everywhere and in all situations. Sense this Light within you and call it forth into expression.

The key: Ask . . . Believe . . . Receive!

It is also vital to understand that healings take many forms. Entering into a healing consciousness unleashes currents of Divine Right Action— the "upper progressive movement of the Spirit" to reveal the highest and best. Sometimes the sought-after or obvious surface changes are neither highest and best nor the essence of true healing. It is crucial to stay profoundly open to all that is seeking to unfold in the body and in the body of our experience. Full and genuine healing can, indeed, take form as the regeneration of the body. Healing can also emerge as clear guidance, life shifts, and transformational encounters. Healing can reveal itself as forgiving, as inner wounds finally resolved. Healing can show up as the magnetizing into one's life of opportunity and new relationships. Healing can express as innovation and breakthrough. And, healing can come forward as the releasing of the body, the freeing of the soul to express in new and more appropriate dimensions. Forms of healing are many, and every person's process of revealing their wholeness is unique. One thing, however, always remains the same: Spirit's eternal and ever-unfolding Wholeness is a gift that can always be revealed and celebrated.

Wholeness is who you are. Let it be.

– The Experience –

Cancer Vaulted Him into the Spiritual Life

Mark Nepo, acclaimed author and poet, openly shares how his journey through a life-threatening cancer experience opened, expanded, and deepened him. His path is a beautiful example of embracing soul messages gleaned through the messenger of disease. In *The Book of Awakening*, he writes, "It is no secret that cancer in its acuteness pierced me into open living, and I've been working ever since to sanctify that open living without crisis as its trigger."

In another place, he adds:

> As a teenager, I wanted very badly to be a professional basketball player. My gifts were enough to hide my limitations for a while and I played in high school and in college. But when I stopped playing my sophomore year in college, I discovered my calling as a poet. This carried me for almost eighteen years until cancer opened me to the uncovered life of spirit. I did not fail at being a basketball player nor did poetry fail me.

*More accurately, my inwardness evolved with enough life expe-
rience, so that moving bodily in the air evolved into the poet's
dance of feeling which then evolved into the spirit's grace
of being.*

Into a Deeper Love . . .

Rabbi Lawrence Kushner tells of his anguish at receiving the news that his
four-year-old son had a disease called progeria, the early-aging disease. He
was told that before his son was ten years old, his body would deteriorate
to that of a person in his nineties . . . that his son would be shriveled
up, crippled, and in great pain—an unimaginable nightmare for any parent. Rabbi Kushner writes that there were, nonetheless, gifts in the situation . . . that in going through that experience with his son, he was drawn
into levels of loving that were more profound than words can adequately
express. It became clear to him that this journey was providing experiences that were more touching and powerful than anything life could
have presented in any other way.

She Fully Embraced the Opportunities!

In the early 1990s, I had the pleasure of joining the ministry team of
Dr. Peggy Bassett for a three-year period. Years earlier, I had gone through
ministerial training with Peggy, so I was a trusted friend. She had developed an extremely large and vibrant ministry in Huntington Beach, California, and now she really needed my help. Peggy had been falling at
unexpected times . . . sometimes while playing tennis, other times off the
speaking platform in her sanctuary. The diagnosis was chilling: ALS, also
known as Lou Gehrig's disease.

I worked with her as an associate minister for one year. Her disease progressed so rapidly, however, that by the end of that year she was forced

to retire. At her request, I assumed the position of senior minister and began a two-year personal-growth experience of a very high order as I sought to build up the church again and assist the multitudes who, given her immense popularity, were either in great grief or immense anger . . . oftentimes both.

What I so deeply respect about Peggy's handling of her experience with ALS was her absolute determination to continue to grow through the experience. She befuddled many people by asking them not to pray for the dissolving of the ALS but, instead, to establish the acceptance in their prayers that she was being empowered to learn, to grow, and to continue to deepen spiritually. She took on the situation as a transformational journey and was quite clear that it had come into her life to bring her needed realizations and opportunities. Many thought she was deserting them and her faith. In truth, she was offering all who could embrace it a clear and compelling example of elevating oneself to a superior position in relationship to a difficult experience. She was doing some of her finest teaching. For her, it was not about praying away the situation. It was about receiving the gifts it was bringing her and continuing to shine her Light—no matter what was going on.

I remember a conversation I had with her near the end of her earthly life expression. It was a labored sharing since the disease had greatly impaired her ability to breath and talk. Despite this challenge, she shared the core insights she'd been gleaning from the whole experience. They had to do with controlling. She openly admitted that she had been a supreme controller most of her life, and especially in her ministry. Now she was being given the experience of being out of control of everything but her own thoughts and feelings—her consciousness. Furthermore, she told me she was discovering the hidden power in being reliant on others, the deeper strength it gave her amid overwhelming and progressive weakness. She was feeling a profound peace, she told me . . . an even more rapturous connection with Spirit and with Life, Itself. Through the last several years of her life and by means of the ALS experience, I am certain that Peggy Bassett achieved and maximized the crowning realizations that this particular lifetime was offering her.

She Dove into Her Bucket List!

Susan Spencer-Wendel was a journalist for more than twenty years, but left her job as a courts reporter for the *Palm Beach Post* when she, too, was diagnosed with ALS in 2011 at age forty-four. How did she respond? She immersed herself in the love of her husband and three children, and began filling her moments as fully as possible with powerful and meaningful life experiences. She went to the Yukon to see the northern lights; then to Cyprus to meet family for the first time; she helped her daughter try on wedding dresses; she got kissed by a dolphin; she got a new dog; she built a splendid hut in her backyard; she traveled with her family extensively. And then she wrote a book, *Until I Say Good-bye*. It is a memoir about the year she says she wanted to devote to love and joy . . . before the ALS claimed her abilities and her life. She wrote the entire book on her iPhone using her right thumb, the only finger she had use of as the disease progressed. Asked at one point how she was doing, she responded, "As well as can be expected. My body and voice become weaker every single day, but my mind becomes mightier and more quiet. You do indeed hear more in silence."

He Let It All Go

J. Sig Paulson, better known simply as "Sig," had an illustrious career as a New Thought minister, author, and teacher. Sig also embraced the opportunities and insights of a life-threatening experience. After returning from an extensive trip in Europe, he couldn't get out of bed the next day. A medical evaluation showed that he was on the brink of a heart attack. Complete bed rest was prescribed. Surgery might also be necessary. He lay in bed recuperating and reflecting on his life. Critical times like this have a way of opening up deep questioning and unavoidable realizations. He wrote the following:

> Then a strange thing happened. I began discarding the roles I had been playing, the images I had projected to the world. I saw my husband image dissolve and drop away; my father image, my brother image, my son image, my family image, my social images all dissolved and dropped away; then my business image, my professional image, my work image followed the same pattern and dropped away. I saw the whole pattern of my life dissolving and dropping away, and suddenly I started to laugh because I saw the humor in my whole experience; how seriously I had played those roles; how diligently I had supported and insisted on many things that had seemed so important and essential at the time, but now were being seen in a new perspective. And there I was, stripped naked, shorn of my roles and images, with only my inner self to face the Love that had created me.

Humor Was Her Freedom!

In *Love, Medicine and Miracles*, Bernie Siegel tells the story of Joselle. He writes that she was a hefty woman but nonetheless came to meetings of their therapy group in a tight shirt, shorts, high socks, and an outlandish hat—all as a performance to give everyone a laugh, but also as an expression of her joy despite her cancer. One day, she declared, "My chest X-ray shows that the cancer is going away, and I know why." Everyone in the group leaned forward to hear a wise and lofty insight. Joselle concluded, "It's because no self-respecting cancer would appear in an outfit like this!"

– The Expression –

1. Move Past Struggling and Forcing.

The most conducive state for healing is allowing. Remind yourself that Wholeness is the Truth of your being and that you are clearing the way for the revealing of this basic Wholeness. Take the energy once channeled into forcing and dedicate this energy to developing an ever-stronger sense of assurance and a peaceful acceptance of healing. Believe that wholeness is being revealed.

It is also very important to access the various messages that are being offered through the experience. Do several sessions of "stream of consciousness" writing. After a time of meditation or prayer, pick up a pen and open up a flow of insights by completing sentences like these: *The core messages of this situation are . . . What the universe is offering me through this situation . . . What I am now ready to realize about myself . . . What my body is telling me is . . .* Keep your "figure-it-out mind" silenced and let the deep wellspring flow. You'll begin to channel forth so much that you *know* but hadn't yet realized. Cherish these insights and let them evolve over several sessions. This process can be a mighty component of the healing!

2. Align with Love.

When you experience some form of disease or disorder, it is essential to move beyond the stranglehold of fear and into ever-present Love. Love is the most powerful healing energy. Remember that your fear is a friend alerting you to a critical step . . . that it is time to shift from the assumptions and fears of the worldly mind into the Realities of Spiritual Love and Truth. Don't be concerned about occasional moments of fear. The predominant energy of your consciousness is what matters most. Center yourself in Love . . . feeling divine Love as you also love yourself and others. An awakened heart is a fountain of healing waters!

3. Maintain the "Field."

As you neutralize fear and forcing, and center yourself in Love and deep assurance, you are catalyzing a healing field in and around yourself. The prayers of others can also support the empowerment of this field. The cultivation of your own consciousness is key, yet an immersion in spiritual community can be a great gift of additional support. Be willing to ask for and receive support . . . from a Ministry of Prayer, from a spiritual practitioner or prayer partner, or from your own "God Squad" of caring and high-consciousness people. Intensify your spiritual practices and study, saturating your awareness with inspiration and Light. Do caring and nurturing things for yourself. All these approaches are designed to energize and sustain the healing field in and around you.

4. Let the Light Shine.

Sense the divine Light that permeates you and everything around you. Visualize or imagine this Light flowing throughout your body. Know that it has the Power to neutralize anything unlike itself. It does this automatically and without any forcing on your part. If you are dealing with a "diseased" circumstance, visualize or imagine this Light saturating all aspects of the situation. Do not be taken in by the naysayers or the "doom-and-gloomers." Remember that the Light shines most beautifully in a background of darkness.

5. Live Anew!

Remember that this Now moment is the point of true Life expression. Live in the now and reenter the joys of the moment. Live as one who is so much more than whatever is going on in the body or in the body of experience. Find an outlet to share, to serve, and to give your gifts in ways that uplift others. Sense the larger Love/Intelligence that is freed through your awakened consciousness to guide, uplift, energize, and heal you ... revealing the magnificence and wholeness of who you really are. It is essential to understand that healing is assured because Wholeness is your True Nature ... now and forevermore! Therefore rejoice ... and savor the wonders of the Life in and around you. Live with holy AWE ... "amazement with everything!" Deep Joy is based in the realization that, ultimately, nothing that matters is at risk ... and everything that is of Spirit abides forever.

13. THIS CHANGE IS BIRTH

> Change is always taking place within that which is changeless. Change is merely the play of Life upon Itself.
>
> —ERNEST HOLMES

> To exist is to change, to change is to mature, to mature is to go on creating oneself endlessly.
>
> —HENRI BERGSON

– The Essence –

Change. It is a constant at every level of worldly life that we can observe, experience, or comprehend. However, about the only person who truly loves change is a baby with dirty diapers! Change is the aspect of life that people most fervently wish they could eliminate . . . or, if not eliminate, at least control or modify. It is what many blame for their woundings, setbacks, breakdowns, or losses. Thus it is the facet of life that is most often detested or resented. Change can seem so ominous that many elect the option of lapsing into deep denial that it will, sooner or later, be a force to be dealt with, an experience to be embraced. Then when change does rear its head, the shock, anger, sadness, or resistance is multiplied many times over. All of this is in response to a universal phenomenon, a natural element within every dimension of life as we know it.

A certain man gave himself the great treat of a fishing trip in Scotland. There he was, out in a boat, fishing alone and having a marvelous time experiencing a dream fulfilled. All of a sudden he noticed some movement in the water beneath him. This continued and he became frightened. Whatever was in the water was big and seemed to be right under his boat. In an instant, the man's boat was lifted up out of the water. He couldn't see what was causing this; all he knew was that the boat kept rising higher and higher. Then the culprit flipped that rowboat one way while the man flew the other way. As he flew through the air, the man looked down and, to his shock, there were the huge jaws of the Loch Ness Monster, spread wide and ready to gobble him up. So the man screamed out, "God, oh God, please help me, please save me!" At that instant, the whole scene went into "freeze frame"—him in midair and the jaws open below him. Then he heard a powerful voice: "This is God. You've never called on me before, my child. I didn't think you believed in me." The man shouted back, "Well give me a break, God. Up until a moment ago I didn't believe in the Loch Ness Monster, either!"

This is how most people see change—as a monster lurking beneath the surface, ready to throw them into chaos and gobble up their well-ordered lives. But when change is felt to be an enemy, all that is left is to devise elaborate strategies for self-protection, and these usually take enormous amounts of energy to maintain. Sometimes these strategies, themselves, become problems that sabotage our lives. For instance, many revert to hyper-controlling, somehow imagining that intensifying controlling behaviors can slow or block change. Believing that we can control change in the world around us, however, is a delusion that distracts us from a more effective relationship with change. The same is true for other ineffective strategies, such as denying or trying to resist change. These approaches usually cause additional upset, stress, or even injury.

I remember counseling a woman whose issue was aging. She was fearful and resentful of the aging process and, as a result, was devoting incredible amounts of time, effort, and money conniving ways to resist it. All this was not only making her miserable and worn out, she seemed to be accelerating the effects of her advancing years. As we discussed all this, she arrived at the very clear realization that her problem was not aging, but her resistance to aging. Over the next several months, she eased up on this resistance, redirected her worry thoughts, used her time to play and rest more, busied herself with some hobbies she'd neglected, and spent more time with her friends. Her friends now enjoyed her more since she wasn't always complaining about her age. Ironically, six months after embracing these new approaches, she looked like a new person, like she was ten years younger.

Ram Dass has declared, "When you cling to what changes, you suffer." Where in your life are you fearfully clinging to things as they are? Do you really believe that the force of your clinging can forestall the changes that are inevitable? Instead of clinging, try fully enjoying and savoring things as they are. This will open you and move you into a deeper, richer experience of whatever is going on and of those who grace your life. Ultimately, all that anyone can control is his consciousness—the direction and quality of thinking, feeling, believing, and responding. Life invites us to release fear-based controlling and our resistance to change so that we can enter into the miracles of the moment. And when change ripples through present miracles, we will be blessed with the opportunity to be fully present to new ones. As Henry David Thoreau remarked, "All change is a miracle to contemplate; but it is a miracle which is taking place every instant."

The biggest challenge with change is that few of us were taught much about it until having to grapple with it. Wouldn't it have been nice to have access to a course titled "Change 101"? This course's curriculum would have to cover "the nature of change and what it really is; why change is essential to life and self; how to craft enlightened approaches to change." Learning these things early on would have made my journey of life much easier and more enjoyable. It's never too late, however, to gain these insights and to develop an enhanced and effective relationship with change. This is essential because life is a never-ending river of change. Then there are those experiences that take us into graduate-level change training. Topping this list is loss . . . losing a job or career, losing a personal or physical capacity, losing a dream and, most especially, losing a loved one. But take heart. Change is not a monster, nor an enemy to you, to life, or to God. It is a vital aspect of the way things are . . . and we are wise to have faith in the way things are.

Change 101

ESSENTIAL CONCEPT #1: We have to begin by realizing what change really is, its essential nature. No matter what any change appears to be about at the surface, the core concept of this course teaches us that . . . This Change Is Birth. This immediately challenges us to go beyond appearances at the level of circumstances, conditions, and happenings. Rather than fixating exclusively on whatever is breaking down, falling away, or ending, this core concept invites us to sense that the Universe is always pregnant with potentiality. Life is forever birthing more of Itself. God, the Universal Spirit, is always revealing newness by expressing through vehicles capable of revealing more of the divine Intelligence and Livingness. So rather than fighting or resisting change, we discover a vital opening into life mastery by shifting our approach and becoming, instead, the midwife of a birth unfolding by means of some kind of change.

Yes, there will be times when it is natural and appropriate to grieve the change, especially if it involves a loss. We readily become attached to people and things, and it's seldom easy to let them go. When the loss involves a loved one or a pet, we grieve more deeply. Yet this has a certain quality of beauty, for we grieve because we have first loved. And in our loving also lies an opportunity for the healing of change's impact: *Love always invites us to keep living, giving, and forgiving.* Love always conceives and champions new expressions of life. Like the phoenix rising, something is always seeking to emerge and to proclaim itself out of the ashes of change. Therefore as it is written, "Let not your hearts be troubled" (John 14:1). Remember also, "Underneath are the everlasting arms" (Deuteronomy 33:27). Or as someone has quipped, "For underneath God's cushions is change." What we are realizing is that change is the sacred mechanism of the Spirit that clears the way for the eternal newness of Life to reveal and celebrate Itself.

ESSENTIAL CONCEPT #2: Change is the necessary vehicle for every person's evolution and awakening. If things remained forever the same in our lives, there would be no impetus for growth, no challenges to evolve our awareness, no resistance to increase our strength or to develop our capacities. Ernest Holmes has written the following:

> *Nature will not let us stay in one place too long. She will let us stay just long enough to gather the experience necessary to the unfolding and advancement of the soul. . . . Nature demands change in order that we may advance. When change comes, we should welcome it with a smile on the lips and a song in the heart.*

In essence, he is saying that change is a mask that transformation wears.

In her landmark book *Conscious Evolution: Awakening Our Social Potential*, Barbara Marx Hubbard clarifies the role of change and evolution. This renowned futurist, visionary, and teacher of the leading edge of human advancement explains that evolution raises consciousness and produces beauty and greater freedom. Thus it is critical to learn to cooperate with change and transformation. Secondly, nature loves "quantum transformations"—leaps from one state to the next, rather than incremental changes alone. For example, leaping from gills and fins to lungs and feet . . . from intelligent animals to early humans. Thirdly, she clarifies that chaos and crisis precede transformation. When nature reaches a limitation, it doesn't just adapt; it innovates and transforms. Thus problems are "evolutionary drivers" that are vital to advancement.

Perhaps this is why it has been said, "Never waste a great crisis!" Crisis and chaos are change elements that promote the birthing of a higher order. There is a phenomenon in groups of ants that could teach us a lot: When a large community of ants is seeking something—some food, something to build with, or a way out of or around something—it seems that mass chaos breaks out with ants scurrying in all directions and even over one another. However, when a single ant finds whatever is being sought, this seems to be communicated almost instantly throughout the group consciousness, and all the ants converge on the discovery. A similar experience has been noted among bees. What this illustrates is that "chaos" in any situation, system, or group is actually a form of order we simply haven't understood. Physicist David Bohm has suggested that there is an "implicate order," an ideal pattern and limitless possibility, indwelling every aspect, particle, or expression of life. This implicate order cannot be destroyed or obscured by chaos. In fact, chaos actually stimulates a greater degree of the expression of this inherent order. This is similar to pieces of a holographic plate, all of which contain the entire image originally encoded on the unbroken plate. The "whole" is encoded within all aspects and bits of it.

Another model that shines light on the forces that drive evolutionary change is Spiral Dynamics, a system identified by American professor of psychology Clare W. Graves and further developed by his many disciples. Spiral Dynamics is a complex system with many ramifications, but it offers us a further understanding of the gifts of change and chaos. It suggests that the evolution of human consciousness is like an upward spiral of various value systems and dimensions or bandwidths of awareness, called *memes*. A new, more effective meme is always birthed when the former meme has generated problems that it cannot solve. A bold and totally new state of realization must be called forth to solve a new class of problems and perpetuate the species. Thus chaos is inevitable when a way of thinking, knowing, and relating—though beneficial at its birth—reveals its drawbacks and limitations. A new way of thinking or knowing must be birthed. And as Einstein declared, "We cannot solve our problems with the same thinking we used when we created them."

By understanding and embracing these models of change, we equip ourselves to stand in the midst of great chaos and attune ourselves to the implicate order, the emerging breakthrough, the more advanced meme. We can recognize it as the greater unfoldment of wholeness and evolution sprouting up by means of disorder. We might even be moved to declare, "I now bless this mess!"

ESSENTIAL CONCEPT #3: To create a new and effective relationship with change, it is imperative to cultivate a deep realization that the Divine is always conspiring for our highest and best. Spirit is relentlessly biased on the side of our growth and fulfillment. After all, you are a cherished vehicle for God's greater and more exultant expression! As a Sufi parable suggests, there is an angel hovering over every blade of grass, whispering, "Grow, grow, grow!" Life whispers that same mantra within the stillness of your spiritual nature. You align yourself with this growth principle by embracing change and cooperating with whatever it seeks to bring forth.

When you realize the force of evolution at work at the deepest levels within, you gain the ability to move into a space of conscious willingness to cooperate with and to encourage the emergence of the higher destiny that is woven into the fabric of your being. You awaken to expanded dimensions and qualities of the Higher Self and thus become a conscious cocreator with the Spirit, with divine Life. Understanding these things shines new light on two of Jesus' proclamations: "The Kingdom of God is within you . . ." (Luke 17:21) and, those who grow in believing "will do the works I have been doing, and they will do even greater things than these" (John 14:12).

Barbara Marx Hubbard, in another of her powerful books, *Emergence: The Shift from Ego to Essence*, highlights the urgency of humanity taking this step of enlightened cooperation:

> *The footprint of self-centered humanity is seen everywhere upon the earth—and the life it is creating is not sustainable. Our generation has reached Choice Point. . . . We are finding out that what worked in the past for our survival will destroy us now. . . . We are a slowly awakening planetary giant just beginning to realize that we are one living body responsible for its own future in a universe of unknown dimensions. Our crisis is a birth!*

This is a call to move beyond an outmoded and increasingly dangerous level of expression. It is, as her subtitle suggests, an invitation to move "from ego to essence." This is the most masterful approach to working with change in a more powerful and beneficial way. Hubbard adds:

> The process of emergence involves a fundamental, definite shift in identity. . . . This is a shift from the egoic, self-conscious, personality self—the local self—to the universal, non-egoic co-creative or divine self—the Essential Self. . . . This change of identity we must undergo is marked by the shift from the creature human, who lives life as a self-conscious, survival-oriented person, to the co-creative human, who is inspired by spirit to express and embody divine intent.

Metamorphosis!

The metamorphosis of a caterpillar into a butterfly is a profound expression of the core concept: This Change Is Birth! As Richard Bach puts it, "What the caterpillar calls the end of the world, the rest of the world calls a butterfly." Here is how this familiar process unfolds . . . and how it relates to you and me:

A caterpillar has an immense appetite. It eats far more than its weight every day, which is why it is such a threat to crops and vegetation. Do you see the parallels to our human situation? Our personal and collective appetites are also out of control in so many ways that the earth and our social structures can no longer sustain. However, prior to change, ignorance prevails. We might imagine a caterpillar seeing a butterfly and, if it could speak, declaring, "You'll never get me into one of those things!" Isn't this similar to most of humanity's response to the various guides and enlightened masters who have proclaimed our spiritual abilities, our divine destiny? Most of humankind denies the possibility, even though we've been given clear examples of what is possible in us and for us.

A greater force of emergence begins to exert itself and the caterpillar feels an undeniable call to transform. Soon the caterpillar crawls onto a leaf and, instead of eating it, it affixes itself to the leaf and spins a cocoon around itself. It is then that "imaginal cells" appear . . . cells encoded with the pattern of the eventual butterfly. When this begins to happen, lesser caterpillar cells attack and resist, but the imaginal cells continue to assert themselves. In a similar way, a Higher Impulsion calls each of us to transform, to continue our journey of becoming. But we also resist. Old ways persist and many voices tempt us to stay stuck and limited. We are apt to war against the great gift.

However, transformation is inevitable. In response to the resistance of the caterpillar cells, the imaginal cells form clusters of cells to strengthen their domain. Soon these clusters form bonds over which they pass genetic information to one another. These clusters resonate at a higher frequency than their host, and it's not long before a state of chaotic unrest develops . . . all a result of the caterpillar's resistance in the face of the growing energy of change. Scientists say that the caterpillar reaches a state of "critical unworkability." Now it is no longer workable to maintain the functioning of the caterpillar. The imaginal cells go from being merely a group of like-minded cells to the "programming cells" mandating the creation of a higher design. The caterpillar's destiny is now set: it is pre-butterfly!

I invite you to explore your own resistance to change, especially the transformational shift into higher states of awareness and living-ness. Whenever a vision is conceived, a dream is embraced, a project is initiated . . . resistance is sure to emerge in defiance of the newness. This resistance wears many costumes but it is, to be sure, a perennial opponent to growth and fulfillment. When we receive signals that it is high time for change, a common tendency is to sabotage both this information and our action steps. So things often get worse. "Critical unworkability" is not just a caterpillar phenomenon. It is what most of us require before substantial change is allowed. Economic instabilities, environmental erosion, educational inequities, discrimination and disenfranchisement, geopolitical tensions . . . these and more are indications that we are arriving at critical unworkability at the collective level. It is time to recognize that our chaos is a birth! It is time to create clusters and alliances of collaboration and cocreation, shared energies that will promote more than mere Band-Aid approaches to our problems, but instead . . . inner and outer transformations. It may be the perfect time for you to gather with prayer partners, a vision group, or a spiritual community to lend energy to the birth of your greater yet-to-be.

Now when the imaginal cells overcome the resistance of the caterpillar's immune system and take on the role of programming the caterpillar's higher destiny, a remarkable thing happens: the caterpillar totally dissolves into a liquid. Now the transformational process becomes even more dramatic. In terms of human development, an essential step in the emergence process for us all is . . . surrender—to become fluid and shapeable by the Infinite. The former self with its resistance, attachments, and fears must surrender so that higher Intelligence can have Its way. As was shared in Chapter 6, this surrender is not giving up . . . but "opening to and flowing with" the higher impulse of the Spirit. It is releasing the resistance and embracing a total willingness to move to a greater state of personal and spiritual maturity. It is moving from forcing, fearing, and fighting to aligning and cooperating with a Power for Good within. This becomes the setting for miracles.

Now the cocoon becomes a chrysalis, a home of unimpaired development as the transformation is unstoppable, progressing in a space of quiet resolution. The organism is no longer a caterpillar but it is not quite a butterfly, either. The process must be allowed to run its course. Corresponding to this, there are those times when we have, indeed, let go of what was and have said "Yes" to what is to be. Yet we're still in a formative stage . . . no longer what we were, but not quite what we shall be. Yet something is, nonetheless, forming in the solitude of the heart that is the forerunner of awakened awareness and advanced expression. This chrysalis of consciousness can seem dark and dire, but this is actually a time of deepening. We have these periods because if the intellect and ego could bring fulfillment, we'd never go beyond these lesser ways of expression. So we agree, at unconscious levels, to move ourselves into situations where we will see firsthand that ego and intellect are not enough . . . and we will be caused to reach for the greater life within us—the real Self, the spiritual Self. We will reach for God.

When the butterfly is finally formed, it must go through what might be judged as great struggle to emerge in all its glory into this world. It must squeeze itself through a tiny opening in the chrysalis. In *Lawrence of Arabia*, the story is told of a well-meaning person who saw this struggle going on and proceeded to cut open the chrysalis to afford a butterfly a quick and easy entrance. To this person's shock, the butterfly soon died. Later it was learned that the butterfly needed the struggle out of the chrysalis to squeeze essential fluids into the wings and to balance all aspects of its new body. The lesson is clear: not all struggle is negative. It is quite common for people to seek quick and easy avenues to their goals and to seek security as a buffer against change. However, when the realization dawns that change is the essential vehicle for birthing our higher Good, it becomes clear that change is ultimately a blessing and the surest way, no matter how difficult things get, to be in partnership with the One, with

God. Anything short of this compromises our progress and our blessings. John Lilly confirms this when he states, "Our only security is our ability to change."

As we embody the newness of what Thoreau terms "the license of a higher order of beings," there will no doubt be struggle experiences, times when we feel awkward and are gaining our "sea legs." We should also be prepared to meet a world still anchored in an old paradigm. By working in nonviolent and compassionate ways, we gain the capacity to foster change in our world through collaboration and by "being the change we wish to see in the world." All aspects of adaptation and struggle are purposeful and well worth it. As the butterfly is empowered to see vistas and enjoy experiences of life that the caterpillar could never imagine, so, too, is our metamorphosis into greater life an unequaled blessing.

Robert Raines writes:

> To go with the flow of your life is to live without a map, to be vulnerable to having your plans changed, your heart broken, your dreams unfulfilled. It is to trust that God is in the rapids of change as well as in the rocks of continuity. It is being able to stop digging your heels in against the tide of tomorrow. It is exercising a suppleness of spirit—in which you respond to the nudgings and promptings of grace moment by moment, day by day, in a kind of love-making with life.

As he so beautifully hints, change is our entrée into more of the emerging magnificence of who we are. So this is the question before us all: are you willing to accept that changes in your life are actually births . . . and are you a "Yes" to what the "imaginal cells" of your Spirit know you are destined to become?

The Ultimate Change

A student of Zen approached his master teacher and asked, "What happens to the enlightened man when he dies?" The master replied, "Why do you ask?" And the student said, "Because you are a Zen master," at which the great teacher declared, "Yes . . . but not a *dead* Zen master!" People have always been curious and troubled about the change called death. Without doubt it is the least understood of all changes. Like the Zen master, we don't know definitively or absolutely what happens. There are those who fear that there is no greater life, that death is an extinction. Some imagine that we go to a distant place, maybe in the sky, and dwell there forever . . . that is, unless we have been cast into a torturous hell because of earthly misdeeds. Others believe in reincarnation . . . that we take on life again in some new earthly form. Still others hold that there is an invisible dimension into which we merge and in which we continue to evolve. The conclusion you choose is either a result of your spiritual training, the conclusions of respected peers . . . or the knowingness of your spiritual intuition.

Yet there is compelling evidence that life never dies but simply changes form. We have the reports gleaned from "near-death experiences" that reveal remarkable similarities. Then there are the testimonies of mystics and enlightened masters throughout the ages . . . ones whose consciousness reached beyond the veil of this visible world. The ongoingness and indestructibility of life is even implied in the conclusions of new science and quantum physics. After all, we know that energy and mass are interchangeable, and that you cannot destroy energy, only change its form. Furthermore, we now know that all forms emerge out of an unformed and limitless "consciousness." So there is that "something" that always is and cannot be obliterated. Suppose you think of your life, your essential nature, as spiritual energy, thus ultimately indestructible. If this is true, then what is left is a journey of continual spiritual unfoldment, perhaps across many lifetimes, always aspiring to reveal more of the "implicate order" or inner perfection of what Jean Houston calls "the Godseed" in us ... of that divine Life in which "we live, move, and have our being."

A higher understanding of this thing we call death requires us to make the distinction between the body and the Self. The body is subject to constant change, being a product of this time/space, earthly dimension. Studies assert that all of the cells in our body die and are replaced within several years. Now if we were, fundamentally, the body, we'd already have died billions of deaths. Of course, we survive this continuous dying and birthing at the physical level because there is a spiritual constant that is who we really are. This is the authentic Self, the I Am, your spiritual Nature. Infinite Life brought you forth out of Its limitless potential and boundless Love. At the physical level, we go from infant, to toddler, to child, to young adult, to adult, and beyond. However, none of these changes damages or impairs the True Self. In fact, it seems that this true Essence of us uses all the changes of the body to blossom and to reveal more of that which we really are. Along with every phase and change of the body, we are becoming, more and more. Why would it be any different when we release the body in the change termed death? Perhaps death is just another in an infinite array of passages, a metamorphosis no more damaging to who we really are than the "death" of the caterpillar as it moves into its higher destiny as a butterfly. What if we went beyond bleak notions of "death" and thought of this change as a "transition"?

It has been said that a person's life consists of twenty years of having their mother ask them where they're going ... forty years of having their spouse or partner asking them where they're going ... and, at the end, the mourners wondering, too! In all seriousness, perhaps this is an opportunity to put to rest a lot of time-honored yet unreasonable superstitions and fears about where we go when we make this "transition." How could God, which is Love—a Love more vast and unconditional than our human awareness can fathom—conceive of, much less create, a place of eternal torment—a hell? No person in their right mind would ever consider punishing their children in such a way when they, inevitably, make their mistakes. How much less, then, could the Divine do such a thing?

Heaven and hell are states of consciousness, not actual locations. We have been given the capacity to create our own hell through our destructive thoughts, intentions, feelings, and actions. Whenever we dwell in a sense of fear and separation, we are to that degree dwelling in a self-created hell. Whenever we abide in revenge, judgment, or hatred, we are imprisoned in a personal hell. But what thought does, thought can undo. We also have the capacity to awaken and to offer our receptiveness to being uplifted, to enter into the Presence of Oneness and Love, and thus to reorder our thinking and behaving. When we choose this path, we are freed from these hell states and established in "heaven." After all, Jesus proclaimed that "the Kingdom of God is within you." Whenever we choose to commune with the Divine Presence at our true Center, we are blessed and enlightened. We return to heaven . . . our true home.

It's fascinating how the perspectives of our awareness in this three-dimensional, time/space experience have influenced our notions about the life "hereafter." Since the ego is established in separation, and in time and space, then eternal life is conceived of as "a place" we may or may not go to, depending on how good we have been, or if we happened to be part of the "right" religion. Then it is common to imagine that eternal life is continuing on in time . . . for eternity. However, mystic revelations and spiritual deepening reveal expanded perceptions. Our True Essence, our spiritual Beingness, is not governed by the apparent laws and limitations of this time/space world. As Jesus stated, we are in this world, but not of it.

Eternal life is not going on forever in time, and immortality is not living forever. Instead, eternity is transcending the lower dimensions of time and space, thus experiencing the eternal Moment of Now. Our True Self is pure Being, timeless Presence. The "I Am-ness" that you are transcends time. It is eternal in its fullness, *right now*. Eternal life is the awakened consciousness of those who live in Love and in the Now. Yes, you will release the body when it no longer functions well . . . or when your soul agenda here on this plane is complete. However, this is not a death . . . it is a graduation day for the soul, as the True You steps back into the direct experience that . . . This Instant Is Love.

You are immortality . . . now! Jesus declared, "In my father's house are many mansions." I believe he was using the metaphor of "mansions" as a parable to open people of his day to the realization that "In my father's house are many dimensions" . . . higher frequencies or vibratory rates of being. Perhaps as the frequency of our consciousness is enhanced and empowered, we prepare ourselves to enter into the experience of more refined dimensions of being that reflect this inner growth. Ernest Holmes adds the following:

> It looks as if we were already immortal and need not die to take on immortality. If there are many planes of Life and Conscious-ness, perhaps we only die from one plane to another. This thought seems reasonable. . . . All evidence should prove to us that we are not going to attain immortality, but that we are NOW immortal.

Or, as Goethe puts it, "Life is the childhood of our immortality."
I've also cherished a vignette attributed to a past U.S. president, John

Quincy Adams. It is said that he met an old friend on the streets of Boston. This friend shook his trembling hand and said, "Good morning! And how is John Quincy Adams today?" The ex-president replied:

> *John Quincy Adams himself is quite well, I thank you. But the house in which he lives at present is becoming quite dilapidated. It is tottering upon its foundation. Time and the seasons have nearly destroyed it. Its roof is pretty well worn out. Its walls are much shattered, and it trembles with every wind. The old tenement is becoming almost uninhabitable, and I think John Quincy Adams will have to move out of it soon. But he, himself, is quite well . . . quite well.*

Psychologists have suggested that all our fears are grounded in the one great fear . . . fear of death. Not only is it a relief to release the fear that is needlessly attached to the change we have called death; it is an ultimate freedom. As Paul proclaimed in the Bible, "O death, where is thy sting? O grave, where is thy victory?" (1 Corinthians 15:55). We find an unassailable security in the realization that we are safe—now and always—that, as the great old hymn declares, "It is well with my soul." Freed of the tethers of fear, we can get back to the reason we're here: to express ever more of the potentialities of the soul. Walt Whitman, in "Song of Myself," stated that his true essence was "not contained between my hat and boots." Who could ever express all that is latent within their being within one lifetime? Victor Hugo adds:

> *For half a century I have been writing my thoughts in prose and verse and history and philosophy. But I feel I have not said the thousandth part of what is in me. When I go down to the grave I can say, "I have finished my day's work," but I cannot say, "I*

have finished my life." My day's work will begin again the next morning. The tomb is not a blind alley. It is a thoroughfare. It closes on the twilight. It opens on the dawn.

The various fear-drenched myths about death seem to be another way that we dampen the Joy of the Spirit; another way that we "grieve the Spirit." Mystics and those who've glimpsed the expanded dimensions of Life through near-death experiences often report experiencing an unspeakable Joy and an undeniable Love. Knowing this, our job is to reclaim these higher states now, not later. It seems many are on the "deferred living plan," seemingly waiting to make it safely to death before really opening up to the fullness of Life. Bursting through the illusion of death can bring us into the richness and magic of Life. Death is like taking off a tight shoe and discovering new ways to dance!

In my first ministry in Portland, Oregon, there was a member of our congregation I'll call Sue. I'll never forget her complete change of personality after a conviction of immortality dawned within her. She was a sweet lady, but oh so negative. During her final illness I tried every way I could think of to lift her spirits—but got nowhere. Then one day, "Helen," one of our incredible spiritual practitioners and a beautiful soul, died. A number of us held an informal memorial service for her right in our church office. Immediately after that I went to see Sue, who had not heard of Helen's passing. When I entered Sue's room, I couldn't believe what I saw: she was sitting in her chair, smiling, looking radiantly happy, and she said, "I'm so glad you came! Something wonderful has happened!" And she told me she had suddenly seen a garden, and in this garden there was a woman standing, and as she turned, Sue saw that it was Helen . . . only a Helen who was young and beautiful. Then Helen turned, as if in answer to a call, and said, "I'm Helen. Lead Thou me on!"

She opened the garden gate to go out, and as she did, the whole scene vanished. From that moment on, that radiant happiness never left Sue until she made her own transition some six weeks later. Back in the rest home where she had previously hated every moment, she found everything and everybody wonderful. When I'd go see her, it wasn't about me giving her a lift. She lifted me! It was a remarkable and soul-stirring transformation.

Often a shocking or shattering experience serves as a breakthrough into the heart of Life. A man was driving home from work late at night. His day had been extremely difficult. It was raining and he was generally cross with the world. He could see the lights of a truck coming toward him in the other lane. Then all of a sudden another set of lights began passing the truck in his lane. There was only an instant to react . . . the man swerved just in time to miss the oncoming car, but in doing so, his car careered into the ditch with a jolt. He wasn't hurt and the car wasn't damaged too badly. So he just sat there for a good amount of time while his heart slowed down. Then he experienced a flood of emotions: first fear, next lots of anger, followed by relief. And then he wept. All the pressures and worries of his life didn't matter anymore. Now he thought of his wife and family and recalled their picnic last week. He thought of so many precious things and cried. That rainy night began an ongoing transformation for that man. A brush with death caused him to awaken to the richness and fullness of life.

We don't have to have a close call, or endure some crisis, to embrace life fully and passionately—to experience the fullness of life. We're prone to ask, "Is there life after death?" But there's a more important question: "Is there life after birth? Am I truly, fully living this life?" It's nearly impossible for a person to fully embrace life and live powerfully in the moment—and still be haunted by death.

Epilogue

This Change Is Birth! Whatever the change, in even the ultimate change . . . greater life is seeking to be born. In the tribal wisdom of the Lakota Indians, there is a saying: "If you discover that the horse you are riding has died . . . it is best to dismount!" Where in your life are you riding a "dead horse"? Is it because of some paranoia about change? Understand . . . there is no need to whip a dead horse . . . no need to pray for the horse to be resurrected . . . no need to try to convince yourself or others that the horse is just napping, that the deadness will be finished soon . . . no need to hire a consultant or visit a therapist to figure out why that horse won't get moving . . . no need to go around proclaiming that the horse isn't dead, it's just "living-impaired" . . . and certainly no need to call your friends together yet again to complain about the dead horse. How about getting off it! Make the changes that are shouting from every side. Change can be the healthiest, most life giving of all experiences.

Remember also that the greatest of all changes are the shifts and enhancements made within our own consciousness. To let go of old, worn-out judgments and misperceptions, self-limiting mind-sets, and toxic resentments and burdens . . . and to replace all this with life-invigorating realizations of the joy and power of your true Being . . . this is the path to mastery, and to the life you truly deserve. Something great is waiting to be birthed into your awareness and experience . . . right now!

Ella Wheeler Wilcox captures this in her poem "Change":

Change is the watchword of Progression.
When we tire of well-worn ways, we seek for new.
This restless craving in the souls of men,
Spurs them to climb, and seek the mountain view.

– The Experience –

Some additional life experiences can shine light on the power of embracing change.

Baby Booties

In mid-2008 my beloved mother, Delma Teel, made her transition into the expanded dimensions of Life. She was a vibrant being who lifted herself up by the "bootstraps" and created a great deal of joy and success in her life. She had an ever-deepening inner life and was a tremendous spiritual practitioner. As many children would say about their parents, I owe so much of my life fulfillment to her unwavering love, her strength of character, and her steadfast faith.

When my wife and I were cleaning out her house following her passing, I ran across a cedar chest. In it were numerous mementos of her earlier life, especially her high school years. At one point I lifted up a quilt and discovered that my mom had saved my first pair of baby shoes . . . light blue, lace-up leather booties. I took them home, then inspected them more closely a few days later. The journey, the changes of my life, cascaded over me. The soul I Am incarnated into the fetus in my mother's womb. Another change brought me into my parent's arms. But then came a defining moment: I was placed in these very booties to learn to walk . . . the physical mechanism to support a spiritual passage—the initiation of my journey of becoming. These booties would kick-start my personal evolution. I would learn to walk, then run . . . and my journey would then wend through constant changes.

Those baby booties also represented a space of innocent and total trusting, an innate acceptance of life's invitations and opportunities.

As we grow older, we are not so trusting because we become fearful and attached to the way things are. We forget that we've been walking through and mastering countless changes all along the way.

I inspected my booties more closely and noticed that their tips were very worn. There were even some small holes in the toes. Evidently I had bumped into many things. Yet I kept on, I never stopped. I wondered why I was so often tempted to stop or hide out nowadays, especially when I bumped into challenges. I thought to myself, *I am still the soul who got these booties . . . along with the "boot" to leap forward into choosing, creating, loving, learning, giving, expressing, and celebrating the dimensions of my Spirit. I am still that powerful soul who was in a little body and got booties for the magnificent journey of my life on this planet. Some babies get wheelchairs or crutches . . . but we all get the nudge, one way or another, to unleash the possibilities within us.*

I realized that no one—not even myself—could foresee what my life would become, how it would unfold. Yet the potential was there all along, waiting to be activated. Every soul possesses that same magnificent and amazing potential that was activated when we were placed in our baby booties. It hasn't run out . . . but we have to cooperate, and say "Yes," especially to changes. This is what the journey is all about. It still continues and calls us each into greater and greater glory. "Except you become as little children, you shall not enter into the kingdom of heaven."

A Brush with Death

In 1999 a group I cofounded, the Association for Global New Thought, was concluding our first Synthesis Dialogs, which were held at the Norbulingka Institute near Dharamsala in Northern India. This institute, established by the Dalai Lama, is the cultural center for the furtherance of the spiritual teachings, culture, and art of Tibetan Buddhism. The dialogs brought together more than a hundred authors, spiritual leaders, social architects, philosophers, scientists, and futurists to discuss human challenges and solutions. His Holiness, the Dalai Lama, participated midway through these explorations.

On the final day of the dialogs, the group assembled at the palace of His Holiness for our concluding session. After many discussions with the Dalai Lama and others, there was a pause. Then a ministerial colleague, the Reverend Ed Townley, rose to speak. With tears rolling down his face, he shared that it was exactly twenty-five years ago on that very day that he had been pronounced dead. Ed explained that back then he was down and out, a homeless bum, and an alcoholic also hooked on cocaine. He was living in a sense of total separation, despair, and unworthiness. And on that day twenty-five years ago, his body couldn't take it anymore. He was taken to a Long Island hospital and pronounced clinically dead. The doctor had signed the death certificate and left it on Ed's chest. Ed knew this because he was out of his body watching it all from somewhere near the ceiling. He was also surrounded by beings that were saying he had to go back. But he didn't want to do this . . . that body of his was in too much pain. So he was told to rest . . . and was in a coma for ten days. Then the beings said he had to go back, but they promised him it wouldn't be as painful now. Ed came to and was hospitalized for another month.

This profound experience seeded in Ed the idea that Life is more than he had known, and he made a commitment to a new chapter for his life. He began a program of sobriety, one day at a time. He took additional steps to empower his commitment, and they just kept strengthening him. He began to uplift his life. No longer did he experience the depths of despair, even though there were still times of struggle and pain. He was now experiencing a greater dimension of Life. He told all of us in that assembly, "My life became a growing collection of little choices honoring a greater commitment that was revealing more and more gifts and possibilities to me than I could have imagined."

So there he stood . . . exactly twenty-five years from a death certificate to a new, transformed life. He was obviously and deeply moved: "How could I ever have imagined when I made that new commitment to Life that eventually I would be the minister of a fast-growing New Thought Church . . . that my life would be brand-new . . . *and* that exactly twenty-five years later I would be standing in the presence of the Dalai Lama!"

Embracing change can, indeed, catapult us into unimaginable possibilities!

Lessons in a Movie

The movie *My Life* is about a man named Bob Jones, a very successful executive who works in a public relations and advertising agency. His wife is pregnant with their first child. But he has received news that changes everything: he has been diagnosed with cancer. The movie then wends through a juxtaposition of life and death themes. Bob, in his time left, decides that he will make the most of his life, to go about the healing of certain aspects of his life, cleaning up his act. You see, his life had been way out of integrity. The people he worked with did not really know him. He held a lifelong grudge against his father. He was not emotionally available to his wife. He had avoided any spiritual experiences. His heart was closed.

By facing his own death and also anticipating the birth of his child, he begins to look at life in new ways. The movie goes on to teach us that our lives are about the heart and about releasing the magnificence within us so that we can become gifts to ourselves as well as others.

The lesson: change is often a process of "unlearning" . . . stripping away whatever layers over the Authenticity and Light within us. We do not need a diagnosis or a life-threatening event to awaken to the original beauty and blessings of our Being. However, we will, very often, find it necessary to surrender the artificial mechanisms we thought were required for success and acceptance.

It's Never Too Late!

The story is told of a married couple who were extraordinarily close. Their marriage was a forty-year epic of tremendous sharing, incredible experiences, and heart-stirring closeness. They were definitely "soul mates."

Then the husband died unexpectedly. The wife was grief-stricken more than most can comprehend. She felt that her life was also over, though her body was still very strong and healthy. In fact, she instructed that a phrase be carved in the middle of her husband's tombstone: *The light of my life has gone out.* Amid her tears at the graveside, she confirmed that these words had been accurately etched.

Several years went by. Quite by accident, this lady met a man at a church social event. She was understandably distant at first, but her new acquaintance was undeniably wonderful. He was attractive, caring, tender, intelligent, thoughtful, and fun-loving. She allowed herself to spend time with this man and, inevitably, fell in love. After a wonderful courtship, this man proposed. She heard a word come out of her mouth she thought she would never utter in such a situation: "Yes!"

But what was she to do with that inscription, *The light of my life has gone out,* on her first husband's tombstone? She thought and prayed and then inspiration dawned. She called the stonemason and instructed him to carve another phrase for her beneath the first phrase. The new inscription: *I struck another match!*

May you allow the endless flow of change to ignite in you ever greater expressions of Life!

– The Expression –

When the Waves of Change Are Cresting in Your Life:

1. Decide to befriend change! In fact, rather than running from it, craft a new lifestyle of running toward it. Welcome change and it will reveal its gifts much more readily.

2. When you are in the midst of the difficulties initiated by some change, remember that these are "labor pains" . . . that something glorious is seeking to be birthed. This perspective can actually shift how things are evolving.

The British author William Macneile Dixon wrote,

> Birth is the sudden opening of a window, through which you look out upon a stupendous prospect. For what has happened? A miracle.

3. Let go . . . Let go . . . Let go! And keep breathing!

4. Rather than shutting down in the midst of change, allow changes to be signals to open your heart wider and to express even greater compassion for yourself and for all involved. Your greatest strength is the energy of your heart.

5. Always remember that you live in the sacred and eternal Now. Amid Life's constant flow of change, anchor yourself in the sacred chalice of the Moment. In this and every moment, you are safe . . . and all is well.

14. THIS UNCERTAINTY IS MAGIC

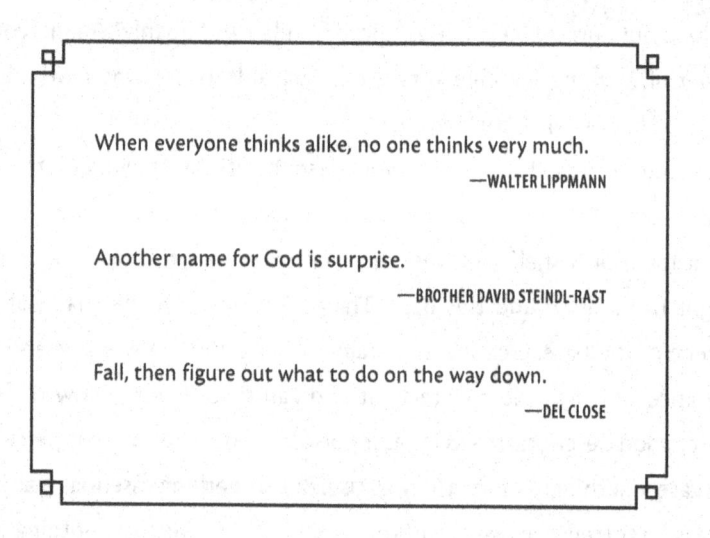

When everyone thinks alike, no one thinks very much.

—WALTER LIPPMANN

Another name for God is surprise.

—BROTHER DAVID STEINDL-RAST

Fall, then figure out what to do on the way down.

—DEL CLOSE

– The Essence –

To be uncertain can feel really uncomfortable. It's fairly typical to avoid not knowing and to scurry to quick conclusions so as to steer clear of such a feared and despised space. Uncertainty is so intolerable to some that they simply elect to make something up instead. Swedish psychiatrist R. D. Laing recognized this when he wrote, "There is something I don't know, that I am supposed to know. I don't know what it is I don't know, and yet am supposed to know . . . and I feel I look stupid, if I seem both not to know it, and not know what it is I don't know. Therefore, I pretend I know it. This is nerve-wracking, since I don't know what I must pretend to know. Therefore I pretend to know everything."

Does this feel at all familiar? I've also heard it said that it's the person who knows everything who has the most to learn. What if we were to cease resisting and demonizing uncertainty? What if we stopped feeling embarrassed by uncertainty and were even willing to befriend it? What if we held our current "certainties" more humbly and openly? An incredibly powerful opening into life mastery is available to us when we realize that . . . This Uncertainty Is Magic!

Imagine a vase. How would you describe it? Most would probably explain that their vase has a flat base so that it can sit on some surface like a table or a shelf. The vase also has sides that rise up to a certain height from all around this base. These sides take on the shape of the outline of the base, creating a container of just about any shape and appearance, as long as it is watertight and can hold flowers. Now this is a pretty good description—as far as it goes. It is a description that perceives the vase as a thing, as something to use. But something essential is almost always forgotten: the essence of the vase is its emptiness, its nothingness. It is just as true that the actual vase is the empty space all the rest of the elements create. This space is a capacity to be filled, so this makes the empty space as important as the boundaries that define it.

Another thing about the vase: it can be filled only because it is open. It is an open invitation. It has to be empty, though it will occasionally hold water, flowers, etc. We would name and define a vase differently if the empty space was always filled up, say with pebbles or cement. Following all this, you may never see a vase quite the same way again! And yet this is an opportunity to remember that what we see creates the space we cannot see . . . and vice versa!

I offer these thoughts because I believe that our minds are meant to be like a vase. The base for our minds is pure awareness, the capacity to be aware of being, of experience, and to entertain perceptions and thoughts.

The sides of the mind could be likened to the fundamental concepts that support us in functioning meaningfully in this life. These "sides" would be a composite of things: core values, essential and universal spiritual principles, a guiding vision, and the components of one's basic identity. Sometimes this composite creates a vase that appears graceful and beautiful. In other instances, the appearance can seem distorted and unsightly. It all depends upon the shape we assign to "our reality."

The "vase of mind" is meant to hold thoughts, images, perceptions, conclusions, judgments, and beliefs, only for a while. They are on display to be recognized, evaluated, sometimes celebrated, then eventually released for something new. However, the tendency is to leave mental material in this vase for far too long. Things can pile up, get stratified, becoming stagnant, even ugly. This is because people tend to become enamored with and attached to what the vase of mind has held, so much so that room for the brand-new can be very scarce. Yet it is the brand-new that represents our growth in understanding. It is the brand-new that opens the way for breakthroughs and transformation.

We can all use some mental housekeeping from time to time. It's refreshing and empowering to let go of junkie ideas or conclusions that are worn out or unworkable. However, one of the greatest challenges in this is that the ego loves to be right, so we don't tend to part with obsolete ideas very readily. Many of us have been taught to remain consistent, at any cost. So if we thought, believed, or said it before, we must continue to do so—even if the ideas are weakening or suspect. We would do well to remember Emerson's classic line "A foolish consistency is the hobgoblin of little minds." Everything evolves; so also should the content of our thoughts and beliefs.

Think of what you absolutely know for sure as a slice of a pie. The more I journey down the road of life, the tinier that slice gets! Then think of what you are clear you don't know as another slice of this pie. I'm very clear that I don't know about calculus or microbiology, how to play the oboe, and things like that. So now you have two slices of the pie, both fairly small. What is the entire rest of the pie? *It is what you don't know you don't know.* When uncertainty of any kind comes along, it is like an engraved invitation into the heavenly "don't know" realms of inspiration and revelation. It is your ticket into radical newness, for universes of possibility open up with the realization of any bold and timely new idea. To honestly "not know" means you're ideally equipped to venture forth as a pioneer of greater knowing. But to be a pioneer, one has to be willing to wander in the wilderness a bit, into the unfamiliar and unconventional. When you embark in this way, there will be those who question your stability, your reliability, maybe even your sanity. They're apt to declare that you're lost. The title of a song by Jana Stanfield makes for a good reply: "I'm Not Lost, I'm Exploring!" Or as I occasionally say to my wife when she realizes that I am without good directions: "Yes, you're right, honey; I don't know where I'm going . . . but we're making excellent time."

Consider the life of Michelangelo, the renowned sculptor, painter, architect, poet . . . and more. He painted the ceiling and altar wall of the Sistine Chapel, and sculpted the heart-stirring *Pietà* and the awe-inspiring statue of David. One of his greatest challenges was that he didn't like to be around crowds of people. In today's language, he was probably an introvert. From what I can surmise, he created defense mechanisms to insulate himself that were not very pleasant. But despite all this, he consistently challenged himself to "leap" into bold, new works. Many he didn't finish because he would succumb to the lure of a new idea or project. However, he continually stepped beyond the known to create out of the unknown. In his later years, Michelangelo was proclaimed to be a genius, and he attained superstar status throughout Europe. When he was eighty-seven years old, he was asked to share his motto in life, some truth that had inspired his creativity for so many years. He replied: *"Ancora imparo,"* which means, "I am still learning."

Now that's the way to court magic. It is to doubt, or at least hold lightly, one's certainties, and to give oneself over to the muse, to the great unknown. To be willing to continue questing and learning, to drink from the fountain of the waters of Spirit's inspiration . . . this is the way to become a creator, to reveal a form of mastery that is becoming childlike before the Infinite. It is to embrace the wisdom of composer Darius Milhaud, who was once asked, "If you had to go to a deserted island, which one of your compositions would you take with you?" Milhaud replied, "I'd take some blank paper. My favorite composition is always the one I will write tomorrow."

Many people doubt their ability to explore, to know more, to rise to new heights of creativity, or to accept significant change and growth in their lives. This is because our culture tends to promote self-limiting mentalities. We recommend against emptying the vase, opting instead for the security of the current arrangement. When we are imprisoned in self-limiting mentalities, we become experts on what we currently know and all that is not possible for us. We act like puppets complying with the opinions and conclusions that others have decreed about our lives and our potential. But who can pronounce limits for anyone else? Teachers said that Thomas Edison was too stupid to learn anything. Louisa May Alcott, the author of *Little Women*, was encouraged by her family to settle for work as a servant or seamstress. Walt Disney was fired by a newspaper editor due to his lack of ideas. One teacher described Albert Einstein as "mentally slow, unsociable, and adrift forever in his foolish dreams." He was even expelled from school and refused readmittance. Winston Churchill failed the sixth grade, and didn't become prime minister of England until he was sixty-two, and only after many setbacks. Luckily these individuals, and others like them, refused the verdicts and kept on learning and growing.

It is so tempting to become a "status quo person." These are people who become deeply attached to their current beliefs, opinions, and experiences. They champion what is, not what can be. They are huge "doubters" when anything new comes along. When Robert Fulton's steamboat was at the dock, people were yelling, "It'll never start." Then it started . . . so they shouted, "It'll never go anywhere." Then it left the dock, and do you know what they shouted then? "It'll never stop!" Such are the ways of doubters and status quo people . . . people like Simon Newcomb, an astronomer, who declared, "Flight by machines heavier than air is unpractical, insignificant, if not utterly impossible." Or like Ken Olsen in 1977, then president of Digital Equipment Corporation, who proclaimed, "There is no reason for any individual to have a computer in their home." But let's not sneer at these folks until we have taken an honest look at our own unwavering allegiance to the acceptable, to the known, to the conventional, to the understandable, to the "impossible." We've all rejected outrageous possibilities when they've knocked on the doors of our awareness; we can all profit by examples of imprisoned thinking.

But there are even greater challenges. There is the unwillingness to challenge a notion because an "authority" established it, and there is the resistance that emerges even when evidence of an expanded understanding or truth is clearly revealed. Aristotle, in his day, taught, "The heavier the object, the faster it will fall to the earth." Since he was Aristotle—one of the greatest thinkers of all time—people believed him for centuries, never questioning or exploring this axiom. In 1589, nearly two thousand years after Aristotle, Galileo dropped both a one-pound and a ten-pound weight off the Leaning Tower of Pisa. They landed at the exact same moment. A few changed their minds on the spot; however, the amazing phenomenon is that most remained caught up in an old belief that was so strong that they denied the evidence of their own eyes and continued to say that Aristotle was right. No wonder humanity has progressed at a snail's pace!

In Plato's *Dialogues*, Socrates is quoted as saying, "The unexamined life is not worth living." This is because to be alive is to grow, and to grow is to question and to explore. The unexamined idea is not worth believing. The unexamined behavior is not worth maintaining. The unexamined mindset is not worth following. The unexamined commitment is not worth keeping. After all, we are not here on this planet to behave like sheep. We are given amazing capacities and abilities, and are being challenged by our Creator to leap into the unknown so that we can become the cooperative vehicles for the revelation of higher understanding and greater livingness.

Einstein wrote, "When I examine myself and my methods of thought, I come to the conclusion that the gift of imagining has meant more to me than my talent for absorbing positive knowledge. Never lose a holy curiosity."

Imagination . . . curiosity . . . both essential equipment in the backpack of a true explorer. In the early 1900s, Graham McNamee was a tremendous singer. One day, he noticed that some huge letters were being hoisted to the top of a building. He didn't block his curiosity. He talked to people in that building and discovered that these were the call letters for a new radio station. Radio was just then emerging as a great avenue for communication. Initially they told Graham that they had no need for singers, but he asked to be shown the control room. He met the manager, who realized that Graham had a good voice. They gave him a test . . . and one of the greatest careers in radio was born.

Glenn Dugger was forced to retire at age seventy. But he still felt great energy and creative skill. He applied for a job with a pharmaceutical lab that was working with natural substances from the earth to cure diseases. They hired Glenn and put him to work studying more than six hundred soil samples. As he studied one sample in particular, he became curious about a golden mold growing on it. It seemed to speak to him: "I'm something!" At seventy-four years of age, Glenn Dugger discovered tetracycline, the antibiotic that in its time helped many, many people.

Luther Burbank's curiosity and wizardry with plants prompted him to develop or improve at least eight thousand plants. Many ridiculed him for dabbling in this pursuit, but he continued on and made many valuable contributions in the fields of horticulture and genetics. I love this message he offers us: "Tell them this is a beautiful world full of wonders. Look for interesting things, learn how to use what you find, and have confidence and faith."

Most important, he declared, "Never let anyone talk you out of your magic!"

Your magic is your willingness to embrace uncertainty and to utilize it as an open arena for discovery. It is to learn to enjoy being freed of limiting notions or situations . . . and to be "firmly in midair."

A Friend Called "Serendipity"

By embracing the opportunities within uncertainty, a new friend will show up. This friend has been wanting to walk along life's path with all of us. This special friend is an integral element of this spiritual Universe. It is too often, however, ignored or turned away. This friend is Serendipity.

What's Going on . . .

- *When a man's car breaks down on the way to an important assignment, so he flows with the situation only to find himself staring into the eyes of a beautiful receptionist at the repair shop . . . the lady who'd eventually become his wife!*

- *When a traveler follows her guidance and agrees to take a different flight than the overbooked one she was scheduled to take, then finds herself sitting next to another lady who shares an opportunity that opens up life-changing new vistas of prosperity and fulfillment?*

- *When a couple who had released the idea of having their own natural child due to a doctor's finding . . . volunteered at a home for pregnant, unwed teens, and a year later meet sixteen-year-old "Angela"—and afterward adopt her baby, creating an incredible family and a beautiful ongoing relationship with Angela?*

Most of us could add to these a similar experience of our own. What's going on within situations like these? Whenever a person is willing to explore beyond the known, beyond stifling certainties . . . and whenever a person believes that something greater than they know can come of it . . . a life-enhancing phenomenon is engaged: serendipity goes to work to guide, enlighten, prosper, and bless.

Over the last several decades, the awareness of the workings of serendipity has had a resurgence. No doubt, this is because of a new wave of higher consciousness emerging across the planet. More people are becoming aware of the field of infinite Intelligence and purposeful unfoldment in which we "live, move, and have our being."

The term comes from ancient Persian tales about "Three Princes of Serendip." They go on great adventures to seek treasures and gain knowledge of how the world works so that they can come back and become kings over their own realms. These three princes experience one mishap after another. They always seem to be on the brink of losing their lives or fortunes . . . when "out of the blue" comes some unexpected opening, some incredible way, and they are saved. They almost never get exactly what they set out to find, but they always fall into something magnificent . . . something greater than the original goal. About those princes it is said: It was as though an unseen Power was guiding them better than they could guide themselves. And they came to know that what was best for them in the long run would be their experience anyway . . . and, consequently, they were very serene.

Let's Explore That Statement More Deeply

- *"It was as though an unseen Power was guiding them better than they could guide themselves."*

This is the major discovery of one who is awakening spiritually . . . that an unseen Power *is* guiding each of us better than our limited human awareness and understanding can at any given moment. Aligning with this great, active resource opens huge doors of possibility.

- *"And they came to know . . ."*

There is a great difference between belief and knowing. We can have a belief about something, but circumstances may cause us to waver . . . we're no longer sure we really believe. However, in knowing—knowing that we know—circumstances don't influence, alter, or diminish such knowing, but instead actually enhance and increase our knowing.

- *"And they came to know that what was best for them in the long run would be their experience anyway . . . and, consequently, they were very serene."*

Serenity is not something we seek. It's a by-product of living in align-ment with the Presence and Power of Spirit, of God. It's realizing, *I can trust the Power . . . I can know that what's best for me is going to happen. A Power greater than my intellect, my ego, is available, and I can yield to It and be guided most powerfully.* Then we take our highest knowing and enthusiastically work toward it, willing to be redirected all along the way. In this approach to life, there can be great serenity. Something occurs and we immediately know that there's a perfection in it—there has to be! This is born of the deep conviction that God . . . Divine Spirit . . . Infinite Intelligence . . . is always conspiring to bring forth our highest and best— beyond what we can ever imagine!

We are all princes or princesses of Serendip! We are all heirs to the King-dom of God. We are all on our own personal quests. And it is critical that we pursue these quests, for without the princes' willingness to be on their quests, they would never have fallen into the incredible circumstances that blessed and expanded their awareness and their lives. But many peo-ple are expert at blocking serendipity because they are fearing and reject-ing their quests . . . opting instead for their security, their certainties, their own designs.

There is a way to move in the grace and flow of the Spirit . . . to be con-scious of the gifts and blessings coming to us from the Great Source in what we often term "accidental or coincidental" happenings. Remember, what the princes found was not what they were seeking. What looks like chance or coincidence is actually part of an incredible weaving . . . an orchestration by our souls in partnership with a Power and Intelligence far greater than we are.

Life asks us to go beyond our own limited understanding and to flow with our quest. It's in our questing that grace and serendipity have room to express! Whether you've got little dreams or big dreams . . . are you questing to forward the great being that you are? By embracing uncertainty, and adding to it an element of expectancy for the revealing of some heretofore unrealized magic, we give ourselves over to the wonder-working powers and options of the larger Life.

Do you remember the story in the Bible of Joseph? He was the favored son of Jacob. Jacob showered him with affection, including making him the famed coat of many colors. Because of his favored status, his brothers hated him. Finally his brothers had had enough, so they conspired to do away with Joseph. When he came out to the pastures to check on them, they grabbed Joseph and were going to kill him. However, his brother Reuben convinced them to just throw him into a deep pit and to let him die there. (Reuben was actually planning to rescue him later.)

However, some Ishmaelites were traveling in the area, so the brothers elected to sell Joseph to them. He was then taken to Egypt and sold into slavery in Potiphar's house—the captain of Pharaoh's guards. Now this was certainly a calamity. However, Joseph prospered in the situation and eventually was running the whole house. But Potiphar's wife took a liking to him. When Joseph refused her overtures, she became angry and proceeded to frame him. As a result, Joseph was tossed into jail—another calamity! Not to worry . . . Joseph maximized this situation as well, getting on the good side of the prison keeper and becoming something of a guard and helper.

Later, Joseph interpreted a dream of Pharaoh and was made Pharaoh's second-in-command to prepare the land for an eventual famine—yet another win. After several years, he had Egypt prepared. But back home, his father and brothers were starving. They had heard there was food in Egypt, so they traveled there. Joseph recognized his father and brothers when they entered the royal court, so he disguised himself, put his brothers to many tests, and eventually they all bowed before him—just as

Joseph had prophesized years ago. Ultimately Joseph revealed himself and forgave them. Then he revealed the philosophy of life that helped him cultivate unimaginable blessings and wins in even the direst of situations. He proclaimed, "You meant evil against me. But God meant it for good."

In his own day and his own way, Joseph was activating the phenomenon of serendipity. Every one of us can do the same. But it all hinges on a choice: the choice of where we will place our sense of power . . . what we will believe is ultimately in charge. Will we be so taken in by intimidating situations or the threats of appearances that we inadvertently worship at their altar? Will we accept the broadcasts of limiting ideas, the wailings of the naysayers? Will we cling to our current ideas and strategies? Or, will we own and bless our uncertainties, and make ourselves fully available to the higher activity and the unlimited Good of the One? Will we, also, proclaim to whatever rears its head, "You meant evil against me. But God means it for good"? This is one of life's greatest adventures: the realization that there is a Power for Good always working on our behalf, whenever we are willing to allow it to take over and to lead us onward and upward.

I realize that to live this way is to expose yourself to being classified as "nuts." I pray that this will never bother you, that you will dive into this radically powerful way of living. I've decided that "nuts" can be a great acronym, so maybe this will help:

NUTS = "Never Underestimating the Spirit!"

It's actually the greatest approach of them all, one sure to grow, bless, and prosper you . . . as long as you're not too attached to your present certainties. Keep exploring enthusiastically. Accept and claim the magic. Allow yourself to be ushered into a radical and wonderful realization of what's true, what's available, and who you really are. You'll experience exactly what T. S. Eliot predicted: "We shall not cease from exploration, and the end of all our exploring will be to arrive where we started and know the place for the first time."

– The Experience –

To realize that This Uncertainty Is Magic is to walk the path of life in a new way. Several experiences on my path drove home this truth very powerfully.

That's Way Too Hot!

In the mid-1980s I agreed to participate in a Firewalk Experience with Tony Robbins. *Why not?* I thought. Scores of friends and members of the church I was serving in Denver were signing up. The experience began with three or four hours of seminar and preparations. Tony was moving us into the shift of "knowing" and "being" that would ensure our safety and success. Through the large windows behind Tony, however, I could see his helpers building one of the largest bonfires I'd ever seen. They added wood to this fire and stoked it for hours. When we all went into the court-yard to begin the walks, the heat from that fire singed the hairs in my nostrils. I mean it was *hot*! But soon lots of people were jubilantly march-ing across the beds of hot embers.

I began to wonder what craziness had prompted me to get myself into this mess. The powerful voices of negation and limitation were raging within me. I was certain that this was both a bad idea and a dangerous one at that. But how could I leave? There were so many people from the church involved, and they were so excited for me to be part of the wins. So, I had to have one of those private moments with myself. I had to face the workings of my mind, the certainties of my rational, worldly beliefs. It was one of those moments of thrusting myself into another paradigm . . . even if it didn't "make sense."

With a great sense of assurance, I walked over those coals—no problem. On the other side was the poignant realization that life is governed by forces more powerful than the physical ones, that there are ways and means available beyond what the "figure-it-out" mind knows at any particular moment. Higher consciousness is miraculous and victorious—if we'll let it be.

That Firewalk became a metaphor for my life. Many times, when I felt that the path ahead would be like walking over red-hot coals, I would remember that it is quite possible to do just that.

A Perfect Saga

By the end of the 1980s, I had served Mile Hi Church in Denver for ten years as an associate minister to my beloved mentor, Dr. Fred Vogt. I had married Erica in 1988 and things were going so well . . . except that I was feeling rumblings of restlessness. Whenever I allowed myself to get still enough, that pesky inner voice would suggest that it would be best for me to leave Denver, to take some next step. The problem, however, was that I had no idea what that next step was; there was no clear direction . . . only the sense that it was time to go. Now this troubled me enormously because I love this ministry and am immensely grateful for all it helped me discover and become. How could I simply leave? It wasn't as though something better was tantalizing me since I had absolutely no idea what would be next. I even sought counseling to help me with this dilemma.

Through this counseling, along with lots of prayer, I arrived at the point of declaring within myself an unequivocal "Yes" to leaving, a "Yes" to whatever the next right place was to be. If you're understanding the message of this chapter, then you won't be surprised that very soon after arriving at this clarity, the next opportunity appeared, and with no effort at all on my part. I was offered a position at our movement's headquarters in Los Angeles. I agreed to accept this position that would oversee all the movement's ministries along with its educational direction. It was a tearful departure.

Although it seemed like a great opportunity, a perfect way to continue to make a difference, I hated the new job—from day one I despised it. Now, some of this was part of my grieving. Not long after getting settled in L.A., I felt inundated with remorse. How could I leave Denver and such a great spiritual community? I grieved so very deeply, and I began to question my choice, my wisdom in the matter, my sensibilities. However, I did soon learn that an administrative, desk job truly is not my calling. I did my best, but I was miserable at many levels.

After a year in this position, my colleague Dr. Peggy Bassett got in touch with me. (I shared her story of dealing with ALS earlier.) I agreed to leave the headquarters job and help Peggy out. She retired a year after I joined her team, and I served as senior minister for her church in Huntington Beach, California, for the next two years. Just when I thought that things had turned around in that ministry and were on the upswing, Fred Vogt called me. He explained that he needed help retiring, and that he had known all along that, if it was right for me, I should succeed him as senior minister. After talking and praying with Erica, I agreed to return to Denver and my home church after a four-year absence.

Much had shifted and evolved for Erica and me while in California. We had worked diligently on our marriage and on our communication methods. We had grown so much closer and had enriched our relationship significantly. I had experienced challenges during that time that had also facilitated tremendous personal growth and spiritual deepening. All of this was the kind of growth work that I now realize couldn't have been accomplished while in Denver. Erica and I both needed to be in a new setting, a different context in which we could really experience and work with ourselves.

The homecoming welcome from the beautiful people of Mile Hi Church was amazing and extremely moving. I was familiar and beloved . . . yet, at the same time, I was different. Over time many people expressed that they sensed the deepening and the growth, my pilgrimage of sorts into new inner territory. I was no longer merely the "fair-haired young man." I had been through the fires. I had leaped into a grand uncertainty and had allowed transformational forces to have their way with me.

I now know my capacity to lead such a large and magnificent ministry was honed and empowered by this arduous four-year experience. Since returning, the growth and development of this ministry has been astounding. This is not so much about me but about the perfect timing and alchemy of the total situation. It is about a tremendously enthusiastic and devoted congregation melding with my personal journey into more effective leadership. A person can only lead from the overflow of their own growth, their woundings and healings, their more activated heart. I was solidly anchored in a greater sense of wholeness, spiritual connection, and inner clarity. These gifts were being cultivated right in the very midst of the "hot coals."

This is the lesson: a perfection, a serendipity, was allowed to grow me, to take me forward in a way nothing else could. Now I am totally grateful for those difficult four years. Spirit grew me and thankfully, despite all the uncertainties, I allowed this magic to happen.

– The Expression –

Here are Some Steps You Can Take to Make Sure That the "Magic" That Can Emerge Through Uncertainties Has Your Full Permission to Expand and Bless Your Life:

1. Stay alert!

Amid uncertainties, and any difficulties involved, be alert to opportunities trying to make themselves known.

Many years ago, Thaddeus and Erastus Fairbanks had a small hemp business. They had a problem, though. They had difficulty weighing the hemp and had to find a better way. They eventually developed something brand-new: a platform scale. This innovation did the trick. The serendipity of this: most of their customers now wanted them to make and sell scales, more than they wanted their hemp. Soon the demand was so great that they gave up the hemp business, and Fairbanks Scales became a famous business, showering them with enormous blessings. It was great abundance lurking within a frustrating problem.

2. Take a stand and keep your heart open!

Do not waver in your acceptance of something unknown, yet really great—even if you've felt hurt in the process. The glory, the answers, the wonder remain. As the Bible encourages: "And having done all, to stand."

Jean Houston writes the following:

> Our woundings tell us that old forms are ready to die, however reluctant the local self may be to allow this to occur, and that hitherto unsuspected new forms are ready to flower. . . . The

wounding pathos of your own local story may contain the seeds of healing and transformation. . . . The wounding becomes sacred when we are willing to release our old stories and to become the vehicles through which a new story may emerge into time. When we fail to do this, we tend to repeat the same old story over and over again.

Arthur Rubinstein, the celebrated pianist, tried to take his own life in his earlier years. Looking back, he realized what a sad thing this was, and that a new and even more powerful connection with life had emerged for him:

When I went out into the street, I came back from death. I was reborn. I suddenly realized what a damn fool I had made of myself. There were people moving through the streets, dogs were running around, flowers were growing in a little park—it was a wonderful, divine show. I learned then that happiness is not smiling or having money or being in good health, although these are conditions worth having. Happiness is really only living, taking life on its own terms. Now, I am passionately involved with life; I love its changes, its color, its movement. To be alive, to be able to speak, to see, to walk, to have houses, music, paintings—it's all a miracle. I have adopted the technique of living life from miracle to miracle.

What a great way to live . . . from miracle to miracle!

3. Get ready!

Anticipate the magic and ready yourself for being surprised. As paradoxical as it seems, prepare not to be surprised by being surprised. Because if it doesn't surprise you, it may not be Spirit's activity!

Hold close to your heart that quote from Brother David Steindl-Rast:

Another name for God is surprise.

4. Some power affirmations:

- Called or not called, God is always here!

- I look for the Good . . . and praise it!

- I expect my unexpected magic!

- It is as though an unseen Power is guiding me better than I can guide myself. And I am coming to know that what is best for me in the long run will be my experience anyway . . . and consequently, I am very serene!

15. THIS DESIRE IS FULFILLMENT

The universal Mind of Creation is in a constant state of supplying. It never shuts down, it takes no vacations, there are no days off, and it's perpetually giving forth. . . . Allowing this all-giving Source into your life means becoming aware of the resistance that you may be placing in the way of the abundance that's always being supplied.

—WAYNE DYER, *THE POWER OF INTENTION*

If I keep a green bough in my heart, the singing bird will come.

—OLD PROVERB

– The Essence –

I believe that every one of us is born to make manifest the glory of God. Try this on . . . speak it out loud:

I am born to make manifest the glory of God!

The most powerful way to fulfill this high calling is to discover and empower your "soul's sincere desire," and to allow this soulful clarity to provide leadership for your choices, intentions, prayers, and actions. This is the way to become an on-purpose being, to experience the very highest levels of fulfillment, and to be a beneficial presence in this world . . . for those who are most authentically on-purpose tend to make the greatest difference. However, none of this potential can be actualized without an understanding of the workings of desire and the dilemmas it can create.

The Dilemmas of Desire

Desire is a tremendously powerful force. It has played a major role in the course of human history and always exerts considerable impact on everyone's personal history. The first dilemma: *misguided desire is often at the core of the weakest and darkest of human tendencies.* This is especially true when desire is fueled by excessive or heartless appetites. Consider just a few of the challenges this is creating: unbridled consumerism that threatens planetary resources and ecology while also contributing to increased poverty around the world; increases in physical and sexual abuse across a wide range of age and gender lines; the tragedies produced by terrorism and ideological extremism of many kinds. These and many other problems are symptoms of raw, misguided desire. They represent an invitation to honestly and compassionately examine the by-products of personal desire and to channel this energy in the most life-enhancing ways, for our own and for humankind's highest good.

Yet, in all fairness, there are other dynamics that can also direct desire. It is simply an energy, and no energy is fundamentally bad. It is a matter of how we utilize or channel it that determines its impact. The same electrical energy that powers up computers or lifesaving medical equipment, if misapplied, can burn down buildings or kill a person. So the problem isn't so much with desire, itself, as with the nature of the personal awareness directing it. What an individual does with their natural force of desire goes a long way toward determining their values and character, as well as the overall quality of their life.

The primary role of human desire is to impel us forward, to evolve us. Desire wells up in human hearts to draw out a higher vision for our experience and expression. It is the soil in which seeds of dreams can put down roots and sprout. It can be the catalyst for inspiration and revelation. Desire is a universal and purposeful human experience, but there's a second dilemma: *The way most work with the energy of desire actually drives away that which they desire, actually thwarts achievement and attainment.* This is because when you desire something, you are most likely energizing even greater feelings of that something's absence. The desiring is allowed to increase the deeper sense of not having. If you have grasped the creative power of our consciousness as explained in Part Two of this book, then it becomes clear that what you most deeply believe is reality for you, in turn sets the tendencies for your experience. If desire makes an absence more acutely real to you, and perhaps more troubling or frustrating to you, then you will tend to manifest more of the absence of whatever is desired. This is desire closing the door to the desired!

In the Book of Matthew, it is reported that Jesus declared, "For to the one who has, more will be given, and from the one who has not, even what he has will be taken away." When I first ran across this, it really troubled me. It seemed like he was saying that the rich get richer and the poor get poorer—and that's just the way it is. But a whole new light was thrown on that statement when I learned about the creative nature of consciousness. And Jesus was one of the greatest teachers of the power and possibilities of consciousness ever to walk this planet. What that great teacher was telling anyone who could understand is that to the one who has a "have" consciousness, more will be given; but to the one who has a "have not" consciousness, even what he has will be on shaky ground and likely fall away—not because this is the will of the Creative Source of all Life, but because this is how consciousness forms experience. It mirrors our dominant acceptance into our experience. So, if a strong desire or yearning produces an even deeper sense of not having, then the accomplishment or attainment is sabotaged.

Notice that in the areas of life in which you possess a genuine "have" consciousness, things flow easily. These areas tend to grow and prosper without very much effort. Greater quality, growth, opportunity, or abundance just seem to be drawn to these areas of your experience. Now honestly take stock of those areas in which you clearly maintain a "have not" consciousness, areas where you continually focus on what's not working or how there's not enough. These parts of your life sadden and trouble you most. You probably pray that things might turn around and start to work for you in these areas. Desire in these areas usually feels very urgent, like a persistent yearning for a breakthrough. No doubt these are the areas in which you struggle, not just occasionally, but most of the time. These are the areas that feel blocked, limited, or impoverished.

There is an antidote to this dilemma. It is found by shifting our relationship with desire, itself. It is a tremendously liberating opening into life mastery . . . This Desire Is Fulfillment.

In a Nutshell

Desire and fulfillment are one. Just as the acorn and the oak are one. They are simply different dimensions of the same thing. A clear desire, rightly understood, is a seed containing the pattern for the eventual manifestation or experience. Fulfillment and accomplishment, then, represent the actualization of the potential held within the heart of the originating desire. *Desire and fulfillment are one!*

Our great stumbling block, however, is that the mind usually separates desire and the fulfillment of the desire. Whenever we do this, we enter into a state of distance from that which is desired. The tendency, then, is to look *to*, or look *for*, the desired thing or experience. We wish or yearn *for* whatever it might be. And we start praying *for* it. All of these approaches are strong messages to the creative Power of the Universe that we are very clear that we *do not* have it. This is the syndrome that so often drives away, that repels, so much of what we seek.

At this point, the worldly, rational mind usually protests: *But you don't have it yet. You desire it, but you don't really have it.* And most of us have learned to accept as gospel truth the reports and judgments from this level of awareness. So we lapse into feeling needy. We walk through our lives feeling like we're needy people . . . desiring, wishing, hoping, yearning, conniving, demanding for more. But what this effectively tells the manifesting Power of the Universe is that, bottom line, we believe we do not have it. And . . . "As thou hast believed, so shall it be done unto you" (Matthew 8:13).

We have also been told, "Judge not by appearances." It might appear that we do not have the fulfillment of a desire, but this is a limited and shallow level of perception. A higher truth awaits our acceptance. This higher Truth was declared in the Book of Isaiah: "Before they call, I will answer" and Jesus proclaimed, "Your Father knows what you need before you ask"; "Ask and it shall be given to you"; and "It is the Father's good pleasure to give you the kingdom." The combination of all this ancient wisdom is designed to lead us to a life-changing realization: *Before I ask, it is already given.* When desire dawns, it is actually the acceptance of something already given. You are simply selecting or appropriating the lovingly given Good of God. But you have to get very clear about the higher Truth beyond appearances. Whenever you have a desire, you must establish and anchor, in your "heart of hearts," the empowering realization: "I already have it. I have it because I desire it, and in my desire is the very seed of the thing or experience itself. My desire is already a reality in the infinite Mind of the One, and it is appearing in my experience in the best ways and time."

Essential Keys

The first key is an indispensable practice:

> Look from *the fulfillment, not for it.*
> Pray from *the fulfillment, not for it.*

In these practices, you are establishing your awareness in the higher reality of the omnipresence of your Good, your Blessings, your Abundance . . . all that is freely offered for your acceptance. Looking and praying *from* the fulfillment builds up a strong mental equivalent of the fulfillment and an absolute conviction that the desire already exists in the Mind/Heart of God, the Universal Spirit. These practices dissolve the illusion of distance or separation from the end result and activate in you the higher reality that the fulfillment is actually seeded within the desire, itself.

To look and pray *from* is to energize the desire as a fulfilled reality within you, right now. Not later, right now. It is adjusting your perceiving from an "out there" viewpoint, to an "in here, right here" viewpoint. It is adjusting your perceiving from a "sometime, someday" acceptance, to a "right now" acceptance. Your acceptance is what needs to be directed and established. Your consciousness of acceptance is the only buffer between the potential and the actual, between the inner and the outer.

The second key is to look and pray *from* the fulfillment . . . and to *do these things with great vividness and feeling.* Few of us are used to looking and praying *from*, so it takes a bit of practice. It is living in the vision of the total fulfillment with great clarity and vividness, aligning yourself fully with this Reality. Relax . . . still your mind . . . close your eyes . . . open your heart. Then begin feeling all the feelings you would feel when the great desire is achieved . . . feelings of attainment, empowerment, and success . . . feelings of deep assurance, profound peace, and abundant blessings. Stay with these feelings and allow them to deepen. Also, see inwardly and passionately what you would see in the full accomplishment. Grasp and embrace the experience; hold it in your heart. Hear within yourself, or actually verbalize, the joyous words that would overflow as a result of the fulfilled experience.

In all of this, make the fulfilled desire absolutely *real* within you. When you have embodied and fully accepted the desire as fulfilled right now, the creative Power of the Universe unfolds and reveals the actuality in powerful, even wondrous ways. As awareness evolves, you will spend less and less time quarrelling with conditions, less and less time involved in what seems absent. The very concept of "absence" will shift. Absence will become nonsense . . . a powerless illusion. What used to seem like absence will simply be invisible potential ready to be invoked into visible expression.

As with the many enlightened masters, I believe that Jesus never bought into lack, disease, or absence. This is why he instructed, "Whatsoever you desire, when you pray, believe that you have received, and you shall receive" (Mark 11:24). He lived in the fullness of the Divine Presence and Givingness. While he may have given brief and passing acknowledgment of the hungry masses, what he *knew* and *saw* was that abundance was right there, starting with a child's loaves and fishes. While he might have given brief and passing recognition of the physical challenges of those who were crippled or diseased, what he *knew* and *saw* was so much wholeness and love that he could proclaim, "Take up thy bed and walk" or "Your errors are forgiven, be whole." While he may have given brief and passing awareness to the appearance of death, he *knew* and *saw* the immortal Life of the Spirit in all beings so unconditionally that he would stand before the tomb and declare, "Lazarus, come out . . ." and to those looking on, "Take off the grave clothes and let him go." Remember that this great Wayshower also proclaimed, "The things that I have done shall you do also; and greater things shall you do." This high prophecy is ready to be fulfilled in each of us in so many ways. Like the man in the cave who finished fighting and discovered his capacity to transcend the limits, our life mastery waits for us to realize . . . This Desire Is Fulfillment!

The Collective Trance

Most of humanity is caught up in a trance state. It is a collective hypnotic trance, and as with the nature of trances, most people have no idea they're living in this trance. It's like dreaming in our sleep. It seems perfectly real . . . until we wake up and step into our waking reality. However, this, too, is just another dream state, another trance . . . for there are higher, more powerful states into which we can also awaken! To heed the call to greatness we must at some point liberate ourselves from trance states of human ignorance and illusion.

This is a good description of our collective, worldly trance state: *Not okay . . . Not enough . . . Not likely!*

These acceptances articulate our shared trance: *I am not okay . . . There's not enough . . . and "It's" not likely: my dreams, desires, goals, purposes . . . they're not likely.*

After all, so many of us have been trained since early childhood that we need to be more or better to receive love and acceptance—that we are basically *not okay*. And we are trained to fear for our supply, and to worry about scarcity . . . so we buy into the illusion of separation from our Source and our Good—*not enough*. Then we join with the multitudes who have decided that a magnificent and successful life is . . . *not likely!*

Do you notice how deep this goes . . . that it's like second nature? It's so pervasive that merchandisers and advertisers hook into these themes and go to great lengths to try to dupe us into thinking that their product or service will fill the void and heal it all.

When we buy into "not okay . . . not enough . . . not likely," this trance state then develops into more specific limitations. I call these Life Limiting Lies, lies that are spawned by the trance. They become more specific rules of limitation . . . ways the trance runs our lives. Here's just a facetious sampling of lies we're apt to hear or tell: *I'll only be a minute . . . This will be a short meeting . . . The check is in the mail . . . Money cheerfully refunded . . . We service what we sell . . . This will hurt me more than it hurts you . . . I'll start exercising, dieting, and forgiving tomorrow.* What Life Limiting Lies are keeping you in this trance? Ernest Holmes wrote, "The sum total of all erroneous human belief binds UNTIL the individual mentally lifts himself above the law of averages into the higher law of Spiritual Individualism." He is saying that we must find a way out of the trance, find an opening into life mastery.

Radical Acceptance

How are you at accepting abundance and blessings into your life? I love a story that takes place on a street corner in a major city. A woman had a cardboard booth where she sold pretzels for 25 cents each. Every day a well-dressed young man would hurry by and toss a quarter into her cup without taking a pretzel. One day, as he rushed off yet again, the woman called out to him, "Just a minute, young man!" "I know, I know," he said. "You're wondering why it is I leave a quarter every day, but never take a pretzel." "No," the woman answered, "I just wanted to tell you that the price has gone up to fifty cents!" Now *that's* a healthy state of acceptance!

This is one of the greatest challenges for lots of people, something that contributes to separating fulfillment from desire: *the genuine ability to accept something more, some greater prosperity* . . . from God, from Life, from others . . . accepting openly and increasingly. In the book *The Joy of Living*, Rick Prigmore writes about the choice he and his wife made to dispose of most of their worldly goods and take off in a motor home. They decided that instead of selling their possessions, they'd just give them away. So, they invited about forty friends to a potluck farewell dinner, and after dessert, they gave each one a pack of labels and instructed them to go through the house and place their labels on items they'd like to have. He then shares an interesting phenomenon that unfolded: "We noticed that one person gazed lovingly at an oil painting and said, 'I've always loved that painting. But, I'll take this vase.' We said, 'No, take the painting!' Another said, 'I've always admired that tea cart ever since I've known you. But I'll just take this picture.' Again we said, 'No, take the tea cart.' The scene was repeated time and again. People were willing to settle for less than what they really wanted. They felt they should pay us something or 'hold it for us' until we returned. It was so difficult for them to accept the abundance of life!"

Life offers us so much, but we either don't believe it or feel unworthy. So it's typical to close off, to not accept the Good, the possibilities, the creative ideas, the wealth that is offered. Do you find yourself regularly settling for less? And then wondering why you don't seem to be as blessed as others? Part of the answer is in learning to receive and accept!

For years I couldn't receive and accept much love. It wasn't that there weren't loving people available. My heart was closed to them. I hadn't healed some things from the past. I thought I was inviting them in, but the deeper impulse was to shut them out. As I have shared, it was a glorious breakthrough when I did some inner healing and opened my heart. Then the love that Life was offering me rushed in from every direction.

In helping us to receive the Good of God, Jesus shared a parable about a king who'd arranged for his son's marriage. Then he sent his servants out to call all those invited to the wedding, but they wouldn't come. So he had his servants go out again and tell of the great feast that was prepared. But those invited made light of it and had other things to do. The kingdom of abundance is like a wedding feast where a great supper is spread for all to enjoy: nourishment for the mind ... answers to every problem ... strength for the exhausted ... hope for the discouraged ... confidence and peace of mind for the troubled. And all are invited to partake in what the Creative Source has already given!

But, so often we don't attend. The Principles of Life are here that have been taught for thousands of years ... the truths, insights, and laws that we can use to live in peace, abundance, and happiness. But we allow ourselves to become distracted and immersed in our worldly concerns and agendas. We make excuses and turn our backs on our higher Good. Many people have gone to church, synagogue, or their spiritual community, but have never gone to the true feast! It's easy to go through the motions of religiosity with little feeling or inner vitality ... never moving into that Oneness Consciousness ... avoiding entering the indwelling Kingdom of God ... the dynamic awareness that opens hearts, uplifts souls, and prospers lives.

After some consternation and conflict, the king decides to have his servants invite anyone who'll come. So the wedding was furnished with guests. But then the king saw a man who wasn't wearing the proper wedding garments. The king had this man bound and taken away, and the parable says, "And he cast him into outer darkness: there shall be weeping and gnashing of teeth. For many are called, but few are chosen." A better translation might be: "Many are called, but few accept." Our minds wear garments, just like our bodies. These garments are the dominant ways we think, feel, see, hear, and judge—our attitudes and patterns of thoughts. Most of these mental garments are not appropriate for the "spiritual wedding feast," the feast at which our minds and hearts are united with our true desires. We can't show up with unseemly or toxic garments such as doubt, pessimism, unworthiness, separation, condemnation, resentment, guilt, and skepticism. We have to shed these garments and put on wedding garments . . . beliefs and attitudes that facilitate and celebrate our union with the prosperity we are accepting! Are you willing to surrender the worn-out, unacceptable attire of the mind, and don the true fabric of your soul—the realization that you are God's beloved child, a spiritual being made in the image and after the nature of God . . . here to have as much of the Good of life as you can accept and share?

It's been said that we all approach the wellspring of God with different containers of acceptance. Some bring a thimble, and that's all they get— not because our Source hasn't provided, but because of that limited acceptance. Others bring a cup; others, a bucket. I say we bring a swimming pool . . . or even greater! We can rest assured that Life will fill the cup of our acceptance if we are clothed in those attitudes and realizations that open us to our true Good.

Wealth in Consciousness and Experience

I remember a time when I was enjoying an afternoon on the patio deck of a condo I'd rented in the Colorado mountains. This deck overlooked an expansive valley with a range of peaks in the distance. As I sat there savoring the view, two hummingbirds arrived and hovered around a feeder that was hanging from the covering over this deck. There was only a little bit of that red liquid these birds adore in the feeder, so they began to fight with each other to get the final sips. As I watched this go on, it reminded me of the collective human trance, our deep belief that there is seldom enough and our lack of acceptance of the givingness of Life, of Spirit. I wished I could send a message to those small but amazing birds: *I have more of that food. I will refill the feeder. Just enjoy. There is plenty.* I believe that Infinite Spirit has been trying to convey this very message to humankind.

So I offer you these foundational principles that can develop a greater acceptance of unlimited abundance. They are key to the shift of perspective that unites desire and fulfillment.

FIRST: God is Source!

We are living in a universe that is formed out of the Life, Love, Intelligence, and Substance of the One Life, God, the Universal Spirit, or whatever name you prefer. This is not a distant or disinterested deity but a spiritual Presence and Power at the heart of all creation. This One Life has created all things, all beings, out of Itself . . . *and* this Divine Life provides all. There is no limit to the Good of God, for God is all Good, freely offered. The quantum physicist might say that this abundance is the "field of pure, unlimited potentiality." It is written: "Ask and it will be given you, seek and you shall find; knock, and it shall be opened to you" (Matthew 7:7). "It is your Father's good pleasure to give you the kingdom" (Luke 12:32). "My God will supply all your needs" (Philippians 4:19). "All things the Father hath are mine" (John 16:15).

So, we can let go of the idea of a reluctant God with limited resources and contemplate the Divine as Infinite Intelligence and Givingness. Therefore, our Source for whatever we seek is God, the all-giving Spirit and Intelligence—not people, institutions, jobs, or things. God is Source unlimited!

Affirm and accept "God is my instant, constant, and unlimited Source!"

SECOND: We are all heirs!

If there is only One Life, One Spirit, One Love, then the only thing we could be created out of is this One Life . . . God! So we are coming to understand that we are *spiritual beings* . . . children and offspring of God, here to express the Life of God with ever-increasing wisdom, productivity, and love. The good news: as heir to God, you have an unlimited inheritance! "In God, we live, move and have our being" (Acts 17:28). "Thou art my beloved child in whom I am well pleased" (Matthew 3:17). "My child, thou art ever with me and all that I have is yours" (Luke 15:31).

Ernest Holmes adds, "In the unity of humankind with Spirit, there can be no lack or limitation; each of us is entitled to all that our Father has. The realization that God is an infinite Source is dawning upon our awakened thought, expanding our acceptance of greater abundance and dispelling all lack. This impartation of livingness to everything is the very nature of the God who gives."

Affirm and accept "I am designed and destined to prosper!"

THIRD: Consciousness is access!

Spiritual wisdom has revealed that, as heirs to all the good of God, our access is through our own consciousness. Our Good must be accepted and seeded in consciousness *before* it can be manifested or harvested in our experience. Our consciousness is the avenue for the flow of our Good. So we can't demonstrate greater abundance if our awareness is permeated with fear and beliefs in scarcity and limitation. The seeds of greater Good must be planted in our consciousness. This is the foundational realization that supports us as we unite desire and fulfillment.

The flow of greater abundance is always initiated by a new or bigger idea. The worldly mind might think that what is needed is more money, friends, opportunities, resources, etc. However, a higher perspective reveals that what we really require is a greater idea, for ideas are the genesis for all creation, the catalyst for our ever-increasing abundance. As we open in genuine receptivity to the infinite sea of divine Intelligence, as we let go of our certainties and forgone conclusions, we can become the vessel for a new realization born from the vast repository of Divine Mind. When we embrace this seedling idea, the next step is to realize that its fulfillment is already within it, just as the oak is already within the acorn. As we practice experiencing this fulfillment in all the ways recommended, our consciousness becomes the fertile soil from which we shall reap an abundant harvest.

When we realize that God is our unlimited Source . . . that we are all heirs to the kingdom . . . and that we are becoming masters in the revealing of the Spirit's unlimited ideas . . . all this brings us to the realization that our oneness with God makes us outlets for the continuous expansion and evolution of Life. It's not just given to us; we are this Life, this Good, this divine Expression. The I Am is the ever-unfolding Good of God!

Affirm and accept "I *am* prosperity!"

Your Soul's Sincere Desire

This chapter could be summed up by this Bible truth: "Do you not say, 'There are yet four months and then comes the harvest'? Behold, I say unto you, lift up your eyes and look on the fields, for they are white already to harvest" (John 4:35). Yes, let us lift up our eyes, our spiritual vision, and perceive the All-Good of our Source. Let us listen deeply to that Inner Voice that whispers of our personal magnificence and the contributions each of us is designed to bring to this earth. There is a calling at the heart of you, a service to render, gifts to give. Life is never fuller than when we discover this calling and commit ourselves to it.

Sometimes it seems daunting to take on these inner directives. Yet the message of this chapter is that fulfillment and desire are one. By opening your heart to the glory seeking to unfold through and as you, a desire will well up that is the portent of its own fulfillment. All Life asks of us is to stand forth as a "Yes." The creative Power and divine Intent for greater and greater Good will lead us forward and provide all we need . . . all along the way. The fields of expanded living are white *already* for your harvesting!

– The Experience –

I offer you these experiences to deepen your realization that . . . This Desire Is Fulfillment.

A Wise and Loving Mentor

In the mid-'70s, when I was in the first three years of my ministry in Portland, Oregon, I was blessed by the friendship and mentorship of a retired minister who lived close by in Camus, Washington. His name was Ezra Ellis, such a beautiful soul. He had a gentleness and wisdom that were enormous blessings and guideposts for me. He and his wife often attended my church services and take me to lunch afterward. Inevitably, each of these lunches gifted me with some nugget of insight or inspiration.

At one of these lunches, Ezra was asking me about the growth of the church, how I felt it was going. I was so "green" in the ministry at that time that I often felt insecure and inadequate. That day, I told him that I felt frustrated that the church wasn't growing as fast as I had hoped. I shared that I was praying for greater numbers of attendance at the services and the classes. Ez, as I called him, just smiled lovingly . . . then, as we walked to the car after lunch, he whispered to me, "You know, Rog, when the numbers attending are no longer an issue for you, the church will probably grow!" He said this almost in passing, so gently and lovingly. But it definitely registered with me, and I pondered it deeply for days. It seemed contradictory. After all, wasn't it important to have a clear intention for growth, with clear metrics in terms of people who were showing up? Wouldn't letting this go be cavalier, a sign of not caring?

However, a more powerful realization eventually emerged. It was about the nature of my desire . . . my desire for church growth. First of all, the desire for expanded attendance was a frustrated yearning for what I actually believed wasn't happening. Again, if the desire is couched in the sense that "it's not here," then it can't come forth, whatever it is.

Second, the desire was not a "soul's sincere desire," a desire born of love and genuine purpose. At that time, in all honesty, my desire wasn't really for more people to attend, but for this attendance to validate me, to prove my abilities, to dissolve my fears and make everyone proud who believed in me. This was a humbling realization, but also a freeing one. It is the height of self-deception to believe that achieving or getting anything at all in this world will serve as validation and confirmation of personal worthiness. Where in your life is this at work in you? Nor are any fears healed, or security guaranteed, by acquiring or accomplishing things, no matter how great or lofty. I was being guided to give up my neediness, so that my deeper desire to love, serve, and grow could reveal and manifest itself. When I got in touch with this "soul's sincere desire," I let go of longing for more people to be there, and it wasn't long before they *were* there. That church began to grow steadily, because my desire was now congruent with my heart, *and* I was living out that desire as fulfillment day by day. Try this—it works!

There was another of these lunches that left an enduring impact. I can't remember if it was before or after the one I've just shared. It was Ezra's and his wife's anniversary, and as part of their celebration, they asked me to join them for brunch after my services. We ate at a really nice restaurant overlooking the Willamette River. When we were finished eating, Ezra's wife excused herself to go to the ladies' room. As we sat there, Ezra leaned over and said, "I really enjoyed your message today." That was all it took. My fledgling insecurities took over once again. I replied, "Ah, Ez, I wasn't too happy with it. I got off track a couple of times, and I just didn't feel like I was into it, that it was really much good." Ez paused, then looked me straight in the eye, and spoke like I didn't think he ever could or would. He firmly declared, "Who the hell cares what you think?!"

I just about fell off my chair. Then he smiled, and here's the essence of what he went on to tell me: "Rog, some things you said really did touch my heart. They really did help me. Understand that the experience you're having delivering your message is not necessarily the experience the listeners will have. Each will hear what they need to hear. Even if you don't feel 'into it' or good about it, don't underestimate the message. It is probably creating more blessings than you know. And also remember that we who listen are part of creating our experience of that message. Do your best, trust the message and remember that your love and sincerity are the most important things."

Well, I also spent weeks reflecting on that exchange. It was another lesson about how we can imbue our desires with our own neediness. I needed confirmation and reassurance. I had fallen into the habit of ruthlessly judging my heartfelt efforts to share and serve. And all of this was interfering with what I was trying to do. So it was another opportunity to let go of what could no longer go with me on my journey. I started offering myself the very compassion I was encouraging people to give to themselves. I made it a practice to put my message in the file drawer when I was done on a Sunday and, with that, to put it out of my mind. There would be another Sunday, another chance to dive into my soul's sincere desire to share my undeniable sense of the Presence and Power of God— in, through, and as every one of us. God bless dear Ez!

Two Whose Desire Was Unstoppable

Let me tell you about Honoré de Balzac. He desperately wanted to be a writer, a novelist. However, his father was vehemently opposed to this path for Honoré. Nonetheless, he chose as he wished, and Honoré de Balzac became one of history's greatest novelists.

Then there's Mary Macleod Bethune. As a courageous and determined girl, she declared that she wanted to read and to learn. But as one of seventeen children of former slaves, she was told to forget it. A soul's sincere desire is not easily turned away, however. She made her decision: *I am going to read.* And soon life delivered the opportunity through a traveling teacher, who encouraged the family to let Mary make the five-mile walk to school. In later years she received scholarships to college and then began teaching. Eventually Mary McLeod Bethune started her own college: Bethune Cookman College. Inscribed above the entrance is the phrase *Enter to learn.* On the inside of the entrance, which you see when leaving, are the words: *Depart to serve.*

The Power of Believing

A lady I'll call Julie graduated from the foundational course we offer in the transformational teachings shared in our ministry. At the end of the course she shared a very moving example of unifying desire with fulfillment . . . through believing:

It all started in 1999 when I held in my hand a picture of myself when I was twenty-five years old. I said, "One day I will look like this again." In that picture, I weighed 115 pounds and wore a size 7. But at the time I held that picture I weighed over 350 pounds, couldn't fit in a size 30, was in a wheelchair most of the time, took twenty Advil a day, was in constant pain, and struggled through life. But I said, "I will look like this again one day, somehow." And I stuck the picture on my refrigerator. Sure enough, it took a few years, but my path to being slim again led to a real result. On this journey, I found out I had a twelve-pound tumor that was killing me, I was bleeding most of the time as organs ripped inside me, I needed surgery on both my knees, had multiple hernias, and diverticulitis, which caused more bleeding.

Today things have changed dramatically. I know exactly how I got here. It's about having a deep-seated BELIEF which reflects itself into our experience. Start with an idea, a new state of being—which, for me, was to be slim and healthy—the creative process works on this idea, and things begin to manifest. Spirit flows within you so it can attract the resources you need, and guide you down a golden path. It's about believing you can be whatever you want to be and Spirit's Divine Presence will express your desire. Then things begin to happen!

I start next week teaching my own weight loss seminar . . . and the Number ONE secret is BELIEVING—You have to believe you can be slim. See it, believe it. Belief leads to commitment, which leads to knowledge, which leads to action. And then you get to enjoy the manifestation of your heart's greatest desires!

– The Expression –

1. I invite you to follow the three steps of this program fully and devotedly.

- **First:** Before moving down the path of some desire, establish a genuine sense of inner fulfillment *now* . . . before seeking the attainment of anything else. The best background for growth and success is to make your peace with yourself as you are and as things are, right now. Remember that accomplishing or acquiring something cannot give you self-worth, validation, peace, or joy. Spend some time loving yourself, reflecting on your positive qualities and actual accomplishments, and then determine that your new desire is not about proving or justifying yourself but, instead, celebrating and expressing yourself.

- **Second:** Get clear on the experience you wish to have as a part of manifesting your desire. Make sure that you energize this experience now, realizing that attainment of desires never guarantees the experience you will have. You are in charge of your experience; it's not brought to you from people or experiences "out there."

- **Third:** Activate and practice "the experience of the experience" you seek. Reread the earlier section of this chapter that explains the importance of vividness and feeling within your desire and the process that I've shared. Practice experiencing *both* your desire as fulfilled now *and* the experiences you expect to have through the ultimate accomplishment and manifestation of this desire. Remember to look, love, and pray *from* the desire . . . and course-correct when you lapse back into looking or waiting *for* it. Maintain these practices diligently and passionately—several times each and every day.

2. I encourage you to study each line of this powerful quote by the great spiritual author and teacher Joseph Murphy. It will anchor you in the abundance consciousness that unites desire with fulfillment.

> *Wealth is a state of consciousness;*
> *It is a mind conditioned to Divine Supply, forever flowing.*
> *Wealth is your idea, desire, talent, urge for service, capacity to*
> *give to humankind, your ability for usefulness to society, and*
> *your love of humanity in general.*

3. Open up the flow!

It is essential to create total congruence within an abundance consciousness. One who truly and genuinely *knows* that they "live, move and have their being" in limitless abundance will automatically enter into the joy of sharing from their overflowing Good. This means establishing a systematic giving practice as further evidence of living *from* greater prosperity instead of longing *for* it.

The child within us all loves to give . . . not just occasionally but continually. Thus it is supremely powerful to give of your time, talents, and treasure in principled and joyous ways. Many people are entirely willing to give of their time and talents, but feel resistance and fear when it comes to giving of their treasures . . . especially money. Money, however, is God in action! It is meant to stay always in a flow . . . that is why it's called currency. To hold back in giving—and giving as readily and abundantly as we wish to receive—is to demonstrate that we are still stuck in the "I don't have it yet" mode of awareness, thus sabotaging increased supply.

God, the Infinite Spirit, is *the* great Giver . . . and each of us is made in the image and nature of this great Giver. Thus it is our deepest nature to care, share, and give unendingly. Luke 6:38 says, "Give, and it shall be given unto you; good measure, pressed down, shaken together and running over. . . ." and "As you give, so shall you receive." These statements articulate the universal Law of Circulation that must be honored if we are to anchor ourselves in the consciousness of "having" and if we are to experience the increase that comes naturally as a result of our sharing.

Here Is a Program That Can Greatly Expand Your Abundance

- *Choose a percentage of your total weekly income before expenses that you would find fulfilling to share . . . perhaps a bit of a stretch as well.*

- *Commit to sharing this percentage every week—even if it's .5 percent or 1 percent—before paying for or buying anything else. Maintain total consistency in this systematic giving. You don't want your receiving to be haphazard or occasional. Therefore maintain this program with great and loving devotion.*

- *Share these gifts where the Light of Spirit's Presence and Love are being radiated into the world—with some activity, organization, or person that is uplifting humankind—and wherever you are receiving your spiritual "food." Share it with love and joy. And give it with no "strings" attached, no expectations or demands.*

- *As you receive your income—or any unexpected income—celebrate it, give heaping thanks for it, then share from it at the established level, or more if you ever desire.*

- *Stay in touch with the giving impulse deep within your heart. After maintaining these practices, be alert for the nudge to increase the percentage being shared. Commit to the new percentage and enjoy it until expansion taps you on the shoulder again. Aspire to reach—or even exceed—the 10 percent level of sharing from all you receive. This is called your "tithe," and most who have entered the realm of masterful living are totally committed to continuous tithing. Remember, always stay in the flow . . . because you can't out-give God!*

Establishing this kind of program creates and empowers a "spiritual covenant" at the center of your financial and consciousness life. As you maintain these practices, you will probably discover that your income is growing along with your joy. You are in the flow of Life and Life's Good. The funds that remain after your principled sharing or tithing will seem to go further than the former 100 percent did. You will feel that you are moving forward on an upwardly inclined ramp of increase. You will feel that you are in partnership with God as a distribution center for Life's blessings. You are placing yourself in alignment and integrity with spiritual Principle . . . and you will be profoundly and continually blessed . . . just as you will be a great blessing.

4. Own Your Fulfillment . . . Now!
Totally embrace and own your fulfillment now. Also recognize that how and when this fulfillment becomes formed or manifest in your experience will probably be different than you are expecting. Stay the course

and do not falter! I love the spunk and commitment shared in this widely circulated "Refusal of Rejection Letter":

Dear Professor Millington, Whitson University:

Thank you for your letter of March 16. After careful consideration, I regret to inform you that I am unable to accept your refusal to offer me an assistant professor position in your department. This year I have been particularly fortunate in receiving an unusually large number of rejection letters. With such a varied and promising field of candidates it is impossible for me to accept all refusals. Despite Whitson's outstanding qualifications and previous experience in rejecting applicants, I find that your rejection does not meet my needs at this time. Therefore, I will assume the position of assistant professor in your department this August. I look forward to seeing you then.

Best of luck in rejecting future applicants.

Sincerely,

Chris L. Jensen

Though there is uncertainty surrounding the author and recipient of this letter, it still makes the point: Own Your Fulfillment . . . Now!

16. THIS RISK IS GREATNESS

Sometimes we are asked in our hearts to do something and we have trouble understanding why. We have a choice. We can either skip that direction, or we can trust that the voice of our heart is a master designer of our life.

—JOYCE VISSELL

Twenty years from now you will be more disappointed by the things that you didn't do than by the things you did do. So throw off the bowlines. Sail away from the safe harbor. Catch the trade winds in your sails. Explore. Dream. Discover.

—MARK TWAIN

– The Essence –

That word *risk* seems to be imbued with a certain ominous energy. For many, it evokes a sense of foolhardiness and, certainly, danger. Just like change, risk is an experience that many seek to avoid at all costs, or at least strictly control. Yet this seems to be a denial of the inbuilt risks of being human and of living on this planet during these times. In truth, we

THIS RISK IS GREATNESS

face and deal with risks every day—and more so in this day and age than ever. New power and greater possibilities emerge in our lives when we realize that risks in life are not merely unwanted experiences thrust upon us by chance or carelessness. Risks have always been essential for advancement. Risks have always been essential for unleashing bold creativity. Risks have always been essential for greater aliveness and fulfillment. As with fear, risk is our friend.

Dawna Markova, also quoted in Chapter 3, was diagnosed with cancer at the age of thirty and later was pronounced dead on an operating table. While she was being wheeled down to the morgue, she felt like she was "falling upward." She began to have a vast experience of the greater dimensions of life. She writes that nagging questions were answered and things seemed to come together. Moreover, she realized her true nature, her spiritual Self, as an indestructible Love and Light. As this experience continued, a voice asked her several questions, concluding with asking her over and over, *What's unfinished for you to give?* When Dawna was resuscitated, her understanding of life deepened dramatically. She shifted her orientation from getting to giving and embraced a radical new commitment to engaging life courageously. Among many pursuits, Dawna went on to become a PhD, a CEO of a company teaching organizational learning and growth, and a cofounder of Worldwide Women's Web. She also has become famous for a short but powerful passage titled "I Will Not Die an Unlived Life":

> *I will not die an unlived life. I will not live in fear of falling or catching fire. I choose to inhabit my days, to allow my living to open me, to make me less afraid, more accessible; to loosen my heart until it becomes a wing, a torch, a promise. I choose to risk my significance, to live so that which came to me as seed*

goes on to the next as blossom, and that which came to me as blossom, goes on as fruit.

This expresses the beauty and energy of embracing risk as a core element of a life well lived. The seeker in the opening story accepted the risk of being thrust into the unknown, into the epitome of limitation and frustration and, through all that, discovered new power, possibilities, and freedom. He began to realize openings into life mastery that were within him all along. This lesson is, itself, an opening: This Risk Is Greatness!

A school principal received a phone call one morning. The voice said, "Tommy Jones won't be in school today." The principal asked, "Well who is speaking?" The voice replied nervously, "This is . . . my father." How many times have you tried to "play hooky" from life . . . and especially from those key moments when it's time to risk, to move into purposeful, dynamic action? As you consider the higher visions and dreams that call to you—and the necessity to move them into action—have you ever wished that you, too, could call the principal . . . call God and declare, "I don't want to do this. It's too much. Count me out!" Whether we'll admit it or not, there comes a time for action, and this often feels like a risk. Then all the fears and avoidance efforts click in, and we're apt to end up "missing in action."

So how do you feel about risking—taking purposeful leaps? If your honest feelings are fear and dread, is that the great Self of you . . . or the little self? The little self is always trying to play hooky from responsibilities. It seldom wants to be a doer, but would much rather be a complainer or a spectator. The little self in us is forever waiting for other forces to bring about change and to make things happen. But, as the saying goes, "If it is to be, it's up to me!"

It helps to remember the words of chemist and author O. A. Battista:

"Nothing is more important to the future of an idea than the first step you take to try it out." Let's be clear: We are here in this schoolroom called "earth" to grow through regular risking, to learn through leaping! Evolutionary leaps got us to where we are as conscious beings. Now it's up to us to leap beyond our fears into the vast, unformed realms of our potential. And the Great Self within us knows that this is our design *and* our destiny.

Several years ago I had a conversation with a man who felt that his life was really stuck, and he was very discouraged and unhappy. At one point I asked him, "When in your past have you felt most alive?" He reflected for a moment and told me about the summer he overcame his fear of heights and learned rock climbing. And when he finished, there was a smile on his face from ear to ear. We used that experience as a launchpad for getting unstuck. I've asked that same question in a class I offer called Breakthroughs . . . and I've noticed some themes: Nearly everyone describes a scenario in which they pushed themselves out of their comfort zone. The outcome of taking the risk is seldom the main thrust of their story. When people finish their story, there's an unmistakable light in their eyes and they, too, are usually grinning. I've come to believe that this is a "God-smile"—the Great Self in us rejoicing and celebrating!

The great Helen Keller wrote: "Security is mostly a superstition. It does not exist in nature . . . Life is either a daring adventure, or nothing."

How true this is . . . but what I also know is that people tend to talk risk more than do risk, talk change more than do change! Can you imagine where your life would be if you had resisted all your leaps? What if you had refused to risk walking . . . riding a bicycle . . . going to school . . . kissing your first girlfriend or boyfriend . . . and all the other signal moments in a life? To be truly alive is to be taking continual leaps. Every time we leave our home, there are risks. Every time a couple walks down the aisle in marriage or in a holy union, it's a leap. Every time we take a deep breath and tell the "fierce truth," it's a risk. Just about everything that takes our lives forward is propelled by a leap, by a risk. Yet within all the unknowns are also the seeds of discovery and greatness. There is confusion about who wrote the following, but it remains a powerful expression of risking:

> *To laugh is to risk appearing the fool. To weep is to risk appearing sentimental. To reach out for another is to risk involvement. To expose feelings is to risk rejection. To place your ideas, your dreams, before a crowd is to risk ridicule. To love is to risk not being loved in return. To live is to risk dying. To go forward in the face of overwhelming odds is to risk failure. But risks must be taken, because the greatest hazard in life is to risk nothing. The person who risks nothing, does nothing, has nothing, and is nothing. He may avoid suffering and sorrow, but he cannot learn, feel, change, grow, love, live. Chained by his certitudes, he is a slave—he has forfeited his freedom. Only a person who risks is free.*
>
> —AUTHOR UNKNOWN

I suppose there are some foolish leaps or risks. But these are merely mis-creations of the ego . . . its games, strivings, and shallow impulses. I invite you to focus on leaps that take you in the direction of your inner Greatness, the deep Wisdom within, the principles that matter most, the true path of your soul. In the moments of your leaps, something is birthed in you. It is only born in the risking, and that's the gift. What you achieve most by risking is in *who you become* as a result: Confident. Engaged. Alive. And more. And it isn't something you do once in a while—it's an ongoing approach to life, a way of being. You see, risks have no shelf life. Yesterday's risks are today's ego trips! Today is brand-new, a fresh opportunity to reengage . . . to risk anew. As Napoleon Hill, author of *Think and Grow Rich*, declares, "It's always your next move!"

Consider the following elements of life-transforming, soul-conducive, heart-enriching risking:

Be True to Your Guidance

By listening to the deep wisdom within you . . . your intuition, your inner guidance, your unexplainable knowing . . . you will catch the energy and direction of the leading edge of your soul's initiative, your True Self's core intention to give, live, and shine. Regular sessions of meditation and contemplation encourage this emerging clarity. Listening or attending to other voices or influences usually distorts and clouds genuine guidance. There can be value in occasionally sitting with a mentor or listening to constructive input. It is humbling, however, to discover the credence so often given to "experts and authorities" other than the Knower within . . . and how seductive it is to become dependent on advice givers and the many opinionated experts that hover around. A fellow in an Asian restaurant paid his bill and then opened his fortune cookie. He was shocked by the message inside: "You are a poor, pathetic, gullible fool who seeks advice from bakery products." The underlying question in all this? Who's in charge . . . really?

Jim Webb is so clear about this: "Before all else, each of us must take a fundamental risk—to be true to ourselves." In 1921 a man started Laugh-a-Gram Corporation in Kansas City, Missouri, with $15,000 from investors. But he was forced to file for bankruptcy two years later when his backers pulled out. Then in July 1923 he left for Hollywood with all his belongings: a pair of pants, a coat, one shirt, two sets of underwear, two pairs of socks, and some drawing materials. It was leap time for Walt Disney! It was time to be true to himself, to what was calling within him.

My wife and I have a friend named Pam. When we met her, she had assumed the lead role in a family-run business in the training and sales of horses. She had built this business over a twenty-year period and it had become so successful that it was generating a six-figure annual salary for her. But then Pam began to move through some "curious and challenging experiences" . . . ones that were actually transformational invitations. She says, "Years ago I had a horse in training named PJ. She started to rear a little when I rode her. I got scared. I fretted, stewed, called some close friends, and did anything BUT ride the horse. I have a friend in a wheelchair from a horse falling over on her, and this image would keep going through my mind. 'It's not worth getting hurt over,' I would tell myself."

Then Pam began attending our spiritual center and studying the spiritual principles we teach. She was guided to take her next step:

> Well finally I made a DECISION. I would ride that horse. Nothing could be worse than the feelings of inadequacy that I had, anyway. I realize now that I was experiencing a lack of FAITH. . . . I got on, grabbed a handful of mane, and smacked her to go. She did everything: leaped, reared, bucked, spun. I hung on . . . and about 30 minutes later I deemed the ride a success. I rode her like this for about 2 weeks. And you know what? I COULD handle it! She got trained and won a few shows. BUT that isn't the point of PJ. . . . Riding PJ scared me, but I knew if I gave in to the fear, the next thing would scare me, too. Then the next, then the next, until I couldn't do anything. So, I worked through the fear, and became a better horse trainer for it. . . . PJ made me stretch. PJ made me tap into resources, talents, and abilities I didn't even know I had. They were lying

dormant in me all those years. PJ woke this up in me . . . which
would open me to waves of further change and growth.

What are the fears you've been reluctant to tame?

There's more to Pam's story. After successfully taming PJ, more opportunities emerged to tame the wild horses of her fears. But she hesitated in dealing with them just as she had with PJ. Several years later it all came to a head. She says, "I had felt for a few years that horse training was no longer my highest purpose. I was having some small injuries . . . but I was ignoring the whispers."

Then, while working with another horse, Pam was kicked. It shattered her knee and ended her career as a horse trainer. She explains:

> *I knew in my heart that I wanted to do other things, but I felt*
> *obligated to the family business. I had invested SO much time*
> *and hard work to build my business—20 years! I was earning a*
> *good living. But I knew I wanted more. I had a good prayer and*
> *meditation practice going, and loud and clear was getting the*
> *message: "Do stand-up comedy!" Life knows what's in your*
> *heart and will get you there. You can go easily, full of faith &*
> *expectancy. OR you can wait until you get kicked in the knee. I*
> *chose option two.*

Having been "kicked" out of the horse business, Pam went for her goal of doing stand-up comedy, and the doors flew open for her. She was given an emcee opportunity at one of the best comedy clubs in Denver. She worked hard at it for a year, then was promoted to a feature act. She is now being booked at other comedy clubs all across the country. Yes, she was scared at first, but she didn't give in! She also had to deal with some financial challenges, but now realizes, "They were simply PJ showing up in a different form to help me tap into resources, talents, and abilities that have been dormant. This was a real breakthrough for me!"

Pam is the happiest she's ever been, is in the best relationship of her life, and is living in a great home. "If that horse hadn't kicked me, I never would have left the barn and experienced all of this," she concludes.

What's your PJ? What is staring at you while you just can't bring yourself to face it? This is the thing that you must face. It might not be a crazy horse or a crazy idea like stand-up comedy. Your PJ might be that you need to speak up in your relationship or to change your job. Is it a health crisis? Whatever it is . . . it is Life helping you to wake up and go for it so that you can have the life of your dreams.

Trust Your Invisible Support

Do you remember the movie *Indiana Jones and the Last Crusade*? Our hero, played by Harrison Ford, finds himself at the edge of a sheer cliff with a huge gap between himself and the other side. He has been told that there is an invisible bridge across this ravine. He throws a handful of sand into the air in front of him, and sure enough, it reveals a bit of the bridge. But now he has to summon unimaginable trust and walk the full length of this bridge, which, of course, he successfully accomplishes.

This invisible bridge has become a powerful metaphor for the trust walk that is everyone's life. As we walk on, day by day, we utilize all the knowledge, advice, cleverness, creativity, preparation, and lessons we can muster. But when it comes right down to it, we all have to step out in full faith and trust. We all have to rely on an invisible support, allowing ourselves to be upheld by the Love, Intelligence, and Power of the One Life, of the Spirit. We do this even if we don't know or deny that we do. When we're perched precariously on the steep cliff of a life-enhancing or defining risk, there's nothing more powerful than remembering the presence of this invisible support system.

Throughout the entirety of my career in spiritual service, I have had to develop this "radical reliance" on God, on the Spirit. I know what it's like to forget, to drift into touting my limited personal understanding and resources amid the illusion of a prideful separation from Source . . . only to experience missing the mark, generating mediocrity, or even crashing. Whenever we prepare to leap, there is no substitute for realizing that "underneath are the everlasting arms!"

The greatest difficulty in this for most of us is that we know we are called to leap without having a map for the entire journey. Most of the time all we can see or really know for sure is that which is right in front of us. Most great risks are leaps into the unknown. Thus it's seldom just a single leap; it is moment by moment, day by day, leaping . . . a continual trusting that we will know what we need to know as we need to know it, not before . . . that we will be guided on a need-to-know basis . . . that we must trust and do the best we can with whatever is just in front of our noses. We're very much like most miners who have those little lights on their helmets. Miners have made their peace with not seeing what lies far ahead. They know that what's important is to keep their batteries strong and their lights clean and bright. In this way they will be able to see what's close at hand, that which they are dealing with nearby. The light exists "here," not "there" . . . "now," not "later." Life calls us to trust the light at hand, to surrender the need to know what's up ahead, and to keep our batteries charged by means of trust and spiritual commitment. As we walk on in continual risking, we must be willing to mine our Good in the moment, right where we are.

Poet Thomas R. Smith underscores this reliance on our invisible support in this beautiful piece titled "Trust."

It's like so many other things in life
To which you must say no or yes.
So you take your car to the new mechanic—sometimes the
  best thing to do is trust.
The package left with the disreputable looking clerk . . . the check
  gulped by the night deposit . . . the envelope passed by dozens of
  strangers—all show up at their intended destinations.
The theft that could have happened doesn't . . . the wind finally gets
  where it was going through the snowy trees . . . and the river, even
  when frozen, arrives at the right place.
And sometimes you sense how faithfully your life is delivered,
  even though you can't read the address.

Be Decisive and Bold

This is the hidden power in purposeful risking. We force ourselves to leave the nests, to try our wings. Sometimes it isn't all that pretty—beginnings are messy. But the commitment is empowered and the process is launched. Might as well experience all this temporary discomfort while being about big things, bold things, life-lifting things! It's the bold, seemingly outrageous leaps that activate the greatest magic. Hebrew literature expands on the biblical story of the parting of the Red Sea in a very compelling way. This literature suggests that when Moses led the Children of Israel to the edge of that body of water, that the sea did not part . . . *until* that first soldier, in bold faith, leaped into the waters. Then the sea fully parted. We have to leap even if the seas of challenges or uncertainty have not yet parted. We seldom know until we go!

At age fifty-five, Bryce Courtenay lost his job. He figured that now he had a chance to follow his dream of writing a book. So he planned that he would write four books, and that the first three would be warm-ups. The fourth would be *the* book that would change the world. He went about the business of writing the first book just as practice. He wrote and wrote and wrote—until it was 1,100 pages in length . . . the warm-up book! He didn't know what to do with this first book, so he put it in a shoe box and used it as a doorstop for his kitchen door. He mentioned this to a friend, who said, "Why don't you take it to an agent?" To make a long story short, this first book got published and became the most popular book ever written by an Australian author. It has sold millions of copies and has been made into a powerful motion picture. The book: *The Power of One*. Bryce Courtenay adds, "Before you die, you have to dare your genius to walk the wildest, unknown way."

What's your genius? What's latent within you seeking to get out? What is your soul's sincere desire? Isn't it time to give this seed of possibility your full permission to take root and grow? Don't worry what others might think or say. Be bold. Be decisive. I love another statement by Courtenay: "If you're going to skate on thin ice, tap-dance and go down in style!"

With Commitment . . . Persevere

An acclaimed salesman was asked to share the secret behind his enormous success. He offered just three words: *And then some!* He would do whatever he could . . . and then some. He would give his all . . . and then some. He would help out and share . . . and then some. He would care for the company and others . . . and then some. He was kind . . . and then some. He was creative and courageous . . . and then some. He was willing to give that extra portion, willingly and continually. He was fully committed.

This is a lesson for us in the essence of perseverance. It is bringing our best to the table of our experience with steadfast devotion. It is making the most of situations, predicaments, or opportunities. It is transcending the "immediate gratification" sinkhole that diminishes our personal and cultural richness. It is to be fully and happily willing to keep on keeping on, even if our initial efforts fall short. William Arthur Ward was one of America's most quoted inspirational writers. He had more than two thousand poems and articles published, and he had an interesting practice: he always kept handy a rolling pin around which he wrapped all the rejection letters he received. When one of his students complained about rejected work, William would unwind the rolling pin to reveal yards of his own rejection letters. The roll reached into the next classroom. Ward would then tell the student, "Anytime you feel like you can't carry on, just pull out this roll and look at it. Never give up!"

One of the most inspiring examples of committed perseverance is W. H. Murray. Murray grew up in Scotland and, in his love of the outdoors, took up mountain climbing. He climbed many mountains in his area until the outbreak of World War II. He then enlisted and was sent to the Middle East and North Africa. He was captured, however, and spent three years in prisoner-of-war camps in Italy, Germany, and Czechoslovakia. While imprisoned, Murray wrote and finished a book titled *Mountaineering in Scotland*. The first draft of the book was written on the only paper available to him—rough toilet paper. But eventually the Gestapo found this manuscript and destroyed it. To the amazement of his fellow prisoners, Murray's response to the loss was to start again—despite the risk of its loss and despite the fact that his health was so poor from the near-starvation diet that he didn't really know if he would ever climb again. The rewritten work was finally published in 1947—the first of twenty books he'd write.

You see, Murray possessed a quality that was essential to getting him through the prison camp ordeal . . . essential to finishing this first book . . . *and* essential to him in his role as deputy leader of the later 1951 Mount Everest expedition (the one that successfully discovered the route to the top now taken most often). In the book he wrote after that Everest expedition, he zeroed in on this essential key in a statement that has become very famous:

> But when I said that nothing had been done I erred in one important matter. We had definitely committed ourselves and were halfway out of our ruts. We had put down our passage money—booked a sailing to Bombay. This may sound too simple, but is great in consequence.
>
> Until one is committed, there is hesitancy, the chance to draw back, always ineffectiveness. Concerning all acts of initiative (and creation), there is one elementary truth the ignorance of which kills countless ideas and splendid plans: that the moment one definitely commits oneself, then providence moves too. A whole stream of events issues from the decision, raising in one's favor all manner of unforeseen incidents, meetings and material assistance, which no man could have dreamt would have come his way. I have learned a deep respect for one of Goethe's couplets:

> "Whatever you can do or dream you can, begin it.
> Boldness has genius, power and magic in it!"

Champion the Emerging Good

Human progress has always relied upon bold and timely risks. This is certainly true in our country's history. Consider the risks taken to end the practice of slavery, such a great stain upon our United States' heritage. Lincoln risked the continuance of our young nation, as well as his own life, to stand on the principles of justice, equality, and emancipation. Others did the same in their day and in their own ways . . . intrepid ones such as

William Lloyd Garrison and Rosa Parks, to name just two. A special momentum and grace accompanies risks that align with higher principles and emerging blessings for the advancement of others and life as a whole.

It touches my heart to reflect on that special commitment to the greater good of all, which is illustrated in so many lives. Take David Juritz, a concert violinist. At age fifty, he sought a greater meaning for his life, so he gave up the concert hall to play on street corners and in front of important buildings around the world . . . all to raise money for musical education for children. George Bernard Shaw wrote towering words calling us all to such expansive possibilities:

> *This is the true joy in life, the being used for a purpose recognized by yourself as a mighty one; the being a force of nature instead of a feverish, selfish little clod of ailments and grievances, complaining that the world will not devote itself to making you happy. I am of the opinion that my life belongs to the community, and as long as I live, it is my privilege to do for it whatever I can. I want to be thoroughly used up when I die, for the harder I work the more I live. I rejoice in life for its own sake. Life is no "brief candle" to me. It is a sort of splendid torch which I have got hold of for a moment, and I want to make it burn as brightly as possible before handing it on to future generations.*

In Summary

Five Components in Life-Lifting Risks

Be True to Your Guidance.
Trust Your Invisible Support.

Be Decisive and Bold.
With Commitment . . . Persevere.
Champion the Emerging Good.

The musical group The Eagles made popular a song with a very telling line:

So oftentimes it happens . . .
That we live our lives in chains,
And we never even know we have the key.

Indeed, we have the key. The key is learning that . . . This Risk Is Greatness! To search our hearts for that special purpose, that unique calling, that social imperative, that lofty vision . . . and to commit ourselves so fully to it that we are willing "to risk our significance" . . . willing to walk that invisible bridge . . . willing to be a force of nature . . . willing to begin it, and sustain it . . . willing to leap into the sea even before it parts . . . willing to tame that wild horse . . . willing to keep our batteries charged and our lights glowing . . . willing to trust that, indeed, our lives are being faithfully delivered . . . and willing to realize that Spirit is capable of using us as instruments for inspired and healing works. This, and more, is the richness and greatness of risking. Guillaume Apollinaire wrote:

Come to the edge, he said. We're afraid, they said.
Come to the edge, he said. We're afraid.
Come to the edge. They came. He pushed them . . . and
they flew.

– The Experience –

Log Walking?

In 1992 my two sons, who were nine and twelve years old at the time, and I journeyed to the Pacific Northwest to do some fishing with a dear friend, Bob Trask, a former sailor and fisherman, and an author, transformational teacher, and philanthropist. He lived north of Seattle and knew the best places to camp and fish. We drove about four hours north, found the spot he liked, and set up camp. When we inspected the river, however, we found that it had swollen above its banks from an especially intense spring runoff. The waters were flowing extraordinarily fast. We made several attempts at fishing, but the waters ripped off our bait every time. Even if we were to use lures, Bob explained, the fish wouldn't be biting in these waters.

The next question was what we would do for the rest of that day and the next if fishing was out of the question. Well, there was some exploring to do. So we did that for a while. Then we built a campfire, made a tasty dinner, told a lot of stories, and then bedded down in our two tents for the night. The next day, our final day scheduled for fishing, we made an equally great breakfast—there was nothing wrong with our appetites! "Now what?" we all asked. Bob lit up with an idea: "Let's go log walking!" Then he pointed out that we were in an old-growth forest and that fallen trees were everywhere. Seldom did they fall all the way to the ground since the forest was too thick. Instead they formed a maze of thin bridges connecting to each other. Bob joyously proclaimed that we could walk on this array of bridges for hours.

Now, I wasn't the least bit sure of this idea. But before I could suggest something else, Bob and the boys had pulled themselves up onto a fallen tree and had begun gliding along until another tree lay across it, whereupon they jumped onto it and kept on going. I climbed onto that first tree and stared down its length. By this time the rest of them were way ahead of me. Now this tree was not very wide at all, only about ten inches thick. I stood up on it gingerly and tried to get my balance. Then I looked down and realized that this tree I had climbed onto was about eight feet off the ground. And the other trees ahead that zigged and zagged over this one were sometimes even higher off the ground. Though this didn't seem to bother Bob and the boys, it certainly had my attention! I tried to walk a few feet, but became wobbly and had to sit down on the log. By this time the boys were calling out for me to catch up. Catch up? I just wanted to find a way off that blasted log! It began to feel humiliating as I was reduced to scooting along the tree in a sitting position.

My youngest son had decided to come back to see if he could help. He seemed to float easily and fearlessly along the trees. When he reached me, he said, "Dad, you just have to relax, and trust, and go for it." Just what I needed to hear. But I knew he was right, and I knew there was something for me to learn in this experience. So I stood up again, surveyed my body, and realized how tense I was. I took some deep breaths and began to consciously relax, especially in the solar plexus area around the pit of my stomach. Now that seemed to work like magic. When I kept my mind and that part of my body relaxed, I could move along fine. The moment I tensed up, though, I became wobbly again. After about fifteen minutes, I was moving just fine—maybe not skipping along like my kids, but moving "in a sensible and graceful way," as I soon tried to explain to them. They were kind enough to play along with this.

Risking is a great opportunity to discover equilibrium within, and to trust it. But you can't "look down"; that is, you can't become immersed in the enormity of the risk, the dangers or threats. You have to relax and keep your vision uplifted. "I will lift up my eyes unto the hills, from whence cometh my help." Pretty soon you'll get the hang of whatever it is, and it becomes amazingly easy. Another great lesson is that the real fear is not in the risk itself, but in approaching the risk. Walking the logs wasn't really a big deal; it was thinking about it, looking at how high I was above ground, and imagining what it'd feel like to fall. But the actual walking wasn't scary. Remember this when you're embracing risks that matter to you: the risk, itself, is actually the easiest part; dealing with yourself is what can get very challenging!

Erica's Cloud Talk

My beloved wife, Erica, lost her first husband, who was twenty-seven years old at the time, to leukemia two years before I met her in 1987. Her sons, whom I adopted shortly after we married, were three and six years old when their natural father died. Erica remained in the Houston area, where she and her family had been living. Three years later, she began to feel restless, that she was in a holding pattern amid friends and trappings of a chapter of her life that had completed itself. She had stayed in that area to grieve, adjust, and provide stability for our boys. She had entered into a new relationship with a man who'd worked with her former husband. He was newly divorced and they helped each other through times that were difficult for both of them. They had an "okay" relationship but it was grounded mostly in helping each other through the pain.

But it seemed like life was now calling her to her next steps. She prepared to take one of her life's greatest risks. In her own words, she explains her process:

> During that time, I became unusually interested in spiritual
> things. This was a surprise to me! Not having a deep religious

tradition in my earlier years, I was being drawn to teachers, books, and speakers who viewed life in ways that intrigued me. They spoke of how thoughts create our lives, that life is eternal, that death is not to be feared, that it is possible to heal our lives on every level. That we were born to be happy. That everyone matters and everyone is loved by the Divine. That the Universe conspires for our good and that Love is the one and only power that exists. That we are always at choice!

When Erica shared her expanding spiritual awareness with the man in her life, however, he seemed disinterested. There was no shared enthusiasm. He didn't get in the way of her spiritual pursuits; he just didn't care much about them. Erica would try to rationalize and justify this significant difference in their relationship, reminding herself that he was basically caring and good to her and our boys. But eventually she began to realize that they were not "a forever couple." When she tried to end the relationship, however, it just became too painful, too risky, and too hard to explain. Her inner battles and futile attempts at change went on for quite some time. One day, she took the boys to the beach so that they could play and she could think. She says:

I sat in my beach chair thinking about my growing dissatisfaction with my life and relationship. I was frustrated with myself. I thought it would be hard, if not impossible, to actually leave.

Then, as if in a dream, my sons came into very sharp focus. Everything else around them was blurred. I became keenly aware of their dependence on me to do the right thing for myself and them. They were at my mercy. They were depending on me whether they knew it or not.

It became clear that sometimes we have to make difficult decisions in life, ones that are not easy or convenient. We have to follow our heart and take risks even if we don't know what or where or even why.

Suddenly, I imagined myself as if I had died. I saw myself on a cloud looking down on my entire life. I saw my current relationship. I saw how I was being guided to leave but stayed because I was afraid to leave, afraid of the unknown. I sat there stunned. And then I heard myself say out loud, "All you had to do was get in the car and drive away."

Really, that was all it came down to—getting in the car and driving away.

Yes the emotions would be there and the unknown would be glaring at me, but the reality was, I could do this. Now, I could also choose to stay and have a mediocre life: one that was not fair to me or my sons or this man. But what a dreary existence. After all I had gone through with my husband . . . all the lessons, experiences, growth, deep grief, moving through his disease and subsequent death, was I then going to simply settle? Really?! I knew the answer was absolutely NO!

Energized by these insights, Erica made plans to move to Denver, a city she'd visited as a child. She made good on this promise by the end of that summer. This decision changed the trajectory of her life. She and I met shortly after she arrived in Denver and married just one week shy of a year later. In sharing about the adventure in loving that she and I have created together, Erica concludes:

We have stuck by one another through both good and easy times as well as tough, difficult times. We have seen the world and each other's souls. We have seen both sons fall in love and get married. We have witnessed Roger's beloved mother transitioning from this life and welcomed grandbabies into our arms. We have grown, fallen down, gotten back up, laughed and cried and bonded like nobody's business. We encourage each other, love each other, and insist that the other go for their dreams and whatever it takes to be happy.

I have never looked back with regret for taking that leap into the unknown. In fact, I shudder to think where I'd be right now if I hadn't. Probably living a "not horrible" life . . . yet missing the glory of a life that was far bigger than I could have EVER imagined!

Go Long, Go Long!

When my eldest son, Justin, was preparing to get married, I decided to write him a letter so that I could share my feelings with him . . . a way to let him know how proud of him I am . . . and some thoughts about his path ahead. As exciting as getting married can be—as beautiful as the love is—it can still seem very intimidating. I wanted to reassure him, and remind him of his strengths and wonderful heart. I found the right words in my memories of throwing the football together when he was younger. He's given me permission to share this letter with you.

> *Dear Justin,*
>
> *Remember when you were about nine years old and we played football in the basement, or outdoors when the weather was nice. It was great fun, the best! We made up lots of routes, gave them each a name, and we'd "run" each*

one until we had it down perfectly. Every new play was more intricate and difficult. I remember how hard you'd work at it, never getting discouraged. It was super when we had them perfected and could run various combinations as though we were in a real game.

But no matter how fancy we made the plays, our favorite one was the long and deep route. This wasn't very fancy or intricate. You just took off straight down the sideline as fast as you could run, and I'd launch the ball way out in front of you. To catch this one, you had to pour everything you had into it and stretch as far as you could. After a while, you got SO good at it! We would run lots of plays, but they were just setting the stage for our super long ball. We'd huddle and I'd say, "Go long, Jus!" You'd smile and your eyes would twinkle. You seemed to love to pour everything you had into the challenge!

On this, your wedding day, I want you to know how pleased I am for you . . . and how proud I am of you. You are a wonderful person, and you've become a fine man. You also have all the attributes to become an exceptional husband and father.

At some level, these new roles may seem intimidating. If you even slightly feel this way, just remember the many powerful qualities you possess: You are caring, energetic, hardworking, creative, intelligent, fun-loving and humorous, sensitive, spiritual . . . and so much more. With all these inner gifts, you really can't lose!

Marriage is better than I ever thought it could be. There are so many joys, adventures, useful challenges, and *precious memories. I've found that love keeps deepening. It starts with romantic attraction, but extends way beyond that, if we let it. There's a heart and soul connection, and when this emerges, it's the greatest experience in life. It usually takes a lot of dedication and hard work to get there, though. At times, most of us are tempted to take the easier route and just give up. But that's really the only way we become losers . . . when we avoid opportunities to step up to the personal growth offered within our challenges.*

And then there's fatherhood . . . do I ever cherish it! You and Bobby are such blessings, and I love you forever. You've taught me so much and allowed me to be involved in your lives. Now this path requires a lot of energy, too, but the rewards are phenomenal. You don't have to have all the answers, either. What parenting is mostly all about (and it took me a while to learn it) is lots of listening, respect for the spirit and genius in every child, along with gentle and relentless caring. Major in these, and everything else falls into place.

Please don't forget that, in the game of life, you are a WINNER! You've overcome and become so very much already. Just rely on the best you have in you—the way you used to run routes, especially the super long one—and everything will be great! So, as you find yourself poised before all these incredible experiences, I'm huddling with you in my heart . . . and all I've got to say is: "Go long, Jus . . . Go long!"

This is also my message to you as you face the risks that can grow, enrich, and ennoble you: Go long, dear soul, go long! Reach, stretch, trust, learn ... and always be loving with yourself. As you stand before your risk, whisper to yourself, *This Risk Is Greatness!*

– The Expression –

1. Here is something that is critically important to your new life as a purposeful risk taker:

    It's really NOT about the outcome! Overconcern about how things will turn out is the biggest impediment to risking for most people. Remember this: *it's about the value received—not the outcome!* And you can get value from every outcome if you keep this perspective. Thus you can set it up to always be a winner in every risk by deciding that the ultimate purpose is to get value from the experience ... to learn, grow, strengthen, enjoy, and find great and lasting meaning. This will encourage you to keep on risking so that you can continue to get value. At some point, you'll also arrive at a wonderful outcome. Now it may end up looking quite different than you initially expected. We try to imagine preferred outcomes and often end up becoming attached to them. However, in our leaping, we place ourselves in dynamic partnership with the Divine, with the Infinite One. Our heartfelt commitment and courageous risking allow this All-Originating Spirit to work in and through us to bring forth our highest and best ... beyond what we can usually imagine. Risking makes welcome our greater yet-to-be!

    In our culture, most people have been conditioned from an early age that their personal value is determined by accomplishments and outcomes. It is a radical new approach to accept that value received trumps outcomes every time. For many this realization becomes the basis of a beautiful new relationship with themselves. No longer do they whip and berate themselves when things don't turn out as desired. A new kind of compassion blossoms. Learning and growth can happen most powerfully with this enlightened self-worth. Living becomes a great joy again and risking becomes second nature, just as when we were children.

2. In a college commencement address, Steve Jobs, one of the founders of Apple Computer, gave a simple formula for heartfelt and lifelong risking: "Stay hungry! Stay foolish!"

   To stay hungry is to remain passionate about your discovery and growth. To stay foolish is to remain playful and a bit crazy. This supports amazing creativity in life. Always remember, *Blessed are the cracked . . . for they shall let in the light!*

3. At one point in his life, Henry David Thoreau decided to conduct an experiment by living in solitude for two years at Walden Pond. During this two-year experiment, he wrote an essay titled "Walden." There are some extremely powerful reminders in it:

   > *I have learned this, at least, by my experiment:*
   >
   > *That if one advances confidently in the direction of his dreams, and endeavors to live the life which he has imagined, he will meet with a success unexpected in common hours. He will pass an invisible boundary; new, universal, and more liberal laws will begin to establish themselves around and within him . . . and he will live with the license of a higher order of beings.*

Delving into these ideas reveals some of the most powerful things we can do to overcome resistance and to continue risking and rising into our greatness:

". . . if one advances confidently in the direction
of his dreams"

What is your direction? Are you advancing confidently? This calls us again to boldness and confident action. *And* it calls us to own the future *now!*

". . . and endeavors to live the life which he has imagined"

What is the life you've imagined? In the Bible, it advises us, "Write the vision; make it clear." Spend time in the quiet, listening and allowing your "soul's sincere desire" to emerge from your heart into your awareness. Your concept of life will expand by quantum leaps! And remember, it says "endeavors." You don't have to do it all perfectly! However, along the way make no agreements with lack, struggle, or limitation! We don't deny challenges or limits. We just make no agreement to give them power.

"He will pass an invisible boundary"

This is because our real boundaries are in our concepts and thoughts in the first place.

Our commitment, advancing confidently, takes us beyond resistance thoughts into ongoing action. We are no longer fighting our greatest enemy: ourselves. Our risking is further establishing the possibility as an actuality. We've gone beyond the boundaries of wishing, fantasizing, and resisting. The Universal Creative Process is working in and through us.

". . . new, universal and more liberal laws will begin
to establish themselves"

We are a law unto ourselves according to the content of our consciousness and belief.

As we free our imagination into a greater acceptance, we find things begin to flow, evolve, and *work* in ways they hadn't before. A new law of consciousness is in effect!

> *". . . and he will live with the license of a*
> *higher order of beings."*

You become licensed and authorized to play full out with the manifesting powers of the Universe, knowing that you are a copartner with the All-Originating Spirit for the advancement of your life and life all around you. Challenges are no longer stop signs. They are green lights for healings, breakthroughs, and great leaps forward for God and for Good! Welcome to "Your Greater Yet-to-Be!"

CONCLUSION

This Mastery Is Heart

The ultimate essence of life mastery is heart-centered living. In every person's spiritual heart is an opening into divine Light, Love, and Joy. In moving through this opening we transcend resistances and obstructions and are welcomed into a paradise of answers, innovations, healings, reunions, and untold blessings. Poet, novelist, and mystic, Rainer Maria Rilke, underscored this when he wrote, *The work of sight is done. Do heart work now.*

To do heart work is to make ourselves childlike before the Infinite, for "God is Love" (1 John 4:8). This passage does not assert that God is "loving." Instead, it clearly declares a paramount truth: God *is* Love—divine, eternal, unconditional, all-encompassing Love. Any one of us may return our awareness to this Love and become a conduit for its miracles. Any path or teaching that does not have Love as its ultimate emphasis, or veers from remaining true to this focus, falls short of lasting validity and authentic power. Carlos Castaneda, in *The Teachings of Don Juan: A Yaqui Way of Knowledge*, guides us so powerfully:

Look at every path closely and deliberately. Try it as many times as you think necessary. Then ask yourself and yourself alone one question: Does this path have a heart? If it does, the path is good. If it doesn't, it is of no use.

To do heart work is to accept for ourselves the only genuine and lasting healing energy. It is the divine elixir that not only mends the broken parts of us, it reunites us with the potential and creativity of our souls—our dharma, as Buddhist teachings describe it. Love is the highest regenerative Power. Everything else falls short. Anthony de Mello (1931–87) was a Jesuit priest and psychotherapist who was born in Mumbai, India. He admits that for many years he was neurotic, anxious, depressed, and selfish. He wrote, *Everyone kept telling me to change. I resented them, and I agreed with them, and I wanted to change, but simply couldn't, no matter how hard I tried. What hurt the most was that, like the others, my best friend kept insisting that I change. So I felt powerless and trapped. Then one day, he said to me, "Don't change. I love you just as you are."* De Mello shared that this was his launching pad for radical transformation. He transcended the former patterns and found a sense of wholeness and self-love. He went on to do great things and help many people through his writings and selfless service. It is also generally accepted that he attained mystic consciousness. Such is the healing power of unconditional Love. May we all accept it . . . and allow the metamorphosis to unfold!

To do heart work is to unearth the inner peacemaker and to embark upon a path of nonviolent living in all its many facets: nonviolence toward all people—even our detractors and critics—toward those who are different than we are, toward the earth, toward ourselves.

To do heart work is to unlock the essence of true generosity and joyous sharing. In a Native American rite, young children are showered with food, drink, and clothing. Later on, members of the tribe call out, "I'm hungry. I'm thirsty. I'm cold." Then from their abundance, the children are led to distribute their bounty to the others in need. The child within us loves to give . . . and to give continually and abundantly. Only the fearful ego, dwelling in a sense of estrangement and unworthiness, pulls away from opportunities to share.

To do heart work is to rediscover the honor and power of serving. It is our portal to the realization of our interconnectedness, the essential Oneness of all people, of all creation. From the heart emerges the understanding that each of us bears unique gifts and purposes to this lifetime; yet we all share a common soul-purpose: to lift each other up, to serve as an instrument for the blessings of the Divine. John Astin put this high calling so well in the title of one of his songs: "To Love, Serve, and Remember—Love." To serve readily and openly is to tap the fountain of true compassion and to let the healing waters flow. The Zen Buddhist master Thich Nhat Hanh suggests four questions to open the heart and to empower Love: Do I understand you enough? Do I water your seeds of suffering? Do I water your seeds of joy? Please tell me how I can love you better?

To do heart work is to embark on the wondrous and endless journey of knowing and expressing God—the Infinite, Universal Love/ Intelligence. As I shared in Chapter 1, I found myself immersed in divine Love in the midst of a transpersonal experience when I was six years old. The expanded potential of that initiatory experience, however, had to wait for the opening of my heart decades later. I know what it is to talk about God, about the Spirit. Only when my heart was opened did I return to the pathway of truly experiencing the Indwelling Beloved. This has been the greatest gift of my life. It fuels my passion to proclaim to any who are ready to hear, and especially to those who are hurting or grieving: "God's Gotcha!" There is healing, empowering Love for you, and It is "closer than breathing, nearer than hands and feet" (Isaiah 57:15). Trust enough to let your heart open, and the balm of the Beloved will pour Itself upon your entire being. You will know your innate ability to transcend the lesser through the impulsion of the Greater within you. For what it all boils down to is that your true nature—the I Am of you—*is* Love.

And . . . to do heart work is to realize that, indeed, This Life Is Joy! The Light discovered by the seeker in the opening story was the ember of Love in his heart . . . waiting to be fanned into a magnificent radiance. This became his key to freedom and genuine fulfillment. When we free ourselves from the "belief prisons" of unworthiness, of endless struggle, of separation from Love . . . then an indestructible, ever-present, undeniable Joy is revealed. This Joy becomes the "rock" upon which a new way of living can be built.

While visiting Cape Town, South Africa, I toured an exhibit dedicated to Oliver Tambo, the great anti-apartheid leader. Scrawled across one of the walls was this same realization painted in broad brushstrokes: *In spite of everything, Joy!* May you anchor your precious life in the strength, beauty, and glory of spiritual Joy. You'll find it nestled in your heart!

An Experience of Heart Opening

Find a quiet place. Play some gentle meditation music, if you have it. Take three or four deep, relaxing breaths. Let go of busyness and anything that is preoccupying, distracting, or worrying you. Slow the "gerbil wheel" of the mind. Spend a few minutes becoming very still.

Bring into your awareness the realization that This Instant is Love . . . that beyond the reports of the senses or the assumptions of the intellect, there is a Presence—a universal Spirit—and It is Love. This Love is the Creative Life that birthed you. This Love has always been with you, maintaining and sustaining you. This Love has always offered everything you really need. It still offers a limitless bounty of Truth, Light, and Joy. This Love is your true and eternal Self. "Behold, I have loved you with an everlasting love" (Jeremiah 31:3).

Ask for an expanded experience of Love . . . and proclaim your willingness to open your heart chakra so that the divine Love within this spiritual vortex may be freed into an abundant and healing flow. Believe that divine assistance is supporting you in this beautiful endeavor, and that you do not have to struggle, force, or try to make it happen. Your willingness is the key. Just allow.

Now sense your heart chakra, the area in the center of your chest. Visualize or imagine that there are shutters or doors covering your heart. Or you might prefer to imagine your heart center as a tightly closed rosebud. Begin to allow an opening . . . sense this opening happening—the shutters gradually parting, or the bud beginning to open. Continue to allow this opening. Allow. Don't force. Remember, you are being supported.

As this opening continues, visualize or imagine a light beginning to be revealed and shining forth from your opening heart. As this light is revealed more and more, feel greater warmth at your heart center. Continue to allow this radiance to increase.

Now just bask for a time in this Love. Keep the mind stilled—nothing to analyze or figure out—just a spiritual experience to embrace.

Healing with Love

If time permits and you feel drawn to it, add this healing component to your experience. (If you don't choose to do this, simply move to the conclusion of this meditation.)

Visualize or imagine that there is a glorious altar table in your heart. This is an altar of healing. It is made of a pure and crystalline substance, and it is radiating Heart Light. See your altar clearly.

Now allow images to emerge on this altar table . . . images of anyone or anything that you choose to bless with Love. Know that healing energies abound for each image placed upon your altar.

One by one, allow these images to appear on your altar for a time. Sense the blessings being imparted, then let another image appear. Some images to consider:

- *Loved ones and friends*

- *Those for whom you feel concern*

- *Anyone with whom you are experiencing conflict or anger*

- *Beloved ones who have left their physical bodies and have moved into the expanded dimensions of the Life, Love, and Joy of the Spirit*

- *Groups . . . communities . . . nations . . . leaders*

- *The earth . . . and all sentient beings*

- *And don't forget to place yourself upon this altar for a further immersion in healing Love.*

Know that by activating these images on the altar of your heart, a blessing of healing, empowering, guiding Love is being instantly conveyed. This is a gift of great beauty and power.

Heart-Opening Conclusion

When you are ready to conclude this heart-opening experience, ask if there is anything you need to know . . . any realizations that are important to your growth and spiritual expression. Listen for the imparting of your guidance from the divine Love/Intelligence. *Be still and know.*

Now dissolve all the images and surround yourself in a protective light. Know that this allows your heart energy to continue to extend to others and to life around you, while at the same time blocking any unwanted forces or energies.

Breathe deeply several times. Sense the wonderful warmth and Light coursing through your body.

Bless this experience, giving thanks for the assistance you've received and the progress you've made. Finally . . . declare—silently or aloud—any affirmative acceptances or blessings that are important to you. Know with deep conviction that even before you speak them, they are already accomplished. They are a current reality in your "heart of hearts." They are being made manifest in the highest and best ways and times.

With great gratitude, release the experience.

Go forth into the rest of your day—and your life—warmed and uplifted by the unequaled Light that glows in the hearth of your heart.

And celebrate . . . for This Life is Joy!

ACKNOWLEDGMENTS

Between every line herein, I pray that you will sense my profound appreciation for the multitudes of beautiful beings who have blessed my life and who have provided me with such a wealth of inspiration and support for the writing of this book. Whether you have realized it or not, you have all made enormous, vital, often life-changing contributions!

MY HEART OVERFLOWS WITH LOVE AND GRATITUDE:

For my beloved wife, Erica; our sons, Justin and Bobby, and their beautiful wives; our fabulous grandchildren; and our extended family, including all the Teels, Silkmans, Smiths, and Whites. The grace of your love is my greatest treasure.

For my devoted and loving parents, Royal and Delma Teel, and especially for my mom's spiritual depth and tenacity.

For my teacher and mentor, Dr. H. Fred Vogt, who never ceased to believe in me, who cultivated in me the ministerial heart, and who regularly reminded me not to miss the Joy.

For the phenomenal and loving congregation of Mile Hi Church; for my beloved Mile Hi ministerial colleagues and their spouses, as well as for the dedicated practitioners, staff, and leaders—past and present—of this extraordinary center of Love and Light—all truly a "mile high" in consciousness!

For the staff at Tarcher/Penguin who have assisted me so greatly in designing and publishing this book, and especially for my publisher, Joel Fotinos—a spiritual dynamo in his own right— who persisted for years in pestering me to write a book, before slapping a contract before me and declaring, "Sign it!" Thank you, Joel and all, for your high awareness and expert guidance.

For John of God and the Entities of Light, in whose "current" the outline for this book emerged; and for Heather Cumming, Laura Gwen, and Monica Evon who have lavished me and so many with their wisdom and love at the Casa de Dom Inacio de Loyola.

For my prayer partner of many years, Rev. Howard Caesar, who has been like a brother to me, and for his lovely wife, Diane.

For Dr. Ernest Holmes, and all the pioneers in New Thought and mystic awareness.

ACKNOWLEDGMENTS

For my ministerial colleagues in the Centers for Spiritual Living, in the Association for Global New Thought, and in all Religious Science, Unity, and New Thought centers around the world.

For all, in every faith, who have taken on the mantle of spiritual leadership for our times.

For so many sparks of Light and caring along my path: Marjorie Staum, Patty Luckenbach, Robert "RAS" Smith, Cynthia James, Barry Ebert, Lloyd Barrett, Kathy Vogt, Michelle Medrano, Barbara Fields, H. H. Dalai Lama, John Denver, Barbara Marx Hubbard, Louise Hay, Oprah Winfrey, Michael Bernard Beckwith and Rickey Byars Beckwith, Mary Manin Morrissey and Joe Dickey, Kathy Hearn, Christian Sorensen, Mary Omwake, Wendy Craig-Purcell, Carol Carnes, Tom Zender, Kathianne Lewis, Edward Viljoen, David Alexander, Dennis Merritt Jones, Cora D. Mayo, Bill Magee, Betty Jean House, Barbara De Angelis, Wayne Dyer, Deepak Chopra, Marianne Williamson, Neale Donald Walsch, Mark Nepo, Tom and Deborah Willard, Terry and Kay Johnson, Carma Lytle and Craig Lang, Scott Awbrey, the Freehs, Bob and Diane Beale, John and Carol Swanson, Steve Burton, Claudia Abbott, Laura and Steve Drury, Eileen Flanigan, Ron Benson and Linda McDonald, Jim and Marilyn Cornelison, Kumar and Shilpi Dandavati, Jean Hendry, Anne Achenbach, Megan Gelhar, Peggy Bassett, Ezra and Winston Ellis, "Dodie" Dyrenforth, Marion Borders, Lloyd Tupper, Tom Costa, Paulette Sun and Michael Davis, Michael Murphy and Mal Bruce, Janet Patton, Norm Bouchard, Karen Paschal, Lee Gibson, Brugh Joy, Bill O'Hanlon, Jack and Jill Kastle, Nathan Kennedy, Mary Ann Lynen, John Harris, George and Rhoda Guerin, Rick and Dionne Lewis, Susan Leterneau and Larry Rowland, Bill and Sue Loving, Kent and Kathleen Rautenstraus, Karen Thomas, Gregg and Brita Moss, Myron McClellan, Jim and Dana Melton, Henrietta O'Brien, Phillip Byrne and Judy Noerr, James and Debra Rouse, Kurt and Deborah Roscow, Gerald and Joan Starika, Stephen Starika, Bob and Mary Trask, Sadie Tourtillot, Ralph and Fran Tuchman, Mike Wazny, Terry Cole Whittaker, Petra Weldes, George Wright . . . and many more. You are all emanations of absolute Joy, and this book would not have been the same without the precious gifts extended to me by each of you.

Finally, my heart overflows with love and gratitude for the supreme blessings of the infinite, ineffable One . . . the Love that heals me, the Spirit that deepens me, the Light that guides me, the Power that sustains me, the Peace that renews me . . . and the Joy that liberates me.

Thank you all, . . . Thank you, Life, . . . Thank you, God!

—Dr. Roger Teel